The Angel TREE

The Angel TREE

ALEX DINGWALL-MAIN

ILLUSTRATIONS BY DON GRANT

ARCADE PUBLISHING / NEW YORK

FIRST NORTH AMERICAN EDITION 2004

First published in Great Britain in 2003 by Ebury Press

Library of Congress Cataloging-in-Publication Data

Dingwall-Main, Alex.
  The angel tree : the enchanting quest for the world's oldest olive tree / by Alex Dingwall-Main. —1st North American ed.
    p. cm.
  ISBN 1-55970-711-9
  1. Olive—Mediterranean Region. 2. Dingwall-Main,
Alex—Travel—Mediterranean Region. 3. Landscape
gardening—France—Provence. 4. Gardens—France—Provence. I. Title.

SB367.D55 2003
634'.63'091822—dc22   2003019906

Published in the United States by Arcade Publishing, Inc., New York
Distributed by Time Warner Book Group

Visit our Web site at www.arcadepub.com

10 9 8 7 6 5 4 3 2 1

Designed by Lovelock & Co.

EB

PRINTED IN THE UNITED STATES OF AMERICA

Contents

Acknowledgements

I would like to thank the following:

France: Laurent Croz, Philippa Gauthier and Louis Musichini
Spain: Claudia Hernandez, Josefina Dean and Issidre Calafell
Greece: Christina Alexandrau and Antonios Pangalos
Italy: Antonio Gianno, Nicole Peyran and Alvaro Mythiana

And finally many thanks to Paul Eddy for the introduction.

Author's note

The names and identifying characteristics of people and places have been changed to protect privacy.

For Theo

The Angel Tree

Introduction

The beautiful and faithful old olive tree. One of the most venerable symbols of the Mediterranean and a tree so bountiful that he covers millions of acres of land and produces trillions of gallons of oil in a multitude of varieties. He adds immense beauty to the landscapes of not only Spain, Italy, Greece and even the South of France but also to places as diverse as Croatia, Israel, Tunisia and the new worlds of California and Australia.

He supplies a way of life and income for untold numbers of hard-working people. To cooks the world over he adds immeasurably to the ever-increasing awareness of the healthiness innate to Mediterranean cuisine.

A tree that puts up with drought, fights against wind, tolerates the cold, basks in the sun and lives longer than a thousand million dreams.

These old trees that 'never die' are as much ever-silver as they are evergreen and their magnificent old trunks and barks exhibit some of the best sculpture that nature can produce.

In this book you will meet a special tree. Special not for his ability to produce one of the marvels of the world, his oil, or for the prolific production of his fruit, nor even for his elegant and artistic bark, but special because of his astonishing old age.

This is the story of a quest to purchase the oldest living olive tree to be found and to move it to a new home where he can take up a gentle retirement as a living statue. A cherished decoration brought into a loving estate to trade affection with a man who wanted something exceptionally distinguished for his courtyard garden.

It was never the idea to demean this hard-wood dignitary of biblical proportions by reducing him to a mere landscape feature, but to celebrate his life and to reward him with a peaceful and comfortable retirement.

Over thousands of years of continuous cultivation these trees have never really been considered for their aesthetic beauty, more as tools for emolument.

Things are changing.

CHAPTER ONE

In nature there are neither rewards nor punishments –
there are consequences.

Robert G. Ingersoll

The whispering warmth that had arrived on the early morning wing had
by lunchtime turned into a hard, unrelenting stab of late summer heat. As
the sun advanced towards its zenith, shadows withdrew their service and
a flat blanching light pounded the garden into fatigued submission. In the
absence of shade the cicadas rattled ever louder, bickering their torrid
tales of need while the lizards darted jerkily from here to there, seeking
cover of stone.

Every late-summer day plays this game of Jekyll and Hyde. The
courteous dawn with its soft drops of dew and optimistic ardour is
unable to resist sipping at the violent prescription of high noon madness.
Forgetting its kindly embrace it rages with a terrible fever for a few hours

draining life from the ground and all who live in there. Then, bit by bit, the drug wears thin, the kicking stops and the forgive-me kisses of evening begin again. The shadows lengthen with each passing moment and the tempered sun gains colour; gold, orange-pink and sienna. But soon they too disappear, leaving the fettled air to drift its scented breath over the balmy earth. All is well again.

The office printer was running out of ink and if a full afternoon's work was to be achieved it looked like it was down to me to get into town before twelve to replace it. When the clocks hit on the first note of noon the shops clap shut. There is a small window between the first strike and the last but it's not a sympathetic sixty seconds of benign management bending the rules to allow a speedy purchase from a late runner. More like an efficient evacuation of lingering shoppers. A booting out of ditherers and a tired rejection of hopefuls. Miss it and you are out of the frame for two hours. Add travel time and your afternoon shift shrinks to a near useless semester.

Snagging myself against the hostile environment of the car's steamy interior I got with it. The tyres squelched on the melting tarmac and the thermometer showed 37 °C.

There are continuing major roadworks on the local National 100 that involve an improvement plan that has been hacking itself into the countryside for longer than most people can remember. A proud sign announces the details of the work. Funded by a fifty–fifty split between the regional communes and the government, the words extravagantly declare a finish date that has been scrubbed out or taped over more times than a bookie's board.

I topped out over the crest of a hill hugging the apex in third, pushing hard only to come unexpectedly upon a queue of stationary vehicles. They were patiently waiting for a tired workman to flip his red disc to green. Men have frolicked in space, computers have held entire economies together, surgeons have separated Siamese twins and satellites have tracked down battalions of car thieves, but here on a hot summer morning in the South of France we had a dull man, bored to within a bat's hiccup of barminess, directing a swell of traffic on the perimeter of a multi-billion-Euro road improvement plan. I smashed my foot on to the brake, pulled back the gears and tightened my hold on the steering wheel. The rubber squealed with displeasure but its flabby grip managed to hold the road like a frog on glass. The car committed itself to a discreet skid that terminated with an almost silent smack into the boot of the expensive saloon in front. When it settled, the driver climbed slowly out.

A tall, elegant man in late middle age, impeccably dressed, with a soldier's deportment, moved towards the rear of his vehicle to inspect the damage. I stumbled out of my car and began to apologise to the stranger for my misdemeanour. He held up the palm of his hand, indicating that I should be quiet. He opened the boot, looked inside at a large leather case, the contents of which were hidden from view by his back, and then with apparent confidence that all was well turned to me.

'I don't think you have done anything to improve my wife's car,' he said.

He was French but spoke good English with a soft American accent. He looked remarkably self-possessed considering the belting heat and the shake-up he had just experienced.

'I'm so sorry,' I began. 'I was hurrying a bit, hoping to catch the shops before they closed. More haste less speed I suppose.' I grinned sheepishly and then fiddled around looking for a card to give him with my address.

The passing traffic bleated their horns and made heavy weather of having to drive round us, probably disappointed at the lack of blood.

'You are lucky that the pair of china pots in the trunk were not broken. They are very old and would have had you coaxing your insurance representative to be very understanding. Give me your card, write down the car's number and I will contact you when I have a quotation for the repairs.'

He was extraordinarily together. We parted politely and I sank back into the driving seat, deeply relieved that both cars were still working, mine with its nose slightly out of joint but still running and his with little more than its dignity ruffled. I shuddered to think what the performance would have been if the china had been smashed.

I returned home without ink and went for a swim in a pool that was warmer than the Caribbean.

In line with the rest of France most of my August had been given over to vacation. What's the point in trying to be efficient when nobody else wants to join in? But the summer holidays were now over and that meant back to work. Four weeks is enough to dislocate yourself from the main vein but it also unsteadies the cash flow. When September arrived, overdressed in bills, the reality was to pull things back into line as quick as possible.

With early autumn, school was back and the landscape began to regain its composure. Everywhere was exhausted. The trees, the grass and the plants had given their best for the last few months but in common with all the hard-working paid-up members of the tourist industry, they needed a break. A bit of time to take a deep breath and fill their lungs with a shot of peace. To allow a revenant of tranquillity to infiltrate their overworked being.

Down on the plane the reddish-brown stained vine leaves were turning crispy and the grape was readying itself for harvest. Soon the narrow tractors with their narrow trailers would be weaving themselves in and out of the rows picking up the baskets of freshly picked grapes, mostly red, and carting them off down to the local *vinicole*.

It had rained during the previous night leaving a freshness that had long been absent. It was only a light shower for a garden that really needed to wallow in a deep bath but it was better than nothing.

I looked over towards the *bassin* to see how much the level of water had risen – not much. But there were plenty of signs that wild boar had been in again. The beasts had been digging up the lawn and ransacking the borders and it was becoming a demoralising habit. There had been a quote from a local contractor to run an electric fence round the property but it had yet to be installed.

It's worst when the weather's been very dry for a long time and they find it too much like hard work digging around in the sun-baked earth of their normal habitat, up in the forests. So they come down seeking soft damp ground in which to make a bed and put up their weary trotters. Pigs may not be able to fly but they certainly know how to make a nest. Those of us who either irrigate their gardens, or have natural spring-fed damp areas, get targeted. If it was just a simple snuffle around for something to eat, a tasty root or tuber, a bug or two, that might be containable, but it's not just food that they are after. They want to make a hangout for their extended family of grannies, cousins, in-laws and endless offspring. They work like overexcited digger-tractors and really upset the pansies.

It was one thing to scrutinise the scene from a window in the early morning and shake your fist in the general direction of where the Porkers might be hiding. But going out in the evenings, which were drawing in quickly now, was an altogether different ham sandwich. Taking our middle-aged mutt out to spend-a-cent before calling it a night had become decidedly hazardous.

There she was, quietly smelling the evening air, her tail quivering like a metronome, when her nose started to twitch with a hint of uncertainty. Suddenly out of the undergrowth burst a battalion of hogs with night vision like the Northern Alliance high on western bombing raids. Savvy to the requirements of after-dark warfare, they moved at a controlled trot towards the poor hound that thought she had better protect her human family and see them off. Without horns or a particularly developed streetwise attitude she didn't have much chance. Soon she was surrounded by a group of boars that thought they were extras in a Hannibal Lecter movie and she had to bale out extra quick. Well, that's how she described it.

If you could harness these over-testosteroned hogs, like you do a carthorse for example, you might save a stack on farm machinery. Meanwhile it remains a bit spooky to think of the four-leg-drive, twin-tusked, three-hundredweight pig-powered heavy-duty wreckers snorting, grunting and excavating their way around your garden while you are asleep dreaming of hearts painted on the back of fallen rose petals.

It was time to get dressed. Not a quick process as it happens. It usually involves wrestling with a pint-sized hooligan for at least ten minutes, battling with Megazord for another five and then taking a front seat in a teeth-washing ceremony. Fortunately this part of the proceedings was becoming quicker by the week as more and more of my small boy's milk teeth came out.

'Do you think they will all fall out now?' he had asked one morning sucking in his lips over his gums, aping an old man without his dentures.

'Bit by bit, but you'll have made a fortune from the Euro fairy.'

His little face was alight with the excitement of growing up and at his accomplishment of joining the ranks of those other small people who had lost a tooth or two ahead of him.

Paternal duties completed, I managed to remove myself from the fray in good time to get to the office. It had taken a few dubious promises and a quick ride in the car, but I was there, exhausted, well before the others came in at nine.

Located in a small two-storey stone village house built about four hundred years ago, the office squeezes itself between two bigger houses that perch on top of the hillside looking over the valley. Outside the front door a thin street ribbons its way past *en route* to the top of the hill. Pedestrians, children on bicycles, indigenous cats and dogs and a cloud of pigeons mostly make up the traffic, but occasionally everybody gets a shock from a small white van doing some local business. Windows and front doorways burgeon with flower boxes and pots and the shutters are painted in an assortment of calm colours. From inside I can look down the side of the valley and see our own house and garden. A strong vantage point to keep an eye on things and an inspirational view to boot. Although the various studios I had had in London were good, they could hardly hold a candle to the spectacular panorama I have from this endearing old building.

I was just contemplating the wonder of it all when a silent commotion caught my attention on the windowsill. A butterfly clapped its wings as fast and furiously as somebody who had just seen Maria Callas in *Samson and Delilah* – *mon coeur s'ouvre à ta voix*. For a moment, the deep red velvety sheets dabbed with soft white brush strokes seemed to stick together, then suddenly came another burst of appreciation that usefully dusted the windowsill. Finally the beautiful creature folded its wings and fell over.

'Oh dear,' I thought, 'it's died,' and took a closer look. The wings slowly began to open and then, to my consternation, dropped off completely, revealing some sort of flying carnivore not much bigger than a hornet finishing off the remnants of the butterfly's body. He was eating quickly like a travelling salesman in a fast-food chain. He must have seen me because he moved his pot-bellied little body off his snack and rose slowly up past my chest like an overloaded helicopter climbing up the face of a high-rise building. He hovered a little uncertainly at head height, looked me straight in the eye and with a breathy belch told me to bugger off.

Midmorning and Philippa, my assistant, put through a call.

At the other end of the line was a Frenchman speaking English with a soft American accent. It was my crash acquaintance. He began to speak in measured meticulous sentences.

'I am about to email you the quotation I have received for the repairs to the damage of my wife's car. Sustained, you may remember, when you drove into it last week.'

'Yes, of course, and I'll pay it straight away. I'm really very sorry for the inconvenience it must have caused your wife, I know how irritating these things are.'

'Thank you. By the way my name is Lautour. I don't think you wrote that down when we, er, met. Now, changing the subject completely for a moment, I understand from your card that you are a *paysagist*. A garden designer – is that correct?'

'Yes sir, that is correct. My office is in Lacoste.'

'I have a beautiful old house here in Provence that I have recently renovated with much care and attention to period. There is also an elegant courtyard attached to it but at the moment it looks very empty. It needs something to make it come alive. I have a few ideas but I would like to discuss them with somebody in the gardening business. Would you be interested in having a look?' he asked.

I said that I certainly would and an appointment to visit his Chateau near Ansouis was set up. It was under an hour away.

That small jostle with a German sedan might just turn out to have been fortuitous after all.

The journey from Lacoste to Ansouis cuts deep through the Luberon mountains. The road which winds and turns against a pale grey limestone landscape is inevitably clogged with a queue of crawling tourists dithering on the edge of the bends or worse, oversized lorries in search of a destination. It's a dangerous place to pass and overtakers keep undertakers busy.

From the bosom of the hills the route emerges out on to the approach to Lourmarin. Listed as one of the most beautiful villages in all of France with its fifteenth-century chateau, narrow streets and lovingly restored old houses, Lourmarin is, as any of the denizens will tell you, where Albert Camus lived and died.

Ansouis is another equally attractive small Luberon village, well sheltered from the Mistral, and its narrow streets are dotted with boutiques and artists' workshops. The cafés of the village square are properly shaded by the mandatory plane trees. The Chateau Ansouis, the one that Lautour warned me not to confuse with his place, is a beautiful venerated fortress open to the public even though privately owned. Inside there is a significant collection of seventeenth- and eighteenth-century furniture as well as some fine old masters.

Ten minutes later I turned in through some ornate iron gates that hung heavily from a suitably grand set of well-weathered stone pillars. The camera picked up my car as I approached and the gates swung their weight inwards to allow me entry. The drive fell away in a Roman straight line punctuated by tall, elegant cypress trees every six or seven metres. The grass on either side was neatly mown and verdant. The hidden irrigation system was evidently working.

Just before reaching the house the drive crossed over a small stone bridge that spanned a stream of gently bubbling water pushing its way past boulders and water plants. The parking area swallowed my car without noticing as I drove aimlessly across it towards the north side and presumably the front door. A young man appeared from nowhere wearing black.

'Good afternoon, Monsieur. If you leave the keys in the car I'll make sure it's OK. Head for that door down there. Mr Lautour will be out to meet you shortly,' he said, pointing to a portico halfway down the house.

Being the north side, the windows were smaller and less grand than the south side, mostly with bars rather than shutters. I arrived at the door which was flanked by a pair of neatly clipped pistachio bushes. Their shiny evergreen leaves knitted tightly together promised a harvest of nuts later in the year, but I didn't entirely believe them – they have a habit of complaining. Native to western Asia they are related botanically to both the cashew and the mango. They were introduced to Italy from Syria in the first century BC from whence they spread to other Mediterranean countries. There is evidence that they were used for food in what is now known as Turkey as early as 7,000 years ago but were first grown commercially in Persia in the nineteenth century. They need at least 500 hours above 30 °C and more than 1,000 hours below 7 °C to fruit successfully but it is, however, quite traditional for the pistachio to be clipped into balls and pom-poms.

Mr Lautour appeared just before I rang the bell.

He politely reintroduced himself and ushered me into the hall. A cavernous room with a fireplace on either side, it supported huge tapestries that draped themselves like exalted pantomime props across the walls: scenes of dewy-eyed minstrels plucking on the strings of medieval instruments, of young men gazing adoringly into the eyes of sweet maidens who coquettishly floated through flower gardens. Faded Persian carpets covered most of the floor while the centre of the room was dominated by a simple mahogany refectory table big enough to seat thirty people. The walls – what you could see of them – had recently been repainted a pale dove grey and the plasterwork on the cornice was highlighted in a washed-out maroon. It was smart, expensive and stylish.

The graceful Mr Lautour owned a face that liked to smile. The laughter lines that were woven round chocolate-brown eyes seemed to hint at an easy life with minimal aggravation. He wore a dark blue silk shirt tucked untidily into a pair of beige cotton trousers and dark brown leather shoes. His sleeves were sort of rolled up and he looked reasonably useful. With an easy manner he suggested we go through to the library. I fell in beside him and walked down a long passage with simple kilim runners on the floor. It eventually led to a fine, booklined room that was as much his study as it was a reading room. Very neat and discreet. The sun broke in through the mullioned windows, pouring shards of light across the soft leather sofas and polished floorboards. A dozen ancestral paintings mingled with oils of racehorses and birds of prey. A small fire flickered warmly in the big fireplace. It wasn't really necessary but it was comforting nonetheless. Above, a carved wooden mantelpiece was loaded with silver-framed photographs, invitations, small lacquered boxes and a clock.

Lautour motioned me towards a seat on one side of the spitting logs and then pulled on the old-fashioned servant bell. 'Excuse me a moment,' he said. Nothing happened, he pulled again … nothing. He drew his tiny mobile telephone out of his back pocket, dialled in a number and waited.

It was finally answered. Quietly, but authoritatively, he gave an instruction into the machine and turned it off. He sat down, looking at the flames and said nothing.

I looked at my fingernails and tarried. The room felt calm and the slightly unexpected lull in conversation did not matter a bit. I didn't feel in the least like talking which is something I usually do too much of when I find myself in a situation like this. For some reason I always feel I have to break the silence by chatting pointlessly about irrelevancies. Lautour got up and without looking at me stood with his back to the fire. His hands were in his pockets and from time to time he moved them forwards pulling his trousers tightly against his bottom. He seemed lost in thought and oblivious to my presence. I began to feel like I was sitting in a waiting room with a patient expecting some kind of test results.

After a bit the library door creaked open slowly and in shuffled an elderly butler with a slightly condescending manner, a Mervyn Peake–P. G. Wodehouse hybrid. A half-hearted tail-wag smacked the floor from the old dog under the desk.

Mr Flay-meets-Jeeves carried a silver salver high up on one rickety hand, the thin extended fingers of which pointed up in a neatly spaced ring supporting the underside of the tray. He carefully tucked the other hand behind his back, incongruously clenching his mobile phone. An anachronism in service. He was dressed in a comfortable old red velvet suit that was having a crisis as to whether it was a retired smoking jacket or a decommissioned morning coat. Tight black felt trousers, distressed patent leather shoes and a slightly skewed bow tie completed the uniform. Silver teapots, jugs and bowls perched proudly on the gleaming tray.

'Meet Rottcodd, my redoubtable butler.'

I smiled warmly at the old gentleman whose kindly but thin and wrinkled face held a thousand secrets.

Rottcodd dropped the tray down on to the sofa table with an indelicacy that made Lautour tighten his jaw muscles.

'I'll be Queen,' he croaked with a passable punch at English, his watery eyes much amused by his own colloquial mastery.

'Mother,' I said.

'Hmm?' he said hardly looking at me.

'It's "I'll be Mother",' I said, 'not Queen,' and then apologised for being so pedantic.

'D'accord, I'll be Queen Mother then,' he said, his eyebrows arching while his hand shook the tea out of the pot.

'Well, nobody is going to be Nanny,' said Lautour enigmatically, taking a cup and passing it to me. 'Sugar?'

Conversation turned to gardening, how I had discovered a career in something that most people thought of as a hobby and how long I had been working in Provence.

'We will go and look at the courtyard in a moment,' Mr Lautour said, 'but first I would like to explain what I have been thinking about.'

I nodded and took out my pencil and notepad and settled down to be briefed.

'I am soon to be sixty-five and I have spent the last seven years restoring this house. My wife and I had been living mostly in Paris. Before retiring I had a courtesy posting with the Foreign Office, and we have a house in Manhattan as well which we spend some time in during the winter. But now we want to be mostly down here. My eldest daughter is working in New York so she's living in the house. It's on 63rd and Madison, do you know the area?'

I said I did and explained that a few years earlier I had made a roof garden and smartened up a backyard for a double brownstone on 64th and Park. We digressed with a few exchanges about the terrible change that had hit the city, indeed the world, since that black and blue September Tuesday. We agreed that it was a city of brilliant hues and murky tints. A place that could turn you on as easily as it could turn you off but never ceased to dazzle. After September the eleventh it was like somebody had violated the rainbow.

Determinedly, we returned to the conversation about his courtyard and Lautour went on with his explanation:

'From the early seventeenth century my family had owned this chateau, passing it from father to son, or occasionally a nephew, but it was abandoned in the thirties when an uncle died destitute and without issue. In 1942 the Nazis requisitioned it and treated it with inventive disrespect. The young soldiers would use the beautiful stone statues for target practice, shooting off noses and ears. By the end of the war it had fallen into terrible disrepair and for years it wallowed in a decaying heap. Can you imagine? Three hundred years of diligent upkeep kicked in the groin by a bunch of fascists.'

Lautour shook his head and looked at the flames and then went on,

'The chateau was unable to be sold because of trustee complications and unable to be maintained. It soon slithered behind a damp veil of overgrowth. For nearly forty years it remained a secret and was virtually forgotten. With no one living here there was no need for anybody to visit. No letters, no services, no staff. Stories of haunted rooms and strange goings-on grew arms and legs in the telling. Local gossip had tales of murder, torture and orgiastic soirées that made anything you may have heard about the Marquis de Sade sound like a tea dance in a retirement home.'

'I live just below Lacoste,' I interrupted. 'Our house lies in the shadow of the Marquis' chateau.'

'His great mistake you know,' said Lautour, 'was to try and sleep with his mother-in-law. She was so appalled by his advances she had him locked up without mercy for twenty-seven years.'

'Like Nelson Mandela,' I said.

'I didn't know he tried to sleep with his mother-in-law,' he said, looking worried.

'Shouldn't think he did, but he was still put away for twenty-seven years.'

Another reflective silence rent the room. The glow of the deepening afternoon sun, the rhythmic ticking of the mantelpiece clock, the reassuring snore of the snoozing Labrador and the hearty fire had me near to closing down.

Lautour cleared his throat. 'As I am now the only surviving male in the family as far as I can find out, I suggested to my wife that it might be an interesting project to see if we could claim the house back. She agreed, finding the idea both challenging and genial.'

'Have you started to make any garden yet?' I said.

'A bit, but mostly it has been clearing and cleaning. There are a few fruit trees that must have been planted before the war, some unidentifiable shrubs that have outgrown their usefulness and some bits and pieces that my wife has been trying to nurse back into shape.'

Lautour held out his cup presumably for Rottcodd to take and refill, but Rottcodd had long gone. He had vaporised out of the room while we had been talking. It evidently wasn't unusual behaviour because after a short interlude Lautour put his cup down, slightly absent-mindedly, on the carpet next to his chair.

'We rented a house locally and I commenced. I visited the Mairie, and with the aid of my *avocat*, I sorted out papers of ownership. I contracted *maçons*, electricians and plumbers. An architect friend of mine from Paris who is also approaching retirement agreed to come and help us.'

There was a slurping noise coming from behind Lautour's feet. The old Labrador had managed to shift his body without actually getting up and had planted his head in the nearly finished cup of tea and was very much enjoying what was left. His tail moved without rhythm, just an occasional short burst of guilty appreciation.

'But first I had to build a little house for my hawks,' he said. 'You see, I have sixteen birds and we travel all over Europe shooting. Before we moved here they used to stay in a special sanctuary.'

'Shooting? You mean as in blasting the living daylights out of game birds?'

'Well, no, it isn't shooting of course, it's hawking,' he smiled patiently, 'but I follow the shooting season you understand. It is the only time we can "hawk". Last year I took the birds to Scotland in August for the grouse.'

Not many people go hawking, I thought. 'Had you ever done that before?' I asked.

'Ah *oui*. We went in the seventies to the very North. Caithness. A cold, exposed place but with magnificent grouse moors.'

A slight chill ran down my neck.

'I know it well,' I said. 'One of my sisters was born there. We have a family graveyard perched on the windswept cliffs overlooking the North Sea. And I think it might have been my father's shooting you rented that year, that August,' I said slowly.

'Really! Why do you think that?'

'Because I remember him saying that he had let the shooting to a Frenchman, and how Willie Ben, his shepherd and farm manager, had told him about the procession of five Peugeot estate cars he had greeted. The first one with people in it, the next two with luggage and the last two with hawks on perches.'

'That sounds like us. How extraordinary.'

'Isn't it?'

Old Willie-Ben Mackay had been more impressed by the amount of luggage and the fleet of cars than he had been by the birds. But the thing that affected him most, I remember, was Lautour's wife. He *fair took a hot face*, as they say, when he talked of her. 'A bonny, bonny lass,' he would sigh. I was giving him my best Scottish accent as I told the tale.

'Ah ha, I think I remember him now. He was quite charming. A beautifully mannered man with a ruddy red face who made us very comfortable and gave me a bottle of malt whisky to take to bed.'

'Hoping to swap it for your wife probably,' I trundled out unnecessarily. I kick myself for making such dumb remarks. I don't know where they come from. They are probably clothed in some kind of insecurity, a need to make people smile, not that this man was at all serious.

Lautour took no notice of my facetiousness and continued seamlessly.

'I think the locals were rather upset by our hawks, you know. It seems it was perfectly all right to remove the life from thirty brace with a shotgun but to slay one or two using a bird of prey made them think of you as a savage. Whereas they are the ones who should know the meaning of savage,' he sniffed.

And he was right. I could remember going into a bar at the local hotel about that time with my father, and the locals were definitely at odds with him about the hawks. He was quite upset by their dogged behaviour. He had considered several of them to be his friends but he was disappointed at how fragile the relationships had been. But like country folk everywhere they hated change or things they didn't understand.

'Have you kept the estate? Do you shoot?'

'No, my father sold it. Ignominiously.'

It had been thirty-something years but I still smarted at the loss. 'And the only thing I've shot since then have been photographs.'

Lautour looked at me thoughtfully and nodded. It was a moment to reflect if ever there was.

'*Alors, on y va, mon ami,*' he said, 'let's go look at the site.'

We left the library and once again I fell in beside my prospective client who talked on as we walked briskly through the house.

'At the moment the space is virtually empty. We have rebuilt the stone wall around it carefully and there is a large pile of ancient flagstones stacked in one corner but little else. I want something spectacular,' he said with a sudden passion that surprised me. 'It must be simple, strong, expressive and of course, romantic.' His enthusiasm was infectious. 'I see something special and almost unobtainable, something that people will want to be near or touch,' he said.

'Is it sculpture?' I asked.

'No. Definitely not. I want people to enjoy it without envy, I want it to be not for stealing.'

'You mean not for stealing because it is not worth much or because it is too heavy to pick up?'

'I want value. But the money is not the issue. It doesn't matter if it is very expensive or not. Perhaps we can think of something that is perhaps money-irrelevant?'

I felt perhaps I had rather coarsely introduced the vulgarities of budget quite unnecessarily, but at the same time quietly noted that the point was irrelevant to him.

The Chateau Valois is a grand, tall building of exquisite proportions. A high-pitched roof of hand-cut tiles sat on four storeys of refined structure. The shutters, closed on the south side against the hot afternoon sun, were pale green and flattered the soft ochre stonework. We let ourselves out on to a small balcony in the centre of the south facet from which a courtly set of steps descended from the raised ground floor windows, throwing shadows into the semi-basement below. Beneath us a virtual quadrant was nearly the length of the house and about twenty metres deep. A two-metre-high stone wall that had been restored with loving attention to detail surrounded it.

The large stones at the bottom became gradually smaller as the wall built up to be perfectly finished off with a well-seasoned mitred capping. Opposite the french windows on the far side of the enclosure, a dainty pair of hand-beaten metal gates seemed to be the only way out. Shade came from an elderly, slightly yellowing plane tree set in the north-west corner.

A small clap of excitement from Mr Lautour announced two pale brown and white spaniels into the midst. Up from the basement for a bit of ragging, they ran shoulder to shoulder with their bobbed little tails demonstrating about ten per cent of how pleased they were to see their lord and master. The ground was spattered with dried-out weeds and early leaf fall.

'Now you can see why I must turn my attention, and yours, to my courtyard,' said Lautour, descending into the arena.

He rubbed his hands together and was clearly stimulated by the prospect of what could be done. 'I think it must be simple, chic and thought-provoking,' he continued, 'unusual, while maintaining a strong sense of the region.'

We walked over to the far side and back again. We then walked from end to end. 'It would be good to have something in here that is old – a tree or an antique birdcage. I don't know, something that has a bit of legend perhaps. I'll leave you to think about it.'

I could see he was about to leave so I asked him if the rest of the garden had been renovated. It seemed to me that he was concentrating all his energies into a very small part of the estate. I wondered if there might not be a broader picture. Even some influences to pick up on.

'It is mostly parkland with fine trees. Quite *"anglaise"* actually. There is a lake and a *potager*, both of which have yet to be cleaned and restarted.' With that he announced he was going back to his study and for me to join him when I was ready. The pair of spaniels followed.

A number of images ran through my mind. A veritable reel of possibilities. On one hand I thought about keeping to period. All classical and elegantly correct whatever that might be. On the other maybe a strict minimal interpretation with razor-sharp indications of modernity. Glass, metal, polished steel. Neo-Gardenist? An architectural juxtaposition like I. M. Pei's pyramid at the Louvre. Or something more organic? Less threatening and more liveable with.

If nothing sorts itself out in the mind immediately, leave it to fester. No need to impress the client with mind-wrenching creativity all within two minutes. If it is in there and left in peace to skip around the Elysian Fields of thought, something usually comes up. I paced around consigning the basic measurements to memory and then just hung in there for a while.

The sun was gathering up its belongings and getting ready to head down-under, and a slight autumnal breeze shivered through the plane tree. I sat for a while on the stack of paving stones and tried to imagine things. I felt a bit like Pooh tapping his brow, *'Think Think.'* It is a strange time this. Face to face with your perceived talent. It is a fidgety and lightly balanced pillow fight of the mind.

I scribbled, doodled and notated. I closed my eyes, then opened them wide. Paced around and did some deep breathing. It was soon time to go.

Sleep on it or dance it around the darkness of the early morning hours.

I walked up the steps, along the passage and jauntily presented myself to the boss. I was about to thank him for inviting me to look at the job, assure him I would work on a few ideas and report back shortly kind of a thing, when he said:

'So, what do you think?' He was looking straight at me and beckoning me into the room at the same time. I got the distinct and sinking feeling that he was expecting some kind of an answer there and then. So much for my not caring a shoot about impressing my client, I was on the spot.

'Well, I have a couple of ideas,' I said, trying to sound like I did.

Lautour lifted his chin a little. 'Come in, let's have a drink,' was all he said. He walked over to a circular rent table near one of the windows. The tail of the evening sun flickered farewell and left without ceremony. He picked up a cut-glass decanter and waving it at me asked if I would like to celebrate our meeting with a small Napoleon?

What makes him think it's fortuitous? I wondered but didn't dwell on it. A small Napoleon sounded very welcoming. Imagine a big Napoleon.

'Have you any olive trees?' I asked him as he bade me sit down.

'Sadly no, we haven't. What there was got destroyed in the winter of '56, and after that they were rooted out and the groves were never replanted.'

Nineteen-fifty-six has gone down in the local record books as the worst winter in decades. It was outrageously cold for the South of France and the thermometers recorded a terrible minus 18°C. It wiped out thousands of olive trees, decimated the crop and caused many growers to reconsider their product. It showed up the vulnerability of growing olives in this corner of Provence. All those years ago, before anybody had ever mentioned Global Warming or the Ozone schmowzone.

'A great shame,' I said, 'because olives don't generally die of the cold like that.' A quick sip on the brandy warmed up my thoughts and on I went. 'What happens is that the top growth goes, the crown and branches, even the trunk, but more often than not the roots survive. Therefore if they are *not* grubbed out of the ground like yours were, regeneration begins and before long you see signs of green life starting over. Even burnt-down trees have been known to phoenix out of the rubble.'

'Is this all leading to something?' he asked.

'What about,' I said, pacing myself, 'planting a very, very old olive tree in or near to the middle of the courtyard? Not just old,' I said, 'but the oldest one in the world!'

I knew I was getting out of my pram of course but I needed to build the drama. To put the concept behind footlights.

Lautour raised an eyebrow and a smile slipped on to the surface of his face.

'The oldest olive tree. And how old do you think that is likely to be?'

I had jumped in with a wild card suggestion and had precious little knowledge to back it up. True, I had become much more interested in olive trees since I had moved to the Mediterranean and I knew considerably more about them than I did eight years ago. I had, for example, found a pair quite recently for a client that looked like twins and were about five hundred years old. I had also met a few growers and had seen the fruit being pressed, but when it came to understanding their absolute legend and longevity I was a novice. It was just an idea, something chucked into the pot while waiting for other ideas to make themselves known.

I took a flyer. 'A thousand, 1,500 years, 2,000, maybe more.' I was gaining a false bravado. 'I saw a picture the other day of one that was over 2,000 years old.' I was spinning out of control and praying that I had read the caption correctly. 'Mind you,' I said pulling myself up a little, 'we probably wouldn't be allowed to buy that one. National treasure and all that.'

Lautour turned away from me and walked over to the fire. He lent against the mantelpiece and stared into the hot grate. I noticed how well polished the heels of his shoes were. Being a slightly apologetic ex-public schoolboy I notice these kinds of things. I spent my first year cleaning the shoes of prefects and the heads of house. Well, I suppose I did other things as well but it seems when I look back on that time that I was either polishing the big boys' heels or trying to avoid them getting into bed with me. My little boy will most probably be a Euro-Kid, but if anything changes and he finds himself heading for a British public school I am certain of one thing: it will be co-educational so that he can make his own choices.

'And the other idea?' Lautour asked.

'Hmm?' I said.

'A couple of ideas. You said you had a couple of ideas and I was just wondering what the other one was?'

I have this aide-de-camp inside my head. I call him Fred and he's on call 24/7. Quite often he goes days without being disturbed, then quite unexpectedly there might be a flurry of activity when questions need quick answers. Although he hasn't got as far as demonstrating the art of nappy changing on the inner child, it was he who had put his arm round my shoulder when I thought I had lost some weight only to find I hadn't lost it at all, but it was just hiding round the corner waiting to come back at a moment's notice.

In that stretched moment of Lautour waiting for my reply, Fred had quickly suggested I think laterally. Hit him with some madness – he might like it; if not it strengthens the olive scam.

So I boarded a flight of fantasy and started by suggesting two matching Boule-Rinks. 'They would be long, thin, very shallow water pools that are artificially frozen over and on warm summer evenings you could play the game with very, very soft rubber balls. Tall pink lights would flood the courts with a marshmallow countenance. On certain nights of the year fêtes could be held. Either side of the play areas could play host to stalls selling celebrity kisses, virtual gardens and pomegranate juice. Raffles for upturned table rides around the Venetian canals, a promise from the National Portrait Gallery in London to exhibit a painting of a chosen relative. There might be rides on multi-coloured donkeys sprayed like rainbows, and balloon flights across the Luberon valley with the President of France. Why we could even have …'

'Impractical, intrusive and highly unlikely,' Lautour closed with a sparkle in his eye.

'All right, all right, then what about this? There is a product; a water-based paint that is used for marking out the lines on a grass tennis court or athletic tracks, mostly used by schools or clubs. The paint is harmless to plants and is ephemeral in that it will grow out or be slowly washed off by rain. We could lay a quadrangle of perfect lawns and then employ local artists to paint pictures on the grass? Imagine each season you could have an exhibition. Those that have a thing about Pissarro could paint the leaves on the evergreen bushes. The cypress trees could have pictures of Van Gogh's *Iris* all over them. Bridget Riley lives down here, maybe we could persuade her to do her black and white stripy thing.' I was motoring. 'We could have flat screen loop videos on the wall showing things like the art of lawn-mower maintenance, or sculptors' workshops. We could have a—'

'I'll go with the oldest olive,' Lautour interspersed.

'You will?'

'I adore olive trees,' he said, 'I think they have the most beautiful of leaves and of course are the symbol of friendship.'

'And what about their talented fruit? It can not only dress a cocktail in a dinner jacket but also make the greatest of oils known to man,' I said.

'Very true,' said Lautour. 'Do you know, my mother used to give it to us by the spoonful when we were young, every day. I grew to love the taste and have never eaten or cooked with butter.'

'The best virgin oil,' I told him, 'used to be massaged into Olympic athlete's bodies before a race. Then when they had all successfully done their activity they would return to the changing room all glistening and sweaty, where attendants would scrape wooden blades over their bodies and collect back the oil and bottle it. It would later be sold as a magical potion to give strength and potency to lesser mortals. Young maidens, for example, would rub it into their breasts to keep them forever firm. Young men would rub it into—'

'Yes yes, I can imagine,' cried Lautour, 'their briefcases.'

He paused to draw on his drink; his eyes closing with unashamed pleasure as the rich, warm, velvety liquid spread itself out along his well-honed palette. I did the same and felt myself very nearly purring. Actually I used to have a slight superstition about drinking with a client at the beginning of a job. Too much *bonhomie* as we set out can easily get tainted as the project progresses and a discord creeps in about something or other. It may be as simple as a stone mason or plumber that didn't turn up on time, or more gravely the damaged underground water pipe that leaked and tried to find its way out through the dining room floor, or worse still, the horror of horrors, a dispute about money.

It is much easier to have a fight – or should that be a dialogue? – with your client if you haven't set up any fragile walls of friendship. As soon as you have socialised, become privy to any intimacies or shared stories of dysfunctional grannies, the cards are harder to play.

Here I was slugging back some serious grape juice with a smooth operator that I knew little about. He was professionally interested, hugely engaging and well, heck, for the moment I was happy to surrender to his charisma.

Sitting with my back to the door I was only just aware that someone else had come into the room.

'Ah *minou*, come in and meet Mr Dingwall-Main,' Lautour spoke in English. I started to get up when a soft voice told me 'not to move' which was probably just as well.

'Hello,' she said offering to shake my hand.

She was tall and thin like her father and wore a black crêpe wraparound dress, ruched at one hip, with long sleeves and a deep, plunging neckline.

'This is Danielle, my younger daughter,' said Lautour with understandable pride.

'*Mademoiselle, enchanté*,' I offered.

Her long auburn hair splashed over her bare shoulders, framing an extremely fine and delicate young face from which shone dark chocolate eyes.

'Your father and I were just talking about gardens and drinking brandy, but not necessarily in that order.'

She laughed lightly, her face unconditionally friendly, and said something about not wanting to disturb us, wouldn't be a moment but had to ask her Papa something or other about goodness knows what.

A small conference took place, out of hearing, in which the two of them seemed quite in accord, and was concluded with a parental hug. She turned from him and, heading for the door, said goodnight to me with a minimum of fuss and a great deal of charm.

'What a pleasure,' I said to Lautour after she had gone, leaving a vapour of Balmain misting around the room.

'She wants to take the Bentley to go and meet Francisco, her boyfriend. He's coming down from Paris by train,' he said with a resignation that I took to mean he was an accomplice to her ploy. 'I remember asking my father when I was her age if I could borrow his Hispano Suiza. I wanted to take a beautiful actress out to a club but he said emphatically no, and how I battled with my love for him in that moment of denial.' He looked wistful.

'So she has the Bentley,' I said.

'She has the Bentley,' he confirmed. And for a moment my mind swam in the viscous oils of autoeroticism.

'Now then,' said the great man, 'let's put these glasses to some use.'

Despite my protestations – about as loud as a moth sneeze – he poured me another brandy and asked if I'd like a cigar.

'No thanks, I haven't smoked for twenty years.'

Another quick call on the mobile phone brought Rottcodd rushing in at a centimetre an hour. He clutched a humidor veneered in Tibetan maple with highlights of delicate marquetry.

Lautour took a cigar from the box and offered again.

'Cuban?'

'Scottish,' I said.

He looked at me sympathetically while he snipped off the end and, squeezing it appreciatively under his nose, he seemed about to say something but changed his mind. Then:

'Where will you find this ancient olive?' he asked, bringing the meeting back on to its axis.

'I don't know yet,' I said, 'but if you are commissioning me I'll start checking it out for you.'

'Make me a proposal and if I can afford you we'll get hunting,' he smiled vaguely, 'but I think you need to consider the rest of the courtyard as well. How we plan on showing off this great-great-great-grand olive. He needs to be planted with much dignity and care. We will have to remove a section of the wall to get him in, and lighting, we'll need to light him beautifully, and watering, will he need a lot of irrigation?'

He waved the decanter around as a tool of expression.

As I drove home thinking about Lautour and his family, their place in the order of things, their kindness and hospitality, I couldn't help wondering if there wasn't a tough egg under his genial exterior. He had made me feel wonderfully comfortable and welcome, had mastered another language well enough to share a sense of humour and had been very focused in what he liked and what he didn't.

But nobody with a lot of money is really *nice*. If you have made it yourself you know how to tread on people without remorse, if you have managed to hang on to some inheritance, then you have cracked how to sack a trustee. Perhaps the successful artist, composer, actor, singer or writer might feign a distance from the earthly reality of money dealing, but for sure they will have appointed a Rottweiler accountant-manager to look after their earnings.

Many years ago in one gardening life, Roger Waters, who at that time was the lead singer and bass player for the immensely successful Pink Floyd, backed my company. Early in our relationship he had described himself to me as a cosmic fascist and I had scratched my head on that one for a while. Waters & Co. had recently written and recorded *The Wall* and was experiencing, for the Floyd, the unlikely pleasure of a Number 1 hit. One day we drove around the outskirts of London in a super-car that had been given to him by BMW, with *'we don't need no educashun'* blaring from the in-car speakers. The great man was singing along in tune which I thought was pretty cool. (Elvis singing 'Heartbreak Hotel' in a pink Caddy would have been tops.)

Waters rang me one evening to say that somebody within their accountancy set-up had badly mismanaged their funds. Waters said that if he left quickly before the end of his tax year, which was imminent, they would at least save on payments to the Inland Revenue and recoup a bit of the loss, as it were. His wife, the kids and cars had already left for the South of France and he was off tomorrow. They would continue recording their next album down there and then move on to LA. He assured me that his management team would look after things.

At that time you could save tax by being in the South of France. Hardly creditable nowadays but you just need to remember Bill Wyman singing the frontier folding *'Je suis un rock-star'*, a somewhat lacking satirical song about being a rock 'n' roller in tax exile that rather challenged his credibility as a Rolling Stone.

After the Floyd had departed for their tax-helpful haven I was left to deal with a grim bunch of suits that wanted everything in little boxes including my secretary. With the company's best interest at heart she did her utmost to keep the books balanced with at least two of them.

But it was these grey men that kept the Floyd coffers in the pink. Tough and rational, disciplined and savvy, they would arrange short-term loans of enormous amounts of money at dizzy levels of interest, back small enterprises and drop them unceremoniously if they didn't return a profit immediately. Being around the band was great, being around the accountants wasn't.

Six and three-quarter litres of turbo-powered Bentley Arnage 'T' characteristically purred its way casually through the encroaching night and on to the tarmac at the recently opened Avignon TGV station. The streetlights mirrored off the metallic midnight blue paintwork as the big motorcar searched out an isolated parking bay. The newly completed high-speed rail extension meant that the famous French express train had now extended its run from Paris to Lyon and on to Marseille, cutting the journey from the capital down to well under three hours.

Danielle Lautour parked the car about thirty metres from its nearest neighbour and turned off the engine but left the ignition on. She wanted the sidelights and electrics working. She got out of the driver's side and let herself into the back of the limousine. She slipped discs into the two players and adjusted the surround sound. A compilation of love-stuff burnt on to a CD from an Internet download was on one and a DVD film on the other. The small flat screens that were let into the rear of the seat headrests blushed at the content. It was a movie that she had seen at a friend's house one evening and had thought pretty grown-up. It hadn't been difficult to borrow. He will like this she had thought. She checked the coldness of the white wine chilling in the mini fridge, unfolded the big fake-fox fur that was kept on the parcel shelf and laid it over the leather upholstery of the back seat. She dimmed the lights, peeled off her dress and tucked her naked body up in the rug. Then she dialled the number of her boyfriend's mobile.

Francisco had answered quickly. 'About ten minutes to go,' he had said, 'and I'll be in your arms.'

'You'll be in more than my arms,' whispered Danielle. 'I'm in Row L down at the far end away from the other cars. I've left the side lights on.'

Shwoosh went the speeding train.

As Francisco hurried towards the Bentley, the area was suddenly flooded in a harsh white light that seemed to stream from a thousand points. 'Stop exactly where you are and don't move,' the order was shouted through an electric megaphone and came from a man in a black uniform with a peaked cap standing in front of a small tank. Behind him a platoon of similarly dressed officials were holding machine guns pointing at the young man. Another officer emerged from the shadows and walked quickly towards the big car, snatched open the door and pulled out the screaming girl. Desperately trying to keep the rug around her she was kicked and pushed over to the waiting guards. Next a shattering crack exploded from the tank and the Bentley was blown to smithereens.

I awoke with a jolt. It took me several disjointed minutes to grasp that I had been nightmaring. I lay awake for a while, deeply grateful that the Bentley was in one piece.

The day after being with Lautour I made notes of the client meeting. Notes about what had been said and agreed upon, what he did and didn't want. (No purple grass had been a disappointment.) Notes were made about whom to contact by phone and letter, by fax and email, any of which might lead onwards and outwards. I got on to the Internet and scratched around olive-oil makers, tree growers and suppliers. I searched out books on the subject of old trees generally and olives specifically, and looked to see if anybody out there had any leads that would help me find the oldest olive tree in the world, or at least in Europe.

I also had to make a proposal to Lautour about how I would structure my fees for this unusual quest.

'I have your proposal in front of me, Alex. I am presuming it includes the tree itself?'

' 'fraid not guv'nor, just my fees.'

'But even with a nought knocked off I would consider it too much,' said Lautour evenly.

That old chestnut, I thought. I've met it many times before and bat it with my eyes closed. I had detailed my quote assiduously and precisely, I had clearly indicated how the fee was structured and had underlined the fact that the cost of the tree, its transport and planting was not, could not be included.

'If you want the best ...' I started, but Lautour cut in.

'If I accept your quote I want shares in your company. How much is this golden tree going to cost?' We were getting closer.

'Can't tell you that until I find it, then there is the transport, don't forget.'

'Where in the name of Pan will this thing come from?'

'Unlikely to be France, maybe Spain or possibly Italy. Could be Greece or the Middle East but I'd want big danger money for that one.'

A short silence then, 'OK. Go and find it.'

I smiled to myself.

'Actually I thought you would ask for more,' said Lautour as a parting shot.

I was delighted to be commissioned. It was a different kind of a project, full of promise and one that involved finding arguably the most majestic of all trees. What other plant was instantly recognisable as an international symbol of peace and hope?

CHAPTER TWO

Olive Trees and Sons

In war, whichever side may call itself the victor, there are
no winners, but all are losers.

Neville Chamberlain

A few days later, I received a letter from Regis Lautour confirming his
acceptance of my offer and wishing me good luck with the search. 'But,'
he had written, 'I do not want to be responsible for you digging up any
old trees in the Middle East. Strongly recommend you read the enclosed
and stay clear of the area, they are wielding a bitter axe.'

The clipping read:

Israelis chop down Palestinians' precious olive trees, insisting it's retaliation for rocks being hurled at settlers.

Hares, Israel – 28 November: The Palestinian villagers heard the
power saws at midnight, racketing up the stony terraces to the hill-
perched village of Hares. It is where Joshua, the Hebrew conqueror
of Canaan in the Old Testament, is buried in ancient Samaria, on

the modern West Bank, the 'Timnath Heres' of Joshua 24:30.

When Ali Abed Daoud Jaber, 76, awoke the next morning, he found he was ruined. More than 400 olive trees were cut down by the Israeli army along the highway leading to three Jewish settlements. At least 110 were his. His entire olive orchard lay felled on the stone-strewn ground.

'Where is God?' the old man screamed, gesturing with his cane as villagers tried to calm him. 'They cut down trees my grandfather tended! Trees hundreds of years old! I depend on my trees completely ... What will I eat now? What will I drink?'

'He is become without a brain since he saw this,' said Nasfat Khufash, who belongs to a rural development committee in the vicinity. 'He was sitting in the middle of the road, crying, this morning.'

The twisted trunks of the massacred trees rose as branchless spikes from the loamy brown earth. Lopped olive branches lay in heaps, their feathery silver-green leaves rustling in the breeze, beneath a sky as blue as a gas flame.

The destroyed trees lent an air of Old Testament wrath to the struggle between Israelis and Palestinians. Even olive trees have become targets in the cycle of provocation and reprisal. More than five thousand olive trees had been cut down according to figures kept by the Palestinian National Authority's Ministry of Environmental Affairs.

Hares is in the West Bank, which was captured by Israel in the 1967 Middle East war. Israel has established more than 150 Jewish settlements in the occupied territory.

The village has been roadblocked by the Israeli army, preventing people from taking olives to market or to oil presses outside the village, Khufash said. Losses from destroyed, rotted or unpicked crops in Palestinian areas amount to $120 million this year, according to the Palestinian Economic Council for Development and Reconstruction.

Jewish settlers driving past the felled trees yelled insults at foreign reporters. 'What are you doing here, you rubbish?' one shouted.

'Take pictures! Take pictures!' called another, sarcastically.

Interviewed later, the settlers complained angrily that Hares village children were throwing stones at their cars as they passed by, using the olive groves for cover. One settler showed a deep dent on his van just above the windshield. Another came over, cursing, and tried to kick in the car window of the reporters' vehicle, just for talking to the aggrieved Palestinians.

But the villagers were angry, too. They said the army's response was a devastating blow, out of proportion to the situation and punishing adults for the actions of children.

They took reporters to a site 100 yards from the highway, where 20 trees had been cut down, seemingly too far from the road to serve any security purpose.

An olive tree in these parts is like an interest-bearing bank account, yielding up to 35 pounds of fruit year after year. Olive harvesting is a time-honored family ritual. The velvety-purple fruit is knocked off branches with sticks, or plucked from ladders onto underlying tarpaulins by stroking each leafy branch gently.

One farmer, Abdullah Hamed Suleiman, 62, who lost seventy trees to Israeli chain saws lately, said the destroyed trees represented $4,000 a year in income, from the olive oil he sells to Jordan.

'For us Palestinians, an olive tree is exactly like a son,' Khufash said.

'It is not a matter of money. You do not sell your son for money.'

Distraught at their loss — the villagers said more than 1,000 olive trees had been cut down in recent months — the settlers invited reporters, over coffee and orange sodas, to hear them spin theories about the olive tree massacre and vent their wrath against the Israeli settlers who live in neat, barracks-like apartments on hilltops throughout the region. Three settlements, Ariel, Revava and Burkan, are near Hares, and settlers must pass beneath the village on their way to and from work.

'The olive trees gave us food. Now they are only fit for the fire,' said Nawaf Suf.

'We believe they want to deprive us of our livelihood, drive us off the land and make common laborers of us, so we have to go to the cities and work for Israelis.'

When old Jaber escorted reporters to his ruined grove, he collapsed in a pile of lopped branches and moaned. At precisely this moment, Yona Shay, a 31-year-old Jewish settler who sells plumbing fixtures for a living, pulled over beside the road and began arguing with the Palestinians. The odds — eight of them, just one of him — didn't seem to faze him.

'There are a minimum of 100 stones being thrown every day from beside this highway. By now 200 cars have been hit with stones,' Shay said. 'Men, women and children have been injured by these stones ... I didn't cut down any trees myself, but I would have if I could have.'

The old man clambered across the ditch and went chin-to-chin with Shay.

'It is as if you cut my throat!' he shouted.

'If someone gives you a punch, do you turn the other cheek?' Shay answered calmly. 'If we get hurt, we have damage, we have to do something back.'

In the nearby settlement of Revava, a 38-year-old computer repairman named Yitzhak Hillel defended the army's destruction of the olive trees.

'We spoke to the army many times about the stone-throwing, and they did nothing. My feeling is, every time I come back home from work, I feel like a duck in a shooting gallery.'

An hour before sunset, the rock-throwing resumed. The minarets of Palestinian villages glimmered white at the summits of the brown hills, which rolled into a wide wasteland of rocks, tufted here and there with olive groves.

Two squads of Israeli soldiers took up positions along the highway and began firing sporadically as rocks landed on the road. Just past the stretch of lopped trees, a large white stone bounced defiantly off the asphalt a few yards in front of the reporters' car.

CHAPTER THREE

France

> I am struggling to capture the light of the olive. It is silver
> — sometimes more blue, sometimes greenish, bronze, off
> white, on a ground of yellow, pink, violet or orange to red
> ochre. But it is very difficult. Very difficult.
>
> *Vincent Van Gogh*

I rang Latour to thank him for his letter and the article and assured him
I would be staying well clear of the Middle East. I had no intention in
getting caught up in the tightly strung antics of an Arab-Israeli olive war.

I would start the quest on the home shores although I knew it was
unlikely I would find what I wanted in France. The weather in the South
had not been historically kind enough to allow for the survival of any
really ancient specimens, and I certainly hadn't heard of anybody locally
trading in very old indigenous trees. That's why there is big business
importing from Spain and, to a lesser extent, Italy.

Very often when people buy second homes down here they do so knowing
that it is unlikely to have much in the way of a garden. Unless of course
they buy something that has been highly developed and is ready for
immediate occupation. The problem there is that it may have been

misguidedly designed or decorated. The new owner will therefore want to rip it all out and start again. As you are quite likely to have paid enough for the smallholding to support the vendor, his entire family, plus their in-laws for several generations to come, the thought of then pulling a perfectly functional house and/or garden apart might make your eyes water a bit.

Plots of land bought for building on are another way forward. That allows for the construction of something probably a little plain but undeniably practical. It will have things like roofs that don't leak, floors that don't absorb water like sponges and septic tanks that don't back up. There is a lot to be said for a new house. But not a word about its garden. That will have to be part of the extras. Seldom does a developer or a quick-sale merchant waste any money on the garden. A little tarting up around the immediate house perhaps; after that it's bury the rubble and rubbish, bung down some top soil and let the weeds do the rest.

As it happens our house is old. Built about three hundred years ago, it was bought without a survey and is still standing proud. Think of the hullabaloo that goes on in most places when you want to buy any building, let alone a really old one. Irrespective of whether you need a mortgage or not, you are advised to call in a surveyor to see if the structure of your dreams is sound. He then comes back to you with a shaking head, draws in his breath and hands over an estimate that lists a thousand dreadful problems that will cost more than a million gallons of rocket fuel to put right. And that is only if you can find the inordinately specialised craftsmen required to carry out the restoration. Down here it's a bit easier. If it's stood for three hundred years it will probably go on for another three hundred. No need to get depressed with surveys, no need to shore up walls or dig in complicated new land drains. So what if a little water comes in via the meeting of two walls put up with a somewhat inexperienced hand in 1783? You live a happier life if you accept these little niggles and stop worrying what the neighbours might think if your bathroom walls have a damp patch. It doesn't matter because they have one too. But a new house is something else. It isn't allowed to leak, groan or sweat, and if it does develop a little weakness it must be very irritating and embarrassing. Better cover it up quick.

I met a new house once upon a garden that belonged to a client who had become a tax exile on the Isle of Man. A decent chap who had made his money out of being an accountant to the entertainment industry. He had probably saved a stand-up comic or two from telling jokes in court and found a loophole to push a few football managers through. He was wised up to the benefits of offshore banking and the gains to be had in tax havens. Naturally enough, wanted to have a house on the three-legged island. Trouble was, buying a beautiful old house on the Isle of Man is not easy. Nigel Mansell had snapped up the last one so that he could race caddy-cars round his private golf course.

So our good client, not one to be put off, bought some prime land and built a beautiful, faithfully reproduced Georgian manor. It was an immaculate *doppelgänger* for anything you might find of the period in England. But better. Because the services worked so brilliantly. The heating bills, for example, were a thin slice of the real thing because of ingenious insulation and underfloor heating. It was probably behind the walls too, I dare say, and it all went towards keeping him and his family very comfortable.

His singularity was incredible and his fastidious attention to detail knew no bounds. Having once sent off a series of working drawings, he sent them back, corrected. That is to say he had circled little bits that he figured were out by a millimetre or two. Having checked them closer than a VAT man with a return from a bookie, he felt duty bound to draw my attention to the howlers of miscalculation.

'The hedge is 3.7 centimetres further away from the house on the east side than it is on the west, according to your drawing.'

I would tell him that one of the joys of designing a garden was that there was room for small adjustments, mini realignments and improvisations. It is in the nature of the game. We are not, generally speaking, building precision-fitted kitchen cupboards and it really doesn't matter if two shrubs are planted 40 or 41 centimetres apart. In the end we asked him to mark our drawings out of ten before returning them.

There are some very well-built repro-houses down here. Clever architects aping the rickety rustic farm buildings. No Corinthian columns needed, no Doric crowns or Ionic porticoes required to over-decorate a simple structure. We have a wealthy retired couple building a pretty impressive bit of largesse just up the road from us. It has weaselled its way through planning permission by pretending to be two houses. The fact that they are built as close together as Siamese twins is seemingly irrelevant. The huge cranes tower against the skyline as this prosperous professional's home takes shape. Proud to be new.

Once a house is finished, maybe even before, people begin to turn their attention to the garden, or the grounds. Very often sizeable tracts of land are included in the purchase package and while the initial idea seems rather wonderful, all that space that can't be built on, all those rolling hectares of blessed countryside, can turn into a bit of a trial. The kings and queens of their own estates rejoice in the 'Land is Good' philosophy until the sobering reality sets in.

'Let's have lavender fields, cherry orchards, and of course olive groves' is the collective mantra. If you want to have an acre of lavender, because the idea of all that incredible colour in July and taking it to the local distillery to have your own lavender oil is so tempting, and so very Provence, you need to spare a moment to think about the somebody that has to cut it before 15 August if they are going to catch the distilling process.

The rows need to be two metres apart to allow the tractor to pull its cutting machine down the line and this gives plenty of space for *les mauvaise herbes* to take hold. Besides who's going to do the weeding and cutting anyway? It is difficult to persuade a local farmer that it is worth his while to keep the field looking like a postcard.

As far as he is concerned he only needs to carry out a minimum of maintenance and that is mostly restricted to in between the lavender plants themselves. Big thistles are not a good thing to take to the distillery. But the space between the rows can weed on. There is not much money in this crop so the less work the better to help stretch the meagre profits.

But this is seldom a money thing for the lucky new lavender growers themselves. They will probably find the cost to be less than sending a few bunches of flowers to friends via the Internet.

The point is you can't just march in and blind the local farmers who may be prepared to contract the harvest from you, with silly wages. You must adhere to the local market forces, and they, sadly, are pretty unimpressive.

A client who has a house high up in the hills wanted the fields that they owned on the approach to their house to be laid to lavender. Between us we found a local farmer who agreed to plant and harvest the crop for them. A certain amount of legalities ensued, needless to say. Things like who would buy the plants, would the land be sub-let or was it a once-a-year contract deal? As the clients wanted the fields to look tickety-boo at all times, no weeds allowed, maintenance was clearly going to go way beyond the farmer's basic necessities of maintaining a crop. In the end an agreement was struck, and the clients settled back to await their picture book landscape. First year got off to an inauspicious start. The proprietors arrived down in the summer quivering with anticipation. She had some scented pillows in mind. He thought he might try a watercolour.

As they turned in through the discreet hole in the hedgerow that is their driveway entrance, dismay descended upon them like a bad bank statement. The field was a fizzing conglomerate of feisty thistles, dock and what is locally known as 'mauve', a weed with a 3,000-metre root. It wasn't long before yours truly got a call. A short but friendly exchange about the niceties of life ensued.

'How's the little boy?' she asked kindly.

'Oh he's great, thank you. Growing bigger and stronger by the minute, he's—'

When someone asks about your children it's difficult to resist pouring out paragraphs by the pound. Like the Bob Hope gag: 'I asked him how he was and he told me for half an hour.' Well, I was well on the road to Mandalay when she said,

'Just like the weeds.'

'Sorry?' I said. 'What weeds?'

'The weeds in our lavender field,' she said with a curt tinge to her voice. '*They* are growing bigger and stronger by the minute.'

I was quiet for a moment trying to remember if I had said I would keep in touch with the farmer or not. Maybe I had said I would weed the fields myself. One says things like that when you have spent an evening with Swedish folk. I don't know if it's something to do with the long hours of darkness in the winter or the celebration of eternal light in the summer. It might be something to do with their draconian licensing laws, but I have yet to meet a Swede that couldn't drink a Scotsman under the table. Mind you, having finally slipped gracefully beneath the IKEA the Scotsman can usually sing his National Anthem with such aplomb that it leaves the Swede on the starting line.

'Ah,' I said. 'I spoke to the farmer about that and he tells me there is nothing he can do about it for at least a year. Each of the little plants, about the size of a small collection of pipe cleaners, need to establish a root system before the farmer can either pull his big hoe down the lines or spray with any kind of selected weed killer, politically correct or otherwise. So patience is the game.'

'But why doesn't he weed between the rows?'

I tried again to explain the temporary unsolvable problem but it was falling on stony ground.

It has taken several seasons but now the fields look pretty much like what everybody had in mind, and the maintenance paid to the farmers is just another overhead to be taken into account.

The riddles of contract farming apply to fruit trees as well. There is so little profit that a really satisfactory maintenance programme is out of the question unless subsidised by your own pocket. The only really good thing to go for is carrot. They grow quickly, green up during the winter, can be harvested profitably and before you can say 'cake', another crop is popping its head up all over the place. They even harvest them in the rain, for goodness sake.

But all these are second-row extras and of little importance compared to the main attraction, the star of the show, the Olive Tree.

'Can't live in Provence and not have a few olive trees. And let's get them old so they look as if they have always been there.' So say most of us.

The net result is a stonking great business trading in old olive trees. Old in this case being anything from one hundred up to six hundred years old. There is a local builder who runs his own company, pretty successfully from all accounts, but he has a second string to his bow. He imports olive trees from Spain. He has stumbled on the fact that, for a few pesetas, he can buy an old tree from an equally old farmer who's glad to unload a plant past its fruit-producing prime. He then ships it up to Provence.

Adding on a caterpillar of noughts to the cost, he sells it to the seemingly endless brigade of rich foreigners who have acquired properties locally. They buy them and plant them and move them and, sooner or later, probably kill them and then buy some more. It's money for nothing, trees for free, you pick a few olives and buy a TV.

The sharp middlemen make a mint, the farmers get a winning hand from a dud pack and the ladies have their garden fashion accessory that they wouldn't dare be seen without. It's an all-win ticket. It's also hard to imagine how much more in vogue these trees can become. Maybe there will be a backlash.

Once the hundred thousand dollar tree has broken through, people will realise how inordinately stupid it has all become and back off. The olive tree will be dropped from the agenda. Too vulgar. It will just have to wait another thousand years before it comes back into fashion. But right now it has moved from being a symbol of peace and source of income to the hard-working *paysan* to a kind of exotic pet tethered out in the hackneyed pastures of pleasantsville. What will replace it in the affections of the gold-plated fun-seekers? What affectation will nudge its way into the arena to take up the slack for a few years? An instant eighty-year-old vineyard transplanted from Bordeaux? Ready-grown lavender fields sold by the square metre? Or perhaps we might settle on plane trees? So Frenchly symbolic, reminders of the long alleys of French roads and the stars of Jean-Luc Godard's *Weekend*. The sprawling arms of the pollarded branches that stretch protectively out above our heads giving dappled shade from the intemperate summer sun. As a must-have these elegant trees are already much in demand, and even more so as pairs. Really good ones come so well matched they could be twins. They will take up their sartorial position some five metres from the swimming pool offering plenty of shade for swimmers. Trouble is, decent-sized, good-looking couples are already weighing in at a knuckle-numbing, bum-tightening £15,000–£20,000 and they aren't even disease-free, quick-growing evergreens.

If the new property hasn't got any old planes or olives then you had better buck up and get some quick.

Early autumn and late spring sees many a lorry loaded up with big trees, particularly olives, being transplanted around the place. Being carted from here to there. Usually standing up in the back of a lorry, they take this upheaval with good grace, minimal grumbling and virtually no depression. The stress of being lifted out of the ground, especially when you are getting elderly, is very traumatic for most trees, but the plane seems to suffer it graciously. Providing he is well watered he will usually just get on with life and keep everybody happy. The olive is something of a hermit at heart and will uproot and set off with only the smallest amount of encouragement. Providing of course it isn't freezing cold, cooking hot or too wet where it is planted.

Not long ago I had a phone call from an acquaintance who lived quite near to Avignon. She informed me rather breathlessly that she had had some kind of disaster with her new olive tree. While she didn't think I would be able to help as such, she said she would feel better if I could just pop over and see her and her tree. Reassure her or something. She didn't really know but she needed her hand holding.

'What's happened?' I asked.

'Well, my dear, it really would be much easier if you would just come over and see for yourself. I find it a bit difficult to explain without sounding stupid, you see.'

I was meant to be having a test drive that afternoon in the new Mini-Cooper. I thought it might be fun for Mrs D-M to have a zippy little car for local runs. I also thought it might be even more fun for me to have a zippy little car for local runs. I rang BMW in Avignon and explained that I had to see somebody nearby and would they be happy if we combined the test drive with the visit to the olive problem. Mr Dabord, the sales director in charge of promoting and selling the Mini, clearly enjoyed zipping about on local runs too because he was happy to come to the house and pick me up, take me to see the distressed olive lady, and then return me to base. A round trip of about a 160 kilometres.

On the dot of the appointed time Mr Dabord drifted the wee car on to the gravel outside the house and with a handbrake turn parked the thing three and a half centimetres from my big toe. He emerged from the little packet looking like a man who was used to picking up the Paddy Hopkirk award for advanced driving. He moved his head with a firmness that suggested a confident chicken and that the sale was a mere formality, the car was already mine.

I called up the family including the dog. If this diminutive buzz box was going to join the clan it couldn't be a unilateral decision, everybody had to vote. The kid was first in, wearing a huge pair of shoes that meant he tripped over the ledge getting in, bashed the steering wheel and arrived on the back seat upside down. Mutt hopped in and hopped straight out again. She couldn't bend herself into the form of the bucket-shaped rear seats. Paws down from her.

Mrs D-M declared that she thought it very cute but couldn't really see the weekly shopping, a small boy and a fractious, overweight old dog all fitting in.

I looked at the engine and boggled at how that diminutive BMC wonder-toy of forty years ago had somehow managed a metamorphosis into this slick little piece of action-packed machinery. Mr Dabord was charmingly refusing to hear Nicky's hesitations or doubts about its practicality, blindly ploughing on about how well it would suit her and how attractive she and the mini looked together.

'OK,' I said 'we had better go for our test drive.'

I climbed into the cockpit. But being about two sizes too large for it I was squatting in there with the side of my face pressed up against the lining of the roof when the kind Mr Dabord from BMW adjusted the seat in every direction. I then found myself virtually lying down in a sort of optimistic lover's position ready to go. A perfunctory goodbye was delivered to the family and I propelled us out of there like a bar of soap squeezed from a wet pair of hands. As we skimmed along the lanes with the CD pumping a compilation of early-sixties love songs I warped through the last four decades of my life as they passed in front of my eyes at double speed. 'Poetry in Motion,' sang Johnny Tillotson, 'I love every movement/There's nothing I would change/She doesn't need improvement/She's much too nice to rearrange.' It was a clever tack; I half expected to be passed a joint.

After thirty minutes of high-entertainment driving we arrived at the garden of my distressed acquaintance and found her waiting despondently.

'What's happened?' I asked again.

'It's the new olive tree,' she said, 'it's fallen into the swimming pool.' She began to walk off in the direction of the pool, with me and an intrigued Mr Dabord following.

We rounded the corner of the house and sure enough there was a sizeable olive tree three-quarters submerged in the very muddy deep end.

Its small leaves looked bedraggled and helpless.

'What happened?' I asked again. My vocabulary seemed to have shrunk.

'Well I bought this big, elderly olive tree thinking it would look well beside the pool and had it delivered yesterday. I had arranged for a tractor driver to come and dig the hole for it to go into but he didn't turn up. I couldn't stop the delivery, so when the lorry arrived the driver wasn't the tiniest bit interested in taking it back. He just dumped it as near to the planting spot as he could. He had a sort of crane thing attached to the lorry you know.' I was beginning to see what had happened.

'Anyway he pushed off at double quick time leaving the thing at a precarious angle right on the edge of the pool. I did say to him that I didn't think it looked very safe.' She sighed deeply, and shaking her wearisome head went on, 'As you know there was a terrible wind last night, and it must have blown it over, knocked it off balance or something.' It was true the Mistral had been in a foul mood. 'And when I looked out of my bedroom window this morning the poor tree had fallen into the pool.'

We stood there gawping at the wretched mess for a while. This was a new one for me. I had seen dogs drowned in pools, I had seen Rolls-Royces parked in them by rock stars, I had even seen one used for dipping sheep, but I had never seen a mature tree, olive or otherwise, hanging out in two metres of water. I suggested we get hold of another digger driver without delay. A good strong belt and a working hydraulic should be able to extract the half-drowned tree from its watery bed. I was uncertain as to what damage the tree might have suffered being in chemically treated water. Not being an expert in this area I thought we should find out immediately. We didn't want the poor thing to die from a chlorine or salt attack. This little bit of motivation was all that was needed because the good lady started off to find some telephone numbers.

I told her not to bother, that I knew a very reliable chap and would ring him there and then.

A lot of time is taken up with these small expeditions and are usually not chargeable. But it is part of the job and by being helpful to friends and acquaintances does the word of goodwill travel. Anyway I am a soft touch for elderly ladies in need.

Back in the Mini the patient and bemused Mr Dabord drove hard and I was soon home. He gave me a cheerful wave and said he would fax me a proposal the next day. That night I dreamt I turned into a mini mulberry tree. A sort of bonsai-ed BMW with leaves.

Suspecting that the oldest olive trees would be foreigners, I thought it would probably be wise to chase back through some of the local suppliers that had introduced these trees from abroad. It didn't seem like a good plan to pursue some historical tree that had come up from the south of goodness knows where only to find that it was the wrong variety and wouldn't cut the mustard with the Mistral, that over-excited wind that evacuates itself from up north via the Bouche de Rhone and accelerates out and down across the plains of the Vaucluse. It snorts harder than a racehorse and blows stronger than Dizzy Gillespie.

France only really has olive trees in the south where the climate allows them to grow and fruit in reasonable calm. However, the winters that occasionally attack inland Provence can completely devastate the crop, even knocking out the trees, and farmers are wary of investing too heavily in the olive because of this. The net result is that the South of France lags far behind the other Mediterranean countries in productivity of both oil and edible olives. It also means that finding a special tree to buy is more difficult.

Laurent Croz is a young and successful *pépinièrist* who, when he isn't dealing in mature trees, likes to compete in international four-by-four rallies. The day after our conversation he was off to Tunisia to grind some sand into his differentials.

His nursery is spread out over several hectares in various locations around Avignon. He has a fine selection of old trees: *Quercus ilex* (evergreen oaks) a difficult tree to move when mature, *Celtis* (micocoulier), *Platanus* (plane), *Tilia* (limes), various cypresses and of course *Olea* (olives) in a multitude of sizes. Some of the big planes can cost upwards of ten thousand pounds and weigh forty tonnes or more. He has a clever second string to his bow which is the planting of these trees. If you buy from him, why not take advantage of his guarantee which is only available if he does the planting and this of course is extra. He has the equipment and so one joins the ranks of his captured clientele.

He has supplied me with some excellent trees over the years and I have always been impressed by his professional approach.

I explained to Laurent what the game was, about the client, and asked him what he thought about finding me the oldest tree in captivity. He had several old boys around the shop either potted up in huge wooden containers or resting temporarily in great pits dug into the ground. Fine trees certainly, and impressive on an ordinary day but not as old as I wanted.

'There's a very, very old tree in Vaison-la-Romaine,' he said, talking more to himself than to me.

'How very, very old?' I asked hopefully.

'Don't know, but everybody agrees that it's ancient. I could find out exactly where it is and you could go and see it,' he offered.

'Can you take a long shot and guess how old?'

'It's very difficult to age an olive. It's like it is with ladies; lots of guessing goes on I warn you.'

I nodded understandingly and he went on, 'You can't tell their age by size. Even if you cut it down and count the rings, it plays tricks like: it doesn't have rings to count. Or at least it doesn't after a certain age. The width of their trunk is no indication. Trees grow at different rates depending on their situation. For example, in the valley they grow faster than up on arid, exposed slopes.'

'Do you think it might be for sale?'

'Doubt it, but you can always ask.'

'Well, I'll go and look at it and see. But the bottom line for me at this stage is to try and establish if you think it might have, say, a thousand years under its bark.' I was pushing him and while I didn't want him to feel cornered I had to try and gain more information. I wasn't going to win if I reported back to Lautour that I had found a tree of only, and I use the word advisedly, four hundred years old. It's not that we don't think four hundred is old for goodness sake, but we are age-greedy with this quest. We are aiming high and at this point we want four figures.

'I think it is unlikely,' said Croz, 'most *parcelles* of land of any age in Provence are listed or catalogued at the Mairie of their *commune*. I learn a lot about the trees from the owner who sells his land.'

He went on to tell me how the records might typically show that 'They were planted by his great, great grandfather, or that the olive grove was sold by his grandmother's great-aunt after her stepfather-in-law's great, great uncle had been bequeathed it by his sister's husband's half-brother after he lost everything on a game of boule.'

Nowadays it is considered important information. The more the legend the higher the price. Whether these olive trees gain branches of questionable history or come through as the genuine article is open to conjecture. But these days with people investing up to, and beyond, five thousand pounds a tree for something that lays claim to a few hundred years of history, they want to know something about its past. Any records, stories or ledgers are considered a bonus and make writing out the cheque a little easier.

A bit like the cost of an old Mercedes 300SLR being inflated because it is recorded that Stirling Moss drove it to victory in the 1955 Mille Miglia. Good for another 50,000 Euros on the asking price. Those of us who remember the race when we were just wee chaps in short trousers would sell our bodies to be able to buy an original one of those cars. Not that that would raise more than a wheel nut in my case. But you know what I mean. Moss beat Fangio over the thousand-mile route by 32 minutes, by the way.

I was telling Theo, my five year old, about how Michael Schumacher had equalled Fangio's world championship record when he said irrelevantly that 'Lucozade Lady' was the 3–1 on favourite at Lingfield. It's a bone this one. Not a big one but a bone nonetheless. I come from a long line of petrol heads and do my best to keep the side up, then along comes Theo who thinks cars are 'silly things' and that horses are where it's at. Some kind of generic throwback. I've done my best with horsepower explanations, even brake-horsepower, but it's no good. He just wants to ride beautiful horses. To canter into the mists of immortality, or to gallop out towards the planes of Equus. Such a worry.

'How close do you think anybody can get to dating a living tree?' I asked him, persistently.

I was ready for Laurent to call the interview off at any moment, but instead with an unexpected chuckle he said, 'I don't know, I've never asked one out.'

There was a small pause as we shared the joke. Then he said, 'Oh I suppose I can be pretty exact, give or take fifty years, but like I said it is very difficult.'

Fifty years either way you see is actually pretty near the bull's eye in olive-speak. It is not as if there are some teeth to look at. And with their lack of rings it is pretty hopeless in that respect, like willows, poplars and fruit trees.

'What's the oldest you've ever traded?' I felt like Parkinson talking to Joan Rivers.

'About five hundred years. I have some here,' he said, pointing to a set of three beautiful trees outside his office. Big, bold, spreading examples which he said he loved far too much to sell.

'How much would you not sell those for?' I asked.

'I wouldn't hear a word you said under sixty thousand each and that doesn't include transport.' He was still talking francs.

Transport is a big problem. There is, generally speaking, a width limit of two metres' overhang on the roads. Anything bigger requires military-style organisation with police co-operation plus advance outriders warning the oncoming traffic of an approaching olive with latitude.

Laurent has a licence to carry extra-width loads, up to five or even six metres, within a radius of 60 kilometres of his *pépinière* or nursery. However, any tunnels, bridges or chicanes need to be avoided. Occasionally he has to organise above-ground telephone lines to be lifted or hitched up. Low-slung electricity lines are to be avoided too, of course, unless you want to be fried in olive oil.

If a tree of your dreams has come from far away, it may well end up costing more to transport than it did to buy. Crazy stuff.

Rather reluctantly Laurent told of a tree he knew. 'Spanish,' he said, the word came out with evident distaste, 'that is sitting in a fairly new nursery near to Isle sur la Sorgue (a local town that has a huge reputation throughout France as a hub of antique dealing). The owner claims it to be *the* biggest olive tree on sale in France and he's asking *eighty* thousand francs for it (that's about eight thousand pounds).

Sniffily, he added that 'Biggest isn't oldest remember. It may have a *very* large trunk.' At which point he rolled his eyes and gripped his desktop. 'But have no head worth speaking of. Anyway,' he said pulling himself together, 'they grow extremely slowly and have very little sap in them, which makes them vulnerable.' He looked protectively out of the window.

The olive is quite possibly the one tree that is the most inexorably allied to mankind. Ever since that little bird flew into Noah's ark with an olive twig in its beak it has symbolised friendship and peace. Although that behaviour on the West Bank undermines any romantic theories a little.

But it is not just in the Bible lands that they have established themselves. They have been at the heart of progress in the Mediterranean region for nearly as long, being considered sacred to the Greeks and Romans. The Egyptians even depicted them on the walls of their chambers.

What is it about this gentle fellow that made such an impression? For sure, the lovely soft grey-green leaves, with their silver-white underbelly, that stay firmly attached to the branches throughout the year are as decorative as you could want. The gnarled old trunks that seem to have a hundred sculptures worked into their body and the tormented old branches all contribute to its welcome, but the real value comes from its fruit.

It is such an incredible source of both fruit and oil. Another bonus is its extraordinary ability to regenerate itself from near ruin by producing new shoots from seemingly destroyed roots. No wonder that this made the ancients think of it as some kind of immortal plant, worthy of a sacred veneration.

'Where else should I go to look at some of these old French fellas?' I asked Laurent, getting to my feet.

'There is an olive tree that is over a thousand years old in Roquebrune,' he said, 'and it is difficult to find suitable words to describe it but not so hard for the heart. *Très majestique.*' His eyes looked off into the distance.

Roquebrune is one of the many characteristic villages scattered along the heights above the French part of the Mediterranean coast, and only a few kilometres away from Monte Carlo. Its narrow streets often open out on to stone-paved terraces with magnificent views. However, the tourists and travellers who step out on to these promenades and alleys are all heading towards the same place to see the 'Olivier Millénaire', the jewel of Roquebrune.

'This would be for you to look at only,' he said, coming back from his out-of-body experience, 'to give you an idea of what *millénaires* look like. It is one hundred and ten per cent not for sale. Never, no-how, so don't ask!' he smiled.

'I'll try and meet it,' I said, 'anywhere a bit closer?'

I've heard there are some good trees in Nyons and Sisteron but I don't know for sure. Somebody told me that he knew of an imported tree in Quissac that might be worth seeing.

'Quissac? Sounds like an antidepressant.'

And with that I bade him a fond farewell, promising to come back with a big offer if we couldn't find anything older for sale.

I drove back to the office feeling slightly blasé about 500-year-old trees. I felt that to be really impressive, to fill the goal that I had theoretically set for Lautour, the tree needed to check in at a 1,000- to 1,500-years minimum. But that is a very wintry old age indeed, and I started to think that maybe I should lower my sights. Maybe 500 or 600 years is pretty damned elderly and I should accept it. Especially given the plethora of aspects to consider; the difficulty of transport, the size not being indicative of age, the dozens of different varieties and of course the beauty of the thing.

Ah, the beauty. Would it not be better to have a handsome, well-worked-out torso of a tree in its prime rather than an arthritic old man whose trunk had shrivelled. Whose fine head of glory had thinned out and whose potent produce had withered to a scanty reflection of those primordial days of magnificence. And yet, part of the excitement was knowing that these trees can, and do, live to be so very, very old. It pokes the imagination into wondrous speculation as to what life was like when these olives first started out. Laurent had talked of his half-century-old French specimens, content in the knowledge that these elegant trees were still showing an athlete's determination to score. Hardwoods that wore their crowns with a young tree's sartorial pride determined to carry on for many generations to come.

What were the signs, sounds and events that surrounded these trees when they were young? The Black Death for a start. The disease that allegedly killed over a third of Europe's population, that attacked with gruesome effectiveness. The victims suffered atrocious agony and it came with virtually a guaranteed fatality for those who caught it. The royal surgeon Ambroise Paré was later to note, 'The plague is a mad, tempestuous, monstrous, abominable, fearful, terrifying and treacherous disease.' Add that to the medical profession's only remedy which was to tell you to leave early, go far, come back late, you realise that this was no ordinary sniffle.

Where did it come from? Who started it in France? There is a legend that the Mongols distributed it by catapulting plague-ridden corpses into the besieged Crimean city of Caffa, but more likely it was the

Genoan merchants bringing the disease back with them from that region in the 1350s.

It undermined normal behaviour patterns, and wild accusations of people spreading its vileness were prevalent. There were even vicious pogroms aimed at the Jews who were accused of poisoning the Christians' drinking wells. All this backstabbing, however, later caused a great sense of guilt and provoked hoards of flagellants to wander about the South of France whipping themselves.

Then, as if that wasn't enough, we had the Hundred Years War. Actually it was the 116 Years War as it ran from 1337 to 1453, but who's counting? It all started when Edward III of England assumed the title of King of France. (Imagine our Queen Elizabeth invading France nowadays.) Anyway Edward had a modicum of success on land but it was at sea that he really got cracking. He defeated the French fleet in 1340 at the battle of Sluis outside Bruges. Horrifying downfalls at Crécy in '46 and Poitiers in '56 convincingly followed this. The loss of Calais was another blow and then to crown it all he captured France's King John II (the Good). He demanded such a heavy ransom that in order to raise the cash the people had their already punitive taxes raised and the pressure furthered the discontent. The English not only received Calais but practically the whole of Aquitaine into the bargain. A bad heir day for the French.

But by 1373 most of the lost French territory had been won back under Charles V. Then just as things were looking a bit settled and it might have been the end of the Thirty-Seven Years War, in stormed Henry V of England renewing his English claims.

He took Harfleur and defeated France's best knights at Agincourt. By 1419 he had subdued Normandy with the connivance of John the Fearless, Duke of Normandy. Next, Philip the Good, successor to John, mediated between Henry V and Charles VI of France and Charles recognised Henry as heir to the crown. What names – 'The Fearless', 'The Good'. Now the olive tree lives in the lands of Ronnie the Rat, Willie the Weasel, Mickey the Mouth.

Back at the office there was a quick unpunctuated message on the answering machine from Lautour.

'Call me Regis.'

And that was it.

Did that mean that he considered it time for us to be on first-name terms? I had stuck carefully to Monsieur Lautour, or avoided it altogether. Or was it simply a message to call him. I took it as that and rang.

It's bad enough deciding when to call someone by their Christian name, let alone trying to work out when to move from '*vous*' to '*tu*'. Generally it's best to wait for an older person to start the ball rolling, but quite often I get all fiddled up and cross my bow. I end up shrugging off the problem, explaining that as a Scotsman it is a bit hard to know. No offence meant and seldom any taken.

Lautour answered the telephone and after a nanosecond of niceties asked, 'How many other trees live for a thousand years or more?'

'Um, well let me think. There's the Bristlecone Pine. I have heard of but not seen one that is nearly 5,000 years old, not a thing of great beauty as you might imagine being that sort of age, *Pinus longaeva* or long-life they call it. Then there's the Montezuma Cypress which can go on for 2,500 years or so. There is one at least that age still living in Mexico. Oaks and sweet chestnuts don't do badly. I think I saw a lime or three at Westonbirt in Gloucestershire that had been ring-dated at 6,000 years old. But the papa of them all, as far as I know, is a yew that can be found in Scotland, Perthshire to be precise. Why do you ask?'

'A you?' he said

'Am I what?'

'You said a you.'

'No not a me, a Yew. That's *Taxus*.'

'Texas? I thought you said Scotland. The line is bad I think.'

'Not Texas, *Taxus*. That's the botanical name for the tree. The French call it "If" or "eeef".'

'If what?' he said.

'Eeef — sounds like beef,' I said, worried that this was slipping off the tracks. 'The French call this tree "eef" — don't ask me why but you must have seen them, they are dark green, persistent and lurk around graveyards.'

'How old is it?' he asked.

'About nine thousand years and three weeks.'

'How can you tell about the three weeks?'

'Because when I read about it three weeks ago, it was listed as nine thousand years old.'

'That is very old indeed. Is it for sale? Shall we get it for the courtyard instead of the olive?'

'You think that's old? Let me tell you that with the development of modern carbon-dating techniques, palaeontologists have been able to date yew fossils to nearly two million years ago. Yews have been discovered preserved in peat bogs, which shows they were all over the place before the Ice Age, and that ended some one point seven million years ago.'

'I don't want a fossil.'

'No, I think we should stick to the olive, more suitable,' I said. 'But what makes you ask?'

'What about *Ginkgo*?' he said, ignoring my curiosity and still manoeuvring around the question.

'Ah, a lovely and much-revered tree,' I said. I was beginning to sound like an expert, which of course I'm not. But I have always been interested in old trees and a bit has rubbed off. Ginkgos first caught my attention when I was a teenager with their lizardy-sounding name. They are tall, slim, elegant trees that can reach over 200 feet or 60 metres. In autumn their leaves turn from a soft pale Granny Smith green to a dazzling Golden Delicious yellow. Set against a deep blue sky, it is impressive.

'I gather they can go on for a thousand years at least,' he said. 'They are also highly significant to the religious orders of Buddhists in China. *Malheureusement,* they are listed as endangered. Did you know that?' asked Lautour.

I didn't. What's he getting at? I wondered.

'Your idea of finding the oldest olive tree has got me thinking about all the other trees that survive for a long time. I'm toying with the idea of maybe having a small collection of ancient trees. A kind of living gallery. What do you think?'

I thought it was a grand and attractive idea. I could see that it would be a fine thing to be the curator of a tree zoo that retained magnificent old specimens from around the world. I could also see that it might be a lifetime's work collating it, full of disappointments and frustrations. I knew that finding our olive was going to be no picnic and really didn't envisage stretching the brief to include a dozen or so other players. So I told him so. I added that perhaps he could commission a dozen experts to all go exploring for their particular classification.

'I agree, we must start with the olive,' he said. 'It is the best of them all and I very much look forward to meeting the old chap.' He paused and we had one of our little silences.

Then: 'Of course we might consider another variety if this quest of yours is successful,' he said with a hint of goading in his quiet voice.

Lautour was developing a new hobby.

The following Saturday, on Laurent Croz's recommendation I set off for Vaison-la-Romain to see if the old tree he had told me about really existed.

Vaison is a village with a population of around 5,500 people and is generally considered to be the star of Roman Provence. It lies in a low basin along the Ouvèze river beneath the watchful chateau that is located on top of the *haute ville*.

It was first recorded in 60BC as Vasio Vocontiorum, but its prehistoric traces of ancient civilisation can be checked back to some 2500BC or what is known as the Chalcolithic period. During the 40s BC it was formally allied to Rome and the tribal leaders were granted Roman citizenship under Pompey, Caesar and Augustus.

I was really hoping to find this piece of local history. To experience the atmosphere of a 600-year-old plant, talk to him a bit and see how he's feeling. No sexist, me, but somehow I presumed the tree would be a 'he'. Would it be more polite to refer to him as 'it'? I wondered. Or should we sex the thing before talking? The French have it as a girl but they would. Perhaps as we are in France it would be more diplomatic to think of it as a 'her'. An 'old her' at that. Probably all really old trees are female, being that women live much longer than us boys generally speaking.

As it transpired there was no ancient olive in Vaison-la-Romain. I couldn't even get anybody to admit that there ever had been one. Was the rumour just a conspiracy to lure unsuspecting tourists into the spending trap? Or was it hidden in some secret garden, possible to visit only after an initiation ceremony that involved answering cryptic medieval riddles?

It was certainly interesting to look round the ancient village with its archaeological digs that have revealed immense, luxurious and elaborate Gallo Roman homes. There were floors in mosaic, marble and marquetry while the statues, ponds, atriums and private thermal baths all showed how grand it could be in Roman times, but the whole town had begun to take on an eerie atmosphere.

During the thirteenth and fourteenth centuries the population of Vaison upped and positioned itself on the north side of the river at the base of the chateau. This was to increase their protection against the continuing marauders thrown up by the Hundred Years War who kept attacking and looting their property. During this time the English and their Burgundian allies had become masters of nearly all France north of the Loire. They were heady with success and no doubt planned to push even further. But they badly overlooked a determined peasant lass called Joan of Arc who raised the siege of Orleans and saw to it that Charles VII was crowned King of France at Reims. He rewarded the resolute Joan by doing absolutely nothing to help her when she fell into the hands of the Burgundians. And it was they who duly passed her over to the English who, as we know, had her roasted as a witch.

It was odd that there were no olives surviving from this period especially as there was evidence of them in other regions.

For example some of the old olive trees in Laurent's nursery had been dug up and brought down from the Ardèche, an area not very far north of Vaison. They must have been planted just after the fall of Bordeaux in 1453 when England retained only Calais. But even that was regained by France in 1558. England, torn by the Wars of the Roses, made no further attempt to conquer or keep France.

Around the time that his trees were putting on long trousers and beginning to develop barks, they probably heard about François Rabelais, a man who grew up to be not only an eminent physician but also arguably the greatest comic genius in world literature. Having been a novice in a Franciscan monastery where he managed to acquire the equivalent of a couple of A-levels in Greek and Latin, picked up a Bachelor of Law and a duet of Masters in Philology and Science, he went on to become a humanist and humorist. At one point the smart kid got it wrong and found himself in hiding and being threatened with persecution for heresy. But he reinvented himself when he knocked together a chapbook collection of familiar legends about a giant called Gargantua. It was hugely successful and inspired Rabelais to write a similar history of Pantagruel, son of Gargantua. His work is considered masterful, as gigantic in scope as the physical size of its heroes. Under its broad humour, often ribald, are serious discussions of education, politics and philosophy. After his death in 1553 his name passed into common parlance as a way of describing bawdy behaviour: Rabelaisian.

Did they eat olives in France at this time? Did the strapping young trees offer up kilos of ripe fruit ready for the pressing? Probably. Medieval cooking certainly wasn't a dubious practice of producing inedible dishes filled with strange spices and dangerous ingredients. Medieval cooks used much of the foodstuffs we use today. People knew then, as now, what tasted good and what would satisfy the stomachs of the fourteenth- and fifteenth-century families. It would almost certainly have involved the oil of olives as well.

They would eat meat pies filled with pork, raisins and dates topped with whole chicken pieces. They liked a light soup flavoured with wine and thickened with almonds, olives and vegetables. For afters perhaps a fruit marinated in wine, honey and herbs. If they were throwing a bit of a do and having a few friends round for dinner they might push the boat out and settle down to some savoury sauces and stews, venison pies, rabbit in gravy, beef roasts, stuffed goose, fish marinated in ale, sweet pastries fried in olive oil, fruit confections and sculptures of sugar. Dribble dribble. Sometimes more exotic creations were served such as the

Cockentrice; half capon-half pig or Coq à Grys, a helmeted cock who rides a suckling steed, a grim sight better left undescribed.

Drink still had a bit of a way to go. Wines and ales were available but brandy for example didn't make an appearance until the seventeenth century. Whisky was emerging in Scotland. Mr J. Marshall Robb noted in his *History of Whisky* that it was first recorded in the Scottish Exchange Rolls in the fifteenth century and probably the work of monks who were pretty good at sussing out how to get drunk.

It was unlikely that much whisky found its way over to France though. They were knocking the stuffing out of themselves with the old 'legitimate' absinthe. A drink originally made from wormwood (*Artemisia absinthium*) and soaked in wine. Interestingly, the word absinthe comes from the Greek *absinthion* meaning undrinkable. From all accounts it was a pretty foul-tasting beverage and mostly used medicinally to treat, among other things, bad breath, rheumatism and indigestion.

In the sixteenth century this concoction, made from the silvery-white and greyish-green leaves, changed from being a medicine into a popular drink among the working classes when it was discovered that, if the wormwood was macerated in malmsey wine and then distilled, it made a perfectly passable hooch.

However, when it was found that it apparently caused convulsions, hallucinations, mental deterioration and psychoses, the wormwood ingredient was removed by order in 1915. New derivatives came on the market, known as Pernod, pastis, anis and ouzo, which if taken over-liberally probably had much the same effect but it was your fault and not the manufacturer's.

There was a wealthy wine merchant in England back in the fourteenth century named Chaucer who had christened his son, Geoffrey. And a brave bloke he was too. He actually fought in the Hundred Years War, was captured at one point and later ransomed for £16. That's probably about

£35,000 nowadays. After his mad, bad soldiering days were over, he settled down and wrote first *The Parliament of Fowls* then *Troilus and Cressida*, inventing modern English as he went along. By 1387 he had started the celebrated *Canterbury Tales*, about twenty-nine pilgrims who, while travelling from London to Canterbury, each told a separate story or tale to while away the journey. One story, 'The Wife of Bath', introduced the prototype feminist. The great and much-respected chronicler of the wealthy upper classes died in 1400 and was buried in Westminster Abbey.

Such were the thoughts of a gumshoe tree investigator as he left Vaison-la-Romain quietly and a bit disappointed that he hadn't even sniffed the scent of an antique olive tree.

The dark secrets that might lurk within The Lodge of Oliviers had eluded him. The trail was going to be full of such frustrations.

Spain had been designated as the next leg on the trail into olive land but before plans could be finalised I had to go to London for a few days to meet a Greek contact. He had promised to help me find my way around Crete, quite probably the source of all Mediterranean olive trees. I also had a book-signing session to attend.

Tired from travel I had mental images of sitting at a table with a colossal stack of books and no one coming to buy them or have them signed. The two other gardener authors that were on the gig with me, Dan Pearson and Paul Cooper, had lengthy queues of happy gardening enthusiasts standing in line, waiting patiently for them to answer questions and sign their books.

I needn't have worried though. It was a charity event raising money for dysfunctional adolescents and I had a perfectly healthy crowd at my point of sale and found myself drawn into much garden-speak. One ripe lady approached me who, having clearly had an engaging alliance with one of the many jugs of mulled wine being offered round, told me that she had absolutely no intention of buying my book. She leant forward and, with breath that could have jump-started a barbecue, hissed, 'D'ya know why?'

'No'

'Because I've already got it.' She practically detonated with intoxicated laughter and then leant even closer. I could hear the dribble inside her mouth galvanising itself for the next sortie. Platoons of well-disciplined particles of froth ready to parachute towards their destiny.

Steadying herself and finding a modicum of decorum, she took a deep intake of air, looked left and right and then said conspiratorially, 'I like to write myself, you know.' She came even closer. 'Having read your book I said to myself if he can get that sort of thing published then so could I. Well, anybody could, couldn't they?'

'Um. Yes probably. Just finding the time to do it really, isn't it?' I noticed a chap standing behind her and asked if she would be kind enough to move over a little so he could get in.

'Who's your agent? Will you introduce me?' she asked, spilling the dregs of her wine over one of the books. Looking at her I smiled as sweetly as I could under the circumstances and said, 'No.'

She hovered above me, her stoned eyes squinting through puffy cheeks. 'I hope your book fails miserably,' she spat, and sank away.

After I got home I heard that the evening had raised a lot of money for the cause and everybody was delighted. Good. But I had missed Costas, my Greek contact. He had shipped off somewhere leaving me a note saying where I could contact him when I was back in the South of France. I tried another time but the elusive chap had legged it again. I wasn't going to Greece yet and perhaps Costas and I would meet up when the time was right.

I had Spain to sort out first. I would probably need a deerstalker, bendy pipe and a magnifying glass to find the clues. I was soon to head off into a country I had only ever visited as a holidaymaker. I didn't speak Spanish and it was inevitable, I supposed, that I was going to have to deal with opportunists, rip-off merchants and dodgy dealers. Perhaps if I kept my wits about me and my forensic senses sharp I might meet some genuine vendors. Who said gardening was easy?

CHAPTER FOUR

Spain

The olive grove slowly casts up its silvery waves even at
high noon, and it keeps the cool moondust on its hair
with which night has powdered it.

S. Myrivilis

There is a lifestyle-type programme on French television on Saturday
evenings that is hinged towards commerce and investment. A few weeks
ago it had a small segment on olive trees. First we met a grower from the
Mediterranean area, not far from where we live. He was not trying to
trade big or old trees; he just wanted to flog young ones, about five to ten
years old and an ideal age for farmers to plant as a crop. But he was having
difficulty selling them. Not because farmers didn't want them, it was just
that people had decided to help themselves, nick them rather than pay for
them. He explained that the thieves were very artistic in their approach.
They either removed every other plant, or more ambitiously, every other
row. He reckoned they did this either to delay him noticing that his stock
was evaporating, or they felt it only reasonable to adopt the 'thinning out'
practice of an experienced grower.

The beleaguered farmer would arrive down at the field in the morning to see another couple of hundred little trees had disappeared. The robbers even took the plastic sleeves that were wrapped round the trunks to protect them against animals chewing on the bark. The little ties that held them to the wire lines were untied carefully and the ground minimally disturbed. Occasionally he would find a broken root where the young sapling had been pulled out of the ground too aggressively, presumably by a novice, a new boy to the game of olive-looting. The poor chap had planted thousands of these trees, investing most of his money and all of his energy, in the hope of selling on after a few years of tender loving attention, only to hang his head in sorrow as he told his tale of loss. Over half the crop to date. He had tried putting up a half-hearted electric fence, a few lights, and had even camped out a few times, but it was all to no avail. To properly fence off such a huge area with effective security measures would have been way beyond his means and cost more than he could hope to recoup in the foreseeable future.

The trouble with these sort of programmes is that while it is interesting to learn of such calculated agricultural skulduggery, it must also awaken more unscrupulous, flagitious pilferers to the notion. Exacerbating the problem rather than sorting it out. It is hard enough trying to get the police to come round to your house in the middle of the night when you think there's an intruder prowling around, let alone persuade the men in blue to go tree-thief chasing through the undergrowth at some ungodly hour.

'How to apprehend a forest of hardwood heavies moving around under cover of the night working a twenty acre field. See page 36 sub-section 109E paragraph 92 (reviewed 1907)'.

The programme then moved on to an overweight bald retiree, a kind of plain-clothed Santa, a fervent grandad who whisked us round his immaculate garden on the coast up in Brittany.

Anybody whose garden is so fastidiously tidy is either retired or has paying guests or both. You can always spot them by looking at their garden. It's advert-clean. The earth looks as if it has been sprayed with matt-black paint, the leaves shine like a florist's portfolio and the paths are pressure-depolluted. The grass is not only devoid of doggy mishap but is also a weed-free zone. Any poor unsuspecting wild plant that thought it might like to be beside the seaside is terminated before it even breaks ground.

The best gardens are often the ones that are left to work hand in hand with nature, complementing each other. Weeds will always be there. They need controlling but they can also contribute to the balance by attracting certain bugs, controlling lesser weeds and acting as ground cover. I have never understood, for example, the flap about having a few daisies or a bit of clover in your lawn. We actually encourage it. They give a little extra colour, spread quickly and their roots bind a fragile soil. I've met people who wouldn't give space to a naturalised buddleia, dismissing it as a weed, yet here is a pretty purple plant that is tough as old boots, flowers for ages in the late summer, plays host to butterflies and can be hacked back without recrimination. Nobody would deny that a patch of aggressive dock or an attack of nettles should be expelled, but something like *Centranthus ruber*, red or white, could easily be categorised as a weed because it is invasive, yet I consider it a useful filler. One of Britain's greatest gardeners, Christopher Lloyd, has several dogs but he never worries about a few patches on the lawns at Great Dixter. Life is too short. Go for the allure and the detail can look after itself.

The little polished head took us off on a tour in double-quick time, the cameraman darting after him as if his job depended on it. These handheld camera shots are no longer innovative filming but low-budget hackneyed compromises.

Fleeing past the perfect petunias held in place by the reconstituted stone wall, down on to more flawless grass, past a re-sited windmill and there, moodily mooching about the bottom of the garden, were a small herd of ancient olives.

'These are about 700 years old and cost me 80,000 francs each,' he boasted, immune to the fact that we neither cared nor wanted to know such financial intimacies. He was confident that we must be colossally impressed and deeply fascinated. Actually it wasn't the cost of the tree that was fascinating so much as how this rotund little pirate had the dosh to make such a grandiose purchase. They seemed oddly out of synch with his lifestyle, and the fact that he was more impassioned by the price than the beauty of the tree showed us a hopelessly misguided amateur. He told us that he had bought them from a nursery that deals in Spanish trees, where, as I now know, many of the old fellas we see around here originate.

Laurent had told of how these trees are indiscriminately ripped out of the ground, then butcher-pruned to fit as many as possible on to the transport trucks, their beautiful crowns chain-sawed off by opportunists who readily admit that about only three in ten survive. Our little guesthouse hero had paid a fortune for one of his old trees and it looked as if it had suffered chemotherapy and showed no obvious signs of recovery. It badly needed a wig. Laurent would have wept.

If this was an example of what sort of Spanish tree you could expect for eight grand I wondered what a really fine example was going to cost. There must be some beautiful specimens around I supposed, if one could just break through the rogue dealers, get behind the ambitious Andalusian farmers and find a bona fide vendor. A merchant who was interested in value for money and putting his old olives out to grass in a warm and welcome environment was needed.

I figured it was worth a trip and there might just be something for Lautour's courtyard. I was going to head south for Barcelona first, then

Valencia and if necessary on to the Malaga coast. Late January was pencilled into the diary.

One of the first problems to get round was the language barrier. There are those who think my French is bad but they should hear my Spanish.

In our village we have an Andalusian family who migrated to France about thirty years ago and their children all speak Spanish and French fluently. Josefina, their daughter, can add English having been married to a British West Indian and lived on Dominica. She and her two sons now live in Lacoste. She is a kind lady who looks like she has taken a few blows from life. But we have always passed the time of day and when I suggested that maybe she could make a few phone calls to her motherland, she was happy to help. I briefed her and she set to. After a couple of days, dozens of faxes and emails, she emerged victorious. Or so we hoped. We certainly had an impressive list of suppliers, dealers, crooks and contacts. On the second day of her mission she warned me that one player would be ringing back that afternoon. He had promised her that he could find a thousand-year-old tree for us, no problem.

'How about one thousand five hundred?' she had asked.

'Sí sí sí …'

'Two thousand?'

'A doddle,' he had assured her, or something to the effect. It was too good to be true. He was either distressing his trees to look older than they really were by slapping on a few extra layers of knurled old bark or screwing on some ancient bits of branch he had found somewhere. Or else he was hoping that a Scottish garden designer wouldn't know the difference between a tree that was 500 years old and one that was 2,000, and he wouldn't be far wrong. He would call back and tell us where we could see them.

Later that afternoon, good to his word he rang, and as Josefina, was out I took the call. I asked him if he spoke any English. He said in a sensationally guttural accent that he was Portuguese and couldn't manage the English very well. He might be able to accomplish a bit of French though.

It reminded me of Laurie Lee writing in *As I walked Out One Midsummer Morning* describing how he had, as a young man, been playing his violin outside a café in Toledo. When he passed his cap round had been asked by a rather elegant lady in Italian if he was German and he had replied in Spanish that he was English.

I shuddered to think what kind of deal I might end up making with this wily Portuguese trader, but sensed the adventure was warming up somewhat. Our conversation was necessarily limited but I got it across that I would try to come and visit his trees soon. Meanwhile he would send me directions. It wasn't much but it was a start. As things turned out he never sent the instructions on how to find him and I never felt inclined to call him again. I don't think I missed anything.

I called Regis Lautour to report in.

'I am off to Spain after Christmas,' I told him, and explained the outline of what I thought might be on offer.

The man clearly had a strong affection for '*The Spains*' as he insisted on calling it, explaining that there was no such thing as Spain singular.

'It is a collection of provinces, each of which considers itself definitive Spain. They are intolerant of each other and as different as gravel and grass. Madrid might think of itself as the capital, attracting patronage from all those who wish to make their fortune; yet the capital has a hold on ambition rather than on the affections of the nation at large.'

'Presumably that's because Spain never had the advantage of a fixed metropolis like London, Paris or Rome,' I said.

'It's true,' he said. 'Iberians would never amalgamate, would never, as Strabo said, put their shields together, would never sacrifice their own local private interest for the general good.'

Strabo I think was a pal of Pliny's. Pliny-Gaius Secundus The Elder AD23–79, that is. You may remember he was a Roman history writer from a wealthy background. He has always stuck in my mind because of the extraordinary amount of boring books he churned out, bettered only by Barbara Cartland. His book *Historia Naturalisa* was his lifelong work and consisted of 160 volumes of manuscript. His style was, they say, inartistic and often obscure. You would have thought that his publishers might have mentioned something after, say, the first forty or fifty books. But if he was so rich perhaps he published them himself. His son, on the other hand, Pliny the Younger, did better. He was an orator as well as a writer. His meagre ten volumes of letters gave an intimate picture of the upper classes in the first century.

'Localism creates a strong freemasonry. You'll always find it among immigrants.' Regis was getting it on.

'Like English rock stars having football teams in LA,' I offered.

'What?' said Lautour lost again. But he was determined to push his point.

'The Northwest provinces are as wet as Brittany and the Southeast is as arid as Algeria. When did you say you were going, and to which part?'

'I didn't. Late January, and starting my hunt in or around Barcelona.'

'Barcelona!' he exclaimed, a thousand happy memories apparently coursing through his cosmopolitan blood.

'Come and have dinner before you go, bring your wife, we'll talk more about it. By the way I have some friends who live just outside the city – I am sure they would be very glad to give you lunch. She is the Marqueza of Marquezas and lives in a beautiful *fienca*. Her husband breeds a few fighting bulls that would have made even Hemingway's eyes water. They are the best in the area. I'll tell her to expect a call from you. When did you say you would be going?'

'Late January. Does she speak English?'

'Of course. She *is* English.'

'Oh. When have you got in mind.'

'What?'

'What date for dinner, shall we make a date? It's just that we have to organise a babysitter.'

'You have a baby?' he sounded incredulous.

'Well, he's five but still needs a babysitter.'

'Why don't you have a nanny?'

'Oh, there's several reasons, not least because we don't particularly want anyone living full time in the house with us.'

'I had a nanny. Wonderful woman, came from Vichy funnily enough. Can you speak Spanish?'

'No.'

'The sixth.'

'Fine. The last day of Christmas.'

'The Spanish celebrate Christmas on the sixth, so it's appropriate.'

Thinking of Christmas, I was hardly back from helping the dysfunctional when a return journey to England for a family gathering was announced.

Earlier in the year Nicky's uncle had died and with him came the end of one major strand of the family. He had no wife or children and his Lordship's title was passed to his younger brother.

The two boys had grown up in Tyntesfield, a magnificent house of extended proportions. The core, the old part, was Georgian but this was wholly beside the point. In the late 1860s Uncle Richard's great grandfather, a deeply religious man, bought the building and morphed it with opulent aspirations into a high temple of Victorian elegance. The Machiavellian entrepreneur heaped great dollops of Gothic deceit onto the original house and smothered out any semblance of the comparatively restrained architecture of the eighteenth century.

On went a colossal conservatory, later taken down to help the war effort. Up went a private chapel with towers and spires and stained-glass mullion windows. This privately owned place of worship was built to seat over two hundred well-behaved protestants. Cavernous drawing rooms, bathrooms, bedrooms and hallways in which could be found mighty stone-carved fireplaces that paid homage to the saints with delicate carvings striking devout poses. A fantastic and uniquely designed billiard room with carved oak panelling and a hammer beam roof boasted a vast billiard table with an automatic scoring system, the first of its kind.

Mod cons included hot-air heating and a hydraulic lift, water-wheel fed reservoirs to ensure good pressure and American-style fire hydrants. Inside, the painted and stencilled decoration was the work of John Crace who in the 1850s had redecorated Windsor Castle for the state visit of the Emperor Napoleon III.

The library, with its arched collar-braced ceiling, had fitted oak bookcases packed with leather-bound, marbled end-papered volumes. Terrible tales of the Crimea illustrated by etchings of uniforms stood sharply to attention next to *The History of Europe* in 125 tantalising volumes of bleeding detail. Maps of campaigns and their strategy breakdowns, then lower down a reference division to the firearms of the emerging nations with manuals on weapon training and maintenance. Open the leatherbacks and they creaked and complained of being disturbed. Most likely the publishers had given the books to his

Lordship's predecessors who had probably not managed to read them all. Even for a fanatic it would have been a challenge. For a mild-mannered and highly active politician it may well have sufficed that the titles were visible on the shelves.

Nowadays libraries like that are a rare site and more likely to have been replaced by racks of best-sellers, films and music collections.

Looking through a friend's considerable video tape compilation one day I asked him if he had seen all the films he had catalogued. He replied that he hadn't but he was comfortable with the possibility that on a whim he could pull something down and watch it. Part of the pride of ownership came from it being there irrespective of whether it had actually been watched. 'Did you see blah blah on television the other night?' 'No but I taped it.' This answer means that you haven't seen it but are aware of its existence, approved of it enough to tape it, thus levelling yourself with those who actually saw it. You were in the know without knowing. This aspect of the modern library runs in tangent with those of the old.

I remember buying books when I was an adolescent that I loved the idea of reading but in my heart knew I probably wouldn't get to. *Capitalism in Latin America*, *The Marxist Mess*, *The Thirteenth Commandment*, *Boo to Buddhism*, that kind of thing. I stopped buying such blockbusters when a girlfriend accused me of intellectual masturbation.

'You should realise the parameters of your intelligence and not goad it into an arena it doesn't understand.' she had said, 'there's no point trying to climb up the library ladder if you keep falling off.'

Stung by the analogy, I briefly bewailed the infertility of my brainpower then, acknowledging her wisdom, concentrated on the more comfortable titles of contemporary classics.

It's a hard job putting a library together, especially when people judge one another by their covers. A quick glance through the CDs, a gallop along the dust covers, out across the videos and discs, and people think they know you backwards. After turning a few pages of Tyntesfield's library I wasn't at all sure I knew the man who had inherited them any better than if I had never seen them.

Fortunately the sale of Tyntesfield was steered through to a satisfactory conclusion with the National Trust. It meant that the house and its contents would stay intact and could soon be displayed to a paying public. Before the property slipped out of the family hands it was deemed a good wheeze to have a final party at the house with all beneficiaries, their spouses, offspring, siblings and close relatives taking part. What better time to stage the event than Christmas?

It was a grand occasion, beautifully presented and skilfully organised. The dining room played host to some fifty people in a fashion it must have forgotten and was unlikely ever to do again. The galleried hall flaunted a smartly dressed tree that reached up to forever and beyond. It was dotted with flickering little candles and the small glass balls shone like rubies.

The children ran around in their Christmas clothes tearing off wrapping paper and dancing in and out of the shadows that the tremendous fire threw out. The shimmied flames from the logs that needed two volunteers to move and some big candles was all the light we had. No Victorian painting could have done it better.

Fettled with fine claret most of us took off for a walk around the grounds to let a little air into the system before it clogged up completely.

The southern part of the garden was enclosed from the adjacent parkland by a haha. That clever eighteenth-century device that makes a two-metre deep cut in the ground and retains it with a wall, then gently slopes the earth away from the wall on the other side back up to ground level. From the inside it affords a view uninterrupted by fences or hedges, and from the outside prohibits animals accessing the garden. It is so simple and effective, it hurts.

A tired old lake waited patiently for a bit of help but still acted as home to numerous birds and waterside animals. In the fading light of an English winter it looked forbidding, its black shiny surface rippling with hidden dangers.

Well-worn steps led up to a series of topiaried holly bushes and classical urns that lay within formal flowerbeds on either side of a gravel path. Beyond beckoned a rose garden. A tranquil spot protected by mature trees, yew hedging and a brick and carved stone wall. A pair of heraldic lions on low plinths watched you as you worked your way through the traditionally laid-out borders towards the twin summer houses.

I sat in the wintry evening light for a few minutes taking in the dwindling heritage, looking at the quiet English countryside that was so far from the Mediterranean landscape that I now worked in. I couldn't really imagine an olive tree taking its place here in a northern garden. I felt a long way from Lautour's courtyard.

With a firework display that Buckingham Palace would have been proud of, the gathering said a brave farewell to the home that had been the centre of the family's life for 150 years. As the last burst faded, four generations stood closely together deep in thought.

After a long goodbye to a small boy who was sure that Spain lay just left of Saturn, and that it would be several light years before he would see me again, I was on my way.

Two hours later the Pyrenees came into view. The sun was shining on the eastern face of the higher peaks, picking up the outlines against the snow like an advert for Evian water. The mountain range is enormous and makes an impressive divide of some 270 miles in length. This gigantic barrier which divides France and Spain is connected with the dorsal chain which comes down from Tartary and Asia. It stretches far beyond the spine; the mountains of the Basque Provinces, Asturias and Gallica are its continuation. The mountains are both broadest and highest in the middle sections where the width is about 60 miles and the elevations exceed 3,000 metres. The spurs and offsets of this great transversal vertebra penetrate on both sides into the lateral valleys like ribs from a backbone. The central nucleus slopes gradually east to the gentle Mediterranean, and West to the angrier Atlantic.

Today a stream of expeditious cars and an endless progression of freight lorries without so much as a sniff of difficulty tackle it head on. Well constructed, fast roads keep the traffic flowing.

Just on the French side of the border hunkers a depressing development called La Catalona Village. A deserted wasteland of motorway nothingness, pretending to promise the hungry or tired driver a welcoming hug into its pseudo-Spanish bosom. In January an empty shadow fell over a compound that had been built with the full force of summer tourism in mind. Unsuspecting and ready for a break I pulled off and into the car park. Enough bays for a thousand cars and not an automobile to be seen. I panicked, trying to figure which of the empty rows to go into. Not that I am the sort of person that has to park next to the only other car, or sit at the same table as a fellow passenger in an empty train: it was just disturbing to find the place so abandoned yet quite clearly open for business.

There were no children or playthings, and an empty paddling pool with polluted sand lay uncombed by missing attendants. Terrible bright primary colours dulled by the grey day were pigmenting themselves all over the place. As I wandered up the escarpment following the congested signposts trying to decipher the quickest route to the cafeteria, I realised I was passing through a courtyard of motel-type rooms. These cheaply and unimaginatively built little structures were actually for rent.

So hideously bereft of charm were they that a sensible truck driver would undoubtedly have elected to spend the night in the much more salubrious sleeping quarters of his cab, with all the mod cons that these roadmasters now demand as their right. The thought of being a travelling salesman having to hang yourself up in there for the night would make Arthur Miller wince. I would rather sleep in one of those weird Japanese coffins that they rent out to businessmen on the move. Tight little boxes that fit into the wall like the drawers you find in a mortuary. Once in, you have air conditioning, TV and dimmed lights all wrapped up in a crisp clean sleeping bag. Just don't try to move, that's all. Endless walls holding row upon row of receptacles all filled to the brim with sushied little Japanese business chappies.

Passing through the complex I detoured and bought a paper. The man behind the till was reading a copy of *La Chasse*, or to give its full name, *Plaisirs de la Chasse.* On the cover was a picture of a really cute little doe caught looking straight at the photographer, alert and soft. She was standing in a spring meadow with a mouthful of flowers. Her eyes were as innocent as the eyes of Ephebes. Maybe she would die young because the gods loved her. She was unaware that the thing that had just shot her could just as easily have been a high-calibre rifle and not a camera with a zoom lens. Why couldn't they use something less endearing like a wild boar eating a child, or a fox killing some chickens just for the fun of it?

I arrived into the café to join a queue of nobody apart from a silent couple having a bit of a day out. Their child was perched on a strange adapted trolley that held the little person in an all-embracing cuddle about two metres up in the air. Just about right for the dangling legs to kick the hamburger out of its father's mouth.

The serving lady was a heavy-jowled body of bumps and ill-designed attributes but she had the gift of gentle and tolerant kindness, unexpected in one of society's misfits. She agreeably guided me through her chicken dish that had been flirted with but ultimately ignored by a Catalonian recipe-ist. I took an inner-room table, fearing to look out of the window, dealt with my feast and was soon out of there.

By mid-afternoon I had found my way to the first nursery on the itinerary, near Canovès. It turned out to be one of a chain of highly organised, limited stock suppliers to the trade. A broking house for plants of all sizes imported from various growers local and not so local. I have been into dozens of places like that in my time; they even have them in the UK now. A kind of huge holding bay tempting the professional gardener to buy from them by bringing together a useful if somewhat dull portfolio of mature and semi-mature trees and shrubs.

The sun had come out and the temperature had climbed up into the mid-twenties. Overcoats, jackets and even sweaters were redundant. The assistants were all bouncing around in T-shirts and shorts, and the implacable green fronds of the tall *Washingtonia filifera* palms towered twelve metres above me standing out against a perfect uninterrupted blue sky. Ranks of enormous *Magnolia grandiflora* marched down one side of a loading shed joined by topiaried horses and hunters, little elephants and deer scurrying around their base. It took a while to find the office because the directors of the nursery group had obviously been trained in supermarket psychology. The drive in had been carefully planned to take you the longest possible route, interweaving you between file after file of their stock. Down an alley of *Abies mariesii*, sharp right at the *Arbutus unedo*, or strawberry tree as it is known, through the *Jacaranda mimosifolia*, past the *Morus alba*, that's the white mulberry in case you'd forgotten, and then right again at the *Albizia julibrissin*, an old favourite that has those lovely pink little explosions of flower in the summer, unexpected and very welcome. Finally, a quick dash down a channel of *Liriodendron tulipifera* before finally lapping into the parking area.

I had spotted one big old olive, unfortunately with a 'sold' tag hanging from it. The crown had been cut off and its trunk looked almost cube-shaped. One gnarly-bodied old creature, squat and depressed. Full of holes, rambling roots, empty bowls with dry, wrinkly skin. Like us, getting old seldom makes them prettier. But there seemed to be plenty of young pretenders lurking around.

I walked over to the office, a surprisingly utilitarian little shanty it was too. I hovered outside as the woman behind the desk was on the phone. She talked for a long time to what must have been one of her best friends. They must have had a lot in common and shared many secrets because she laughed and wept, she argued and consoled, she gesticulated, she stood up and sat down, but she didn't stop. I dared not leave and take a look around lest I lost my place in what had now built up into a sizeable file of customers. Finally she reluctantly emerged from her burrow and looked at me impatiently. Yes, she did speak a little English, yes she was in charge of sales and no she didn't remember my fax. Or for that matter, my email.

I started from scratch explaining my mission. That I had an eccentric millionaire client who wanted me to find him the oldest olive tree I could, etc. Afterwards I thought perhaps that she had been pretty unimpressed by the word millionaire considering how many pesetas there are to the pound and one would only need about forty quid's worth to be that proverbial millionaire. Anyway she said that she had a few trees that were about a thousand years old, but not older as they would be too expensive for people to buy and would take up unnecessary selling space. Quite. We piled into a jeep and headed off to look at what she had. I soon realised that I was radically in the wrong place. It was a big nursery with a good catalogue of stock, but olives were only one of its many commodities and not any more important than anything else. They were middle men and would undoubtedly be a very expensive source. If I was to be successful in finding a really old tree I needed to trace back to the actual grower or supplier. I needed to talk trade to an outlet that was exclusively for olives.

After another spin through the conduits of commerce we pulled up in front of a fine double row of tightly planted old olives. She talked me through the trees as if she were a bored waitress reciting the fixed price menu for the umpteenth time in a low-rent restaurant. Rosé, as I discovered her name to be, was in her mid-thirties, had short black hair and looked smart in her tailored grey cotton skirt and jacket. She held her clipboard tightly to her chest and doggedly stuck to her script.

'These trees are between 800 and 1,000 years old, they have been bought in from local farmers and are ready to be moved to their new location.'

She seemed uninterested in my particular request and when I enquired how long olives lived for, she answered 'for ever'.

'Do you guarantee the trees?'

'No, they never die,' and when I asked her 'what variety are all these trees?' she answered 'Big'.

'Ah, the celebrated classification, Olivio Grandissimo?' I teased without reaction.

I thought at the time to say that they never died was a great but wishful bit of saleswomanship. One hears of Spanish olives dying in

France quite regularly. The sharp-shooters swing them on unsuspecting punters without warning them about the change in climate quite often giving them a terminal shock. But having said that, I was later to learn that there was more than an ounce of truth in what she was saying.

Her job was to take people round in a jeep and sell sell sell. It wasn't really on her agenda to waste much time with a gardener like me searching for one of something she didn't have.

Before I could ask much more we were back at the office where she dropped me cold and disappeared off with a favoured customer for half an hour. But I was still there when she got back and cornered her. I asked a couple more questions she couldn't answer, and then I suggested that perhaps she might ask her boss. She didn't much like that, I can tell you. However, this boy was on a mission and he was not about to be easily put off. Sulkily she made a phone call, or pretended to, I don't know.

She put the phone down and said, 'My patron is having lunch and does not want to talk.' It was, after all, only four o' clock in the afternoon and all self-respecting Spaniards were doing the same thing. Maybe that was why Rosé was so off-hand. She felt cheated at having to work at that anti-social time. Anyway she took my card and quite unashamedly stuck it to the bottom of a huge wad of other cards and said, 'Next.'

It ran through my mind to tie her up naked to a palm tree using giant rubber bands, and tickle her to death with magpie feathers.

I pulled out of the nursery, tucked myself back on to the autoroute and headed south to Barcelona for the night. A beautiful city with four rush hours and where the long dual carriageways that lead into the centre pack a thousand cars into a square metre. Cars puking out pollution that hangs in the still, warm air almost as impressively as LA. The inhabitants live late into the night. They enjoy their city and are well trained on how to capitalise its offerings.

I checked into my hotel, conveniently located behind the Cathedral near the Place St Jaume. Well, conveniently located if you're on foot, a whole different bag of tortillas if you happen to be driving and don't know your Quartier Gothique from your Las Ramblas. L'Eixample had been bad enough. An early expansionist scheme on a grid principle built behind the Barri Gothic where, at every intersection, the corners had been knocked off the buildings, making each square into an octagonal. It was clever planning opening up the visibility but if you were looking for a landmark, or a bit of road to remember, it worked best as very big joke. Each crossover appearing identical to the untrained eye to the last one. But like driving in Paris, the knack is to relax into the flow of things, let them hoot and holler but just keep moving in what you trust to be the right direction. There's no point in pulling up and asking the way because even if you could pull out the stops with a few well-chosen Catalonian words, you probably wouldn't be able to understand the directions if you were given them.

I soothe myself in these situations by stopping a cab and asking him to drive to the destination, then follow close behind him. If it works in Birmingham, it will work in Barcelona. But in the end it wasn't necessary and I was soon hiding in a car park close to the hotel. A strange place actually. You take your car into a bay, remove your luggage, lock the car. Press a button, doors swing open and the motor gets dragged into a gaping hole. The doors close and you are left feeling bereft. It is as if the poor thing has just been cremated.

At Reception, the pleasant man handling new arrivals passed me a note. It was from Lautour saying he had contacted the Marqueza and she in turn had kindly sent me an invitation to join her for dinner. She was throwing a small party that night and would be very happy to include me. 'Black Tie. Come early, say ten for ten-thirty.' *Early?*

I rang to thank her and accept. To check on the best way there and how long it would take. She said she would send a fax through to the hotel, 'it was easy and would take about – oh, not very long. It would be best to come for the night, we have lots of spare rooms and it will mean you can enjoy some of the local wine.'

I didn't know much about what the Catalonians could do with a grape but had heard that the sparkling wines were extremely good, clean and very dry.

Having just put the car to bed in its burrow I didn't much want to dig it out again, yet at the same time I rather enjoyed the idea of driving out through a night-time Barcelona. In the end I made a deal with the desk clerk to pull my car back out and have it brought round at nine and to please bring the Marqueza's fax up to my room when it arrived.

For a man on his own there is a routine to be observed on walking into a fresh hotel room. Check out the bathroom; see if it has a secondary lighting circuit so that you don't have to lie in the bath being blanched by something akin to floodlighting. Look out the window and take your bearings. The room happily had a roof terrace with a view over the city and not the back of the fire escape well. Then quickly note if there are any computer and Internet sockets. Flick on the TV and scroll its satellite channels.

I once stayed at The George in Edinburgh. A cosyish hotel well located in the 'New Town' as they refer to the Georgian bit of the city. Channel Z was advertised and I was warned that I could have a free peep at the sweaty action for five minutes, after which it would automatically close down. If you wanted more you simply dialled in your room number, whereupon you could canter on for a modest nine pounds an hour.

This was the Calvinistic Protestant management bending its stiff neck towards the demands of modern-day travellers who obviously liked a little bit on the back before calling it a night. Next, scamper swiftly on to the mini-bar. What an invention. What a cruel little device. Tinkling wee mouthfuls of whisky, gin, vodka and a few local teasers. In this case it was a brandy from Jerez called virtuously, Soberano. It sounded like a TV series; *The Soberanos*. A couple of passes with this bit of rough and you became 'Drunkerano'.

Follow signs to Monserrat, the fax had said. Monserrat, the spiritual heart of Catalonia. The tenth-century monastery remains a pilgrim shrine of profound significance. It was the only church under General Franco permitted to celebrate and conduct weddings in the Catalonian language.

I arrived at Casa Nuova at about 10.15. I would have been there earlier only it took about half a lifetime to get through the gates past security, down the drive and into the garages. I tied the car up in its stall and with bag in hand followed the usher into the house.

Outside, the clear night sky ran deep into the universe helped by a lavish retinue of dazzling little stars. The slightest glaze of frost corrupted the shiny leaves of the big old *Magnolia grandiflora* that leaned tiredly against the house. A dog barked in the distance and a strange quietness hung over the bull paddocks. The boys must be breathing out there but you couldn't hear them, unless you counted the faint throb that tremored over the cold grass like a well-rehearsed warning.

The Marquéz's great grandfather had sailed to California in 1769 along with a coterie of priests, a small body of soldiers and a selection of younger sons of Spanish grandees under the watchful eye of Father Junipero Serra. The King of Spain had decided to firm up his claims to the sunshine state and begin the task of mission-building. The family had received enormous land grants from Spain. The padres erected chapels, hospices and administration buildings in adobe brick and stone.

Considering the limited facilities, tools, technical knowledge and untrained craftsmen, the architectural and decorative results were astonishing. Pedimented facades, colourful tile-roofed towers, belfries and cloistered patios created emotional silhouettes and symbols of peaceful sanctuary in the untamed Californian landscape.

Fifty-two years of Spanish mission settlement ended with the Mexican War of Independence in 1821 when Mexico City declared ownership of all the lands that Spain had claimed. But it was a long struggle for Mexico and came to a head in 1846–48 with the US–Mexican War. Mexico lost ownership of California. Monterey became the capital of the state and with a fast-growing network of roads and railways the population quickly grew. Between 1883 and 1890 the number of residents had increased from 64,000 to over 200,000. The boom brought not only traders, merchants and businessmen, but architects and real estate agents. The Marquéz's family had stayed on and capitalised on their European background and had cleverly developed property in the Spanish style while introducing the immigrants to Hispanic architecture, literature and music.

This carefully clothed if somewhat spurious fable of 'Spanish roots' fitted in well with the architects and property dealers who recognised that the true ethnic origins of Southern California did not provide a marketable tradition. In fact the first American settlers had constructed impermanent dwellings made of perishable materials. The synthesis of imported Spanish style, which owed much to Moorish civilisation encoded by Arab rule, along with imaginative architects, dubious estate agents and the unquestionable geographic connection to the Spanish-speaking peoples of South America, managed to create an entirely bogus background. A fine fiction that reassured and stroked the wealthy residents' burgeoning sense of belonging.

At the turn of the twentieth century the Marquéz's great uncle had died without issue and our host's father had inherited the title and the deeds of the estate. He packed up his life, wife and children, left California and headed back to the family home near Barcelona. His father had been a kindly man and dedicated to his children. He had respected his position and performed his duties punctiliously. But he had also been passionate about bullfighting. A passion which he passed on to all his offspring generally and to the current Marquéz Marcial in particular.

The old man, clearly not in line to become a toreador, had looked for a way to involve himself and had taken up bull-breeding. He had died when Marcial was twenty-four.

As we walked up the balustraded steps, my personal butler pushed open the huge double front doors and bid me enter. The hallway was so vast that a troupe of beautiful flamenco dancers could have stomped and rattled with passion and bravado and hardly been noticed. Actually that is exactly what was happening. Down at the far end of the room a collection of colour and clicks massed itself with a disciplined strut. I couldn't make out if it was a bunch of houseguests just loosening up before changing for dinner, or whether it was an ensemble that had been hired to jolly up the diners. After a short walk, we arrived at a full-length portrait of a horse-borne Spanish aristocrat charging straight towards us, rising out of his stirrups, brandishing his sword and seemingly yelling something about El Cid. As my butler had stopped to gaze dreamily at the canvas I did the same. Quite suddenly the picture swung open and revealed a lift door behind it. Again I was bid to enter and we slid seamlessly skywards. Sponging to a halt, I was downloaded into a silent corridor lined with enormous mahogany doors surrounded by delicately worked architraves. I thanked Pedro for his attention and noted his advice about not taking too long, as we would be going in to eat in about twenty minutes. No need to check this room out. It was a TV-free zone with a candlelit bathroom, towels the size of elephant blankets and a four-poster bed that stood tall on an old tiled floor.

I dumped my small bag down on a delicate chair and went to the loo, a fine old throne it was too, straightened my tie and headed off to the party. Not being one to miss out on a decent bit of exercise, I ignored the lift and descended the wide stone staircase that uncoiled itself down through the many floors like an idle boa. The gently rounded walls had a hundred recesses that held a hundred busts of noble Spaniard warlords. At the bottom, the room throbbed with about forty people. The Flamenco gogos and a small school of waiters padded out the crowd and still there was room for a game of skittles. The music by now was sassy and horny. I hummed as I reached the final step. I guessed it was Satchmo but couldn't name that tune.

'Ahh, my sweet hunk o' trash,' said the Marqueza arriving at my side and looking at me with a quiver of impish conspiracy.

'You really mustn't flatter me,' I said and smiled as winningly as I could manage.

She looked pretty and demure, denying her advancing years with determination.

'The song, darling,' she said. 'It's "My Sweet Hunk o' Trash". Louis Armstrong and Billie Holiday.'

'Uh-huh,' I said, relieved that she hadn't completely unfolded me.

'Do you like Jack Teagarden?' It was a rhetorical question, as she certainly wouldn't have heard my reply. She was too busy leading the way and I followed compliantly. I was ushered into the drawing room where a gathering of another two dozen or so people had gathered. The butler and his assistants moved seamlessly among the guests, keeping their glasses brimming with vintage champagne.

'I want to introduce you to my Colombian goddaughter. She is an architect.'

As we advanced on a small group standing near the huge heavy brocade curtains that fell from metres above, a striking woman with cream-coloured skin and in her mid-thirties stood out. Her long shiny black hair was tied back with a simple diamond clip and her unfussy red velvet dress with black appliqué was beautiful.

'This is Claudia Hernandez, the daughter of my closest friend,' the Marqueza announced and then continued on round the group, Don Victoriano and Doña Loly Bonastro, Doña Arantxa and Don Pepé Cortez, Baron and Baronessa Manolo. I forgot most of the names as soon as I heard them. We all swapped smiles, they very kindly welcomed me to their country in English and I did my best with a couple of well-worn Catalan phrases. Then dinner was called.

Rejoining the stone staircase we all dropped down another floor to find ourselves in a spectacularly decorated vaulted hall. A basement with a formal stone terrace running along one side of the dining room and countless clay pots planted with clipped oleanders, box, yew and *Ligustrum*. The branches of an old *almandier* tree creakily bent over one end and the uplighters showed that the blossom was already starting to come out. Tables had been laid in groups of eight with heavy beige cloths and pale brown napkins. Cut glass shone and winked and the silver glowed. Massive metal chandeliers hung on chains with twenty candles apiece. In the centre of every table was a small bronze statue of a fighting bull. Each in a different pose, caught in a frozen moment of terrible action.

Claudia was on my right and an empty chair waited on my left. Soon a tall, thin lady in her late forties arrived and claimed the vacant spot. She was wearing a long antique dress that had about as much substance as rice paper. The floppy collar lunged towards the shallow bony ravine of her exhausted bosom and a necklace of tiny pearls dangled unsatisfactorily from her neck. Her hair was probably dark and greying but that night it was telling fibs and pretending to be blonde. Her face had a damaged prettiness that refused to give up. It had lost its grip on the surface but was heroically hanging on to the bones. She sort of floated down on to her seat, weightless. She held her cigarette in between a cluster of upside-down fingers and thumb.

She looked at me with tired eyes that looked as if they had been through a washing machine.

'Hello,' I said and introduced myself.

'Are you going to fiddle with the stitches of my corduroy?' she asked in a light Spanish accent, apropos of nothing. I looked back at her, trying to figure out how to answer that. 'I wasn't planning on it,' I said.

'Well, thicken your chicken,' she said, sniffed and turned away.

'OK,' I said and started to turn towards Claudia but she was back a couple of seconds later. She turned rather suddenly and extended her head out towards me on a flappy length of neck, like a stoned vulture.

She put her hand on my knee and squeezed with her long, sharp nails until the skin yelped and then she whispered, 'Do you want to come to candy land on my loosely woven carpet?'

'I don't thanks, no.'

I smiled at her. She was really quite sweet. Silly but quite sweet.

'I never drink the drink of drunks you know,' she went on. 'You'll never find me boring the moon with tearful tales. I am,' she paused for effect, 'an unbottled spirit that seeps into the ether of life.' She pulled back and croaked. Then she started to motion her arms around like a rusty belly dancer, her head disjointedly moving from side to side. She smiled and a light burst into her eyes for a moment then quickly faded along with the fun from her face. 'Take away my heavenly herbs and I am a fairy whose wings have been confiscated, unable to fly to my dying hero and save his soul with feathery kisses.'

'Blimey,' I thought. We hadn't even got to the first course and I was getting webbed in with some dope head.

'What's your name?' I asked gently. Her placement card had disappeared. She had probably used it to make her joints. Her cigarette ash was about to drop into her lap. 'Name?' she said, her glassy eyes staring at something the rest of us couldn't see. 'Give me a name and I will be her for the night.'

'OK, I'll call you Catalana seeing as we are where we are. Do you know the Marqueza well?' I asked sounding more formal than I meant.

'How well does one know how well one knows one?' she answered. 'I know we share a love of big balls, and that is why we stay close to each other.'

'Big balls?' Presumably she means extravagant parties.

'The Marquéz breeds them here in the leisurely land of their destiny.'

'Oh bulls,' I said catching myself.

'Sí, señor, oh bulls. Big bulls, big bad bulls with big balls. Do you love the Corrida de Toros, or are you a squeamish British man who thinks that it is coritically inpolect?' She burped, drew on her cigarette and clanked down some more fizzy water.

'I've never been to a fight, but I would go if I were organised. I'd like to experience the emotion, but I don't know if I want to watch the *faena*. It seems a bit, you know, pagan I suppose. But I wouldn't mind trying on the embroidered outfit, what's it called, the uniform of the toreador?'

'The *Traje de Luces*,' she said, looking at me with a sceptical stare. I wasn't sure if she was trying to imagine how I would look in the skin-tight career-wear of the bullfighter, or was sneering with contempt at my aspiration.

'It's true,' she yawned, 'that the *corrida* is still very close to its origins in religion. It is a religious ritual in a state of slow transition.' She sounded quite different. She had become more lucid and precise. Clearly this was a subject she could manage without dipping into quasi hippie-speak.

'The objective of this shift is pretty much away from the actual kill and more towards the preparation. The cape passes where the man and bull can seem to reach an unlikely communion.

'Does that make it all right then? The ugliness being excused in the name of religious expression?'

'The sacrifice of the bull has always been mixed up with the dogma of old Rome and Spain.'

'But hasn't modern-day clergy intervened, do they condone it?' I asked.

'Ah, the elders of our church. Those dull ghosts who only reveal themselves in parodies of punctilious reverence. They of course dislike being touched on the subject of the ethics of bullfighting. They prefer to turn a shaded eye, *Es costumbre* – it is the custom – they will say. Besides,' Catalana opened her silver cigarette case, pulled out two reefers and lit them almost as well as Bacall did for Bogey. I thought she was going to pass me one of them, but she just started pulling on both of them. 'The *corrida* raises money for charities helping support the sick and wounded. It is the old Jesuitical doctrine that the end justifies the means. And, dear boy,' she let out a double-barrel stream of smoke, 'why not? The game is growing in popularity, not declining as the rest of the world might hope.'

'It doesn't surprise me. It seems the gentler emotions of pity and mercy rarely soften any transaction held by the hard Iberian,' I said a little pompously. 'Certainly in a bullfight they seem to be banished from their hearts all together. They hardly notice those cruel incidents which engross and horrify the foreigner, who, I suppose, in turn is equally blind to those redeeming excellences of skill and valour.'

Catalana looked as if she was about to say something then changed her mind. She turned from me and looking at the two cigarettes decided to separate them. This accomplished, she passed me the one in her right hand. 'Here Britishman, have a joint. The *corrida* is a gory glory.'

'Thanks.'

I attempted to introduce her to Claudia but she didn't help me. She seemed uninterested in projecting more than one place beyond her own. The man on the other side had practically turned his back on her.

At last we were being given something to eat. Mussel soup with a hint of anis. A local twist on a great soup. Catalana didn't touch hers. It didn't seem to matter whether I talked to her or ignored her so I did both.

Next we had beef stew with chocolate. Bearing in mind that Spain uses chocolate in the way other countries use gravy browning, it wasn't a complete surprise. It is not sweet at all but gives the sauce a rich darkness. It was very good and was further enhanced by a good shake of *aguardiente*. Catalana didn't touch hers.

The noise in the room was like being in a concert hall between performances, nothing too boisterous but a solid clamour nevertheless. At least six different languages skipped around the tables with people trading stories in an assortment of European dialects. After a few more crazy rounds with Catalana I opted for an altogether easier proposition and talked to Claudia.

'We were just talking about bullfighting,' I said by way of getting going.

She smiled softly and said, 'Have you seen the beautiful "El Julio"?'

'No,' I said.

'Julian López López. The teenage maestro. He arrived on the scene a couple of years ago, trained in Madrid and is doing seriously well.'

'He's a teenager?'

'I think he went to work in South America for a bit, while he was too young to operate in Europe. But he has made a huge name for himself. The young girls love him like a rock idol. Even the adults have dubbed him "The Mozart of Toreo". He is only seventeen and is electrifying the *corrida*. By the end of last year's Spanish season he had allegedly cut two hundred ears off.'

'Oh I see.' I didn't want to sound too dumb so I didn't ask if that meant both ears off one hundred bulls or one off two hundred. Either way it sounded damned impressive for a boy hardly old enough to ride a motor bike. I was a greenhorn when it came to bullfighting and although we were in a bull grower's domain I thought it best to move away from it, if I could.

We worked the usual behaviour patterns, gaining knowledge about each other's work, families and interests. She was trained as an architect in Colombia but was now practising in Barcelona. Her mother lived further south and her father was an artist back in the homeland. I told her about my third marriage and our subsequent move to Provence from England. I just stopped myself pulling out a portfolio of photographs of my inestimably fine wife and five-year-old boy, hotly pursued by dog, cats and rabbit.

'My husband is a clown,' she said looking wistfully at her fork.

'I am so sorry,' I said. 'I know some of us men are. We just don't seem to be able to help it.' I smiled, I hoped with a sort of sympathetic doctorish look.

'No no, you don't understand,' she said, talking slowly. 'He is a professional clown. He does it for money. He is very good at it.'

'Clowning or making money?'

'Well, both I suppose. I find him very amusing. He is about to start a private tour of California.'

'How do you mean, "private"?'

'He will perform at private parties only. No circuses, theatres or clubs. I think he does a couple of shows for a children's hospital but that's all.'

'Is he a white clown?' I asked having always been drawn to the sad harlequin whose pathos leaks slowly out from behind the mask that hides his soul.

'No. He is a colourful clown. He wears loud coats and silly hats and mop-top hair, that sort of thing.'

'And big long boots that trip him up?'

'Yes,' she laughed, 'but he makes a double edge to the joke and people find they are laughing at themselves.'

'And his act appeals to grown-ups as much as children?' I suggested.

'Definitely. He is a masterful clown.'

A smooth operating crew cleared the plates and filled the glasses.

'Did you see the bulls in the fields?' she asked.

'I heard some on the way in. It was beginning to get dark,' I said, noticing that we were back on bull.

'They keep them in herds because they are much calmer if they have others around them. Part of their aggression in the ring is instigated by the stress of being on their own. They don't like it.'

'I don't much either. Being alone I mean,' I said. 'Are the Barcelona rings considered important?'

'Yes, definitely, but not like Madrid and Seville.'

'I saw one this evening that seemed to have huge eggs sitting on the top of the circular wall. Do you know about it?'

'Yes. In Catalan it's called the Plaça Braus Monumental or, in Spanish, Plaza de Toros Monumental.' This Plaza de Toros is in the Gran via Corts Catalans. It belongs to the *modernismo catalan*, the most important architectural movement at the end of nineteenth and beginning of the twentieth century. In the bullfight milieu, la Monumental of Barcelona is an important place.

The plates were cleared and I managed to talk a little more to Catalana although, as the evening wore on, her bottom lip seemed to be getting looser and droopier, allowing words to totter out of her mouth without any instruction at all. They splintered and fragmented, jumbled and jumped, and finally by the time we were on *crème-brûlée* (Catalana didn't touch hers) the hapless lip was off on a journey of its own. Her eyes bravely stabbed at focusing but it was profitless. As people began to rise from their tables I offered her my arm to steady her progress. She refused and, snatching at the tablecloth, she yanked herself to her feet, very nearly destroying the table in her effort. Thanks to the bronze Toro a disaster was satisfactorily averted.

'The broken ladder of the cherry picker is useful only to the spider with holes in his heart,' she hissed, adding, 'If you pull the chord on my lovely gown you will be covered from nipple to knee in bruises.' She played a cock-eyed wink and disappeared. Unusual gel.

Later we all salsa'd to the music. Some better than others. I had had enough wine to make me start hailing the magnificence of the bagpipes and how wondrous it would be if we could just knock off an eightsome reel, strip the willow and have some fun with a dashing white sergeant. My efforts to convince anybody that Scottish dancing was far sexier than salsa fell on deaf ears. I went to bed.

The next morning breakfast was brought up to my room at about nine. It was placed on the bed by a discreet maid who seemed to understand how a chap might be feeling after a bit of a late night, and withdrew courteously in silence, having wisely left the curtains closed.

On the tray, among other things, was a very large cup of the thickest hot chocolate I had ever seen. You could stand a teaspoon up in the semi-solid brown goo. It came as such a surprise that when I picked it up I managed to sludge about half of it over the sheets. I sat there looking at the terrible mess with disbelief. I couldn't just walk out leaving the bed looking as if a calf without nappies had spent a feverish night in there, so I pulled them off and took them for a bath. It didn't work very well actually; in fact it made it considerably worse. My fine bed linen looked quite shocking. I stood in the middle of the room trying to decide through the unforgiving fog of a royal hangover, just what to do. I had a bright idea, or reasonably bright. I put them back on the bed, sort of, and then spilt the rest of the hot chocolate all over them, arranging the mug on its side, making the whole thing look as if I had had an accident. Which I had.

Then I thought that if I had done that, I would have probably picked things up and just tidied it all away. So I picked up the sheets again, opened the window and slung them over the windowsill to dry. I was just looking for the mug to position nearby as a pointer to the situation, a clue as to why half the bedding was where it was, when I heard an awful crash of glass below. The mug had slipped out of the sheets. I must have picked it up at the same time and, having parted company with its soiled sling, it had managed to go straight through the glass conservatory roof just beneath my window and smash into a thousand-piece jigsaw against a stone table which was proudly displaying an adolescent avocado plant.

I left a couple of dozen guilty Euros on the dressing table and crept out of the still-sleeping house before I dug myself any deeper into the mess and became a key player in a farce. I would call the Marqueza later and thank her for her kind hospitality, and possibly mutter something about the hot chocolate. But right now I had to head off for Lleida or I would be late for my rendezvous with the next olive man.

My car stood in the stable yard looking a bit like a Burberry advert. Thoroughbred stallions, endless grooms and teenage boys pushing strange wheelbarrows with horns on them moved around it. Did I leave it there? I was just trying to figure this out when Claudia came up, looking as though she had had an early night with a good sixteen hours' sleep. I knew of course that she hadn't as she had been busy dancing her heels off when I had called it a night.

'Can you speak Spanish?' she asked.

'Good morning, Claudia. No I can't.'

'So how are you going to get on with the olive tree dealers in Lleida?'

Did I tell her I was doing that? What else couldn't I remember? And with that thought came the uncomfortable muscle-tightening you get when you realise you may have said all sorts of things.

'Oh I take a dictionary, I try a bit of French, I mime and gesticulate, you know,' I said. 'Why?'

'Well, if you want I'll come and help you. I have nothing to do today. I've seen enough bulls to last a lifetime; it will make a change to see some old olives instead. Then I could do the interpreter thing for you.'

'Great, let's do it,' I said and bundled my belongings into the boot and fumbled around for the car keys.

'I have them,' said Claudia. She was wearing jeans and a sweater and her hair was loose.

'Have what?' I asked

'Your car keys. You left them in the ignition so I went for a drive this morning, it is such a beautiful day I couldn't resist.'

We drove along the drive that cut through the fields where bulls grazed quietly in the winter sun. Magnificent big beauties snorting confidently and talking tactics amongst themselves. It was impossible not to pick up the excitement of it all.

We picked up the new autoroute that's nearing completion and will join Barcelona with Lleida and Zaragoza. After which you can push on west to Salamanca or drop south to the big orange itself, Madrid. A mighty bit of road-building that carries endless caravans of articulated lorries moving every conceivable kind of cargo from here to there.

A couple of hours later we arrived at Cultius Calafell. A nursery specialising in olive trees in general and old ones in specific. When we turned into the yard we saw three great big boys being craned on to a low loader about to make the trip up to Toulouse.

We were received by José Victoriano the proprietor, Maria his wife and David their son. There is a daughter but she was in Barcelona busy being a barrister. We explained our mission and over a bottle of water started asking questions. Within a few minutes it was clear that we were with a man who definitely knew his olives. Not just knew them but loved them passionately.

While he settled us on to some schoolroom seats and himself at a desk I asked him if the trade in very old olives was a new phenomenon, or whether people have been selling the retired old trees for ever.

'Ten years ago they used to blow them up with dynamite,' said José. It was a quick way of getting rid of old trees that took up space and didn't yield much fruit. They were in the way. 'I remember one day the dynamite didn't go off so we went to take a closer look and you know what? Exactly, we blew ourselves up.'

José produced a newspaper cutting which had been carefully mounted in an olive wood frame. It was a photograph of a two and a half thousand year old olive, or *millénaire* as any tree over a thousand years old is called, being lifted up out of the ground. It weighed about 35 tonnes and the crane had it high enough for our man to stand underneath it and pretend to be balancing it on one of his fingers, Clark Kent style, the snap being cropped so you couldn't see the rig holding it. The tree's age had apparently been confirmed and certified in Paris. It had clearly been trotted out to impress many a visitor, but it didn't matter – it was pretty persuasive.

It had taken three days to prepare it for transport and they had used a stone cutter on its incredibly hard old wooded roots to free them from the ground.

They had also found shells and bones in its trunk. Many of the old hollowed-out olive trees had hidden soldiers in the civil war, and no doubt some had perished within the desperate and confined space. The scars and breaks in the bark, the bullet holes and bayonet wounds helped shape its legend and lend certainty to its age.

'How much did you sell that one for?' I asked shamelessly.

'Sold to a man in Perpignan,' was the short answer.

'For how much though?' I persisted. I needed to know what Lautour should expect and the undying loyalty to my client made me push in a way that I would ordinarily have drawn back from.

He shrugged, looked a trifle uncomfortable, but looking me in the eye said, 'About 20,000 Euros, that's say £14,000, plus transport.'

It was hugely expensive but at least for the first time I had a feeling I might be in the right place. At least I was talking really old olives with a man that dealt solely with the object my desire.

'Have you any more like that. That old?'

'I'm afraid we haven't,' said his wife rather too quickly, and with a look from her husband that could have strangled olive oil out of a beech tree, and a burst of guttural Catalonian, she soon changed her mind. She stopped mid-sentence and looking down over her bosom busily started to brush clean the front of her impeccable full-length leather coat with her hand. She smiled bravely and complied.

He said that he had some others including another one of about 2,300 years old.

Something was amiss here. Evidently this couple ran the business together, or as a family concern, or else she probably wouldn't have been in the office with us, yet he obviously had some knowledge that he hadn't shared with her. He must have some shady agreement going on somewhere that she was not privy to.

'How do you get a certificate authenticating its age?' I asked, taking no notice of this bit of chicanery.

'By carbon dating,' he said.

'How do they do that?'

'You push an implement similar to an apple corer deep into the trunk, take a plug and send it off for analysis. Then if all works out as you hoped and suspected, back comes a laboratory result corroborating the tree's age.'

'But as most of the really old olives are pretty much hollow inside, the trunk being precariously thin in many places, how can you push this machine into them?' I said.

'Exactly,' he said in agreement. ' It is a very difficult process.'

Señor José was so polished in his display of olivility, so knowledgeable and impassioned by the whole story – he was after all a third-generation olive man – that he had virtually become an olive tree himself. When pushed a little harder on the clearly touchy and uncomfortable absoluteness of age, he finally said in a hushed and endearing fashion that 'they talk to me and tell me'.

He explained. 'I gather together the available information. Where it was grown and under what circumstances. Dry or lusher. We consider the variety of olive and the treatment it has had. Then I wait for the message. It always comes to me, a whispered statement.'

'How do you mean?'

'The tree tells me how old it is.'

'A silent communication?'

'It is in the spiritual mists,' he said.

Here was a man that was prepared to be ridiculed in much the same way Prince Charles had been when he once admitted that he spoke to his plants. He put his professional status on the line and admitted that when in doubt he actually engaged the tree in conversation and asked it to divulge its age. I, too, strongly believe in chatting up trees, shrubs and plants of all denominations, so I was thrilled.

'Do some of them feel indignant at such a leading question? Do they lie about their age?'

He laughed heartily and said that he thought they were very proud of their longevity.

'Perhaps,' I said slowly and a little slyly, 'they pretend to be older than they really are?'

José batted with, 'The oldest and biggest are not necessarily going together,' thus moving us away from the dating game.

'Sometimes you will find very old trees that have been grown on a windswept hilltop with stony ground and they will be small and contorted, while younger trees found on the lusher valleys with richer soil will be very much bigger.'

'Where do you find these old trees? They must be quite hard to locate.'

'Nowadays yes. To get hold of very old ones is a whole new game. Peasant farmers have wised up to the demand from the middle men and will only sell their old trees if you buy land as well, thus inflating the value of both the tree and the terrain.'

'But the land will be a reasonable investment?'

'Yes, the buyers are generally happy. It is a new kind of real estate currency. The field might only have three or four *millénaires* on it and the trees may stay put for ages before being sold but the value of the land will hold its worth or maybe even increase a bit.'

'And those three or four trees will fetch what, some ten thousand Euros each?'

'Probably, if they are really good trees. It is,' he said, 'a bit like oriental or Turkish carpets. A hedge against in- or de-flation. A sound investment that holds its price. Not altogether a bad place to put your money.'

Renoir had done the same kind of thing about 130 years ago. But he had done it not so much as a hedge against inflation but more as an acting conservationist. He bought all the olive fields that surrounded his home in Agnes-sur-mer near Nice to protect them against being ripped out by the locals in the name of progressive construction – the original greenist.

'Please excuse me, I must complete a little business. I suggest you have some lunch in the restaurant over there,' he said, pointing to a modern building across the way. 'Then afterwards I will show you what we have.'

We took a break for a filthy lunch in a motel diner that had recently been built to meet the low-key demands of the lorry drivers. The waiter managed to lay the table without looking at it or us. He didn't look at the food he brought either, but one couldn't blame him for that. He reminded me of a British Rail attendant who worked in the restaurant car when I was going down to Plymouth one night. I had chosen the 'stew' rather than the fish pie, being of the school that steers well clear of anything to do with fish unless I have met it socially.

The so-called stew was shocking; gristly, fatty and of questionable animal origin, and when the steward came round with the bill and asked me what I had eaten for main course, 'Tinned dog food,' I had told him.

'Would that be the beef or rabbit flavour, sir?' he had replied without missing a beat.

Three kilometres up the road and down a track we came upon an orchard of *millénaires*.

Walking silently between these ancient hardwoods that had been gathered together and planted in the rich soil of Lleida was an eerie experience. Most of them had been around for at least 1,500 years longer than me and a few of them even longer. As I moved among them, listening to see if they would mutter anything about how old they were, a confidential confirmation of age, I felt I was in the company of a collective wisdom. Perhaps being in among a heard of old elephants might have created the same mood. The soft, dreamy air felt like it was their breath caught and folded into a small whisper. An almost imperceptible beat of life floated around the wood with a warm sigh and if I could have tapped the sap I might have celebrated an olive oil of greater eminence than you could imagine.

The weight of history was everywhere. Jesus was probably crawling around in nappies when they had been planted. Rome was advancing the frontiers of ego-tripping. Actually at that time the Romans were beginning to lose the plot. Heady with over-confidence and arrogance, they were pushing just a little too hard at the front and getting sloppy at the back. The soldiers flounced around in skirts covered in metal panels, their chests protected with breastplates, while ridiculous feathers nested on top of their helmets. Mind you, the Spanish could puff out their chests just as well as any pontificating Roman. There is an old Castillian saying: '*Si Dios no fuese Dios, seria rey de las Españas, y el de Francia su cocinero*.' ('If God were not God, he would make himself king of the Spains, with him of France for his cook.')

The dress designers had a busy time keeping everybody smart. Already the bikini had made an appearance worn by the Ginnasta. The toga look was hot for both men and women. The boys slinging a silky sheet over one shoulder and letting it wrap itself around their bodies. The girls employing much the same style but often starting with the fabric covering part of their heads, held in place by a tiara which encouraged it to fall in loose folds towards the ground.

Rome had originally come to occupy Spain because it was at war with Carthage, an ancient city in North Africa founded by the Phoenicians in 870BC, who wanted control of the western Mediterranean.

The Carthaginians had arrived in Spain in the sixth century BC. Treacherous, deceitful and faithless as they undoubtedly were, they didn't engage in battle with the Romans until 264BC, the first of three major confrontations in what would become known as the Punic wars. Despite fighting with massive determination for some twenty years, Rome beat them up and took away their islands: Corsica, Sicily and Sardinia. They didn't, however, get the Straits of Gibraltar or south-eastern Spain that the Carthaginians managed to hold on to.

The Iberians, also from Northern Africa, had first settled in the south, creating the peninsula of Iberia as early as the sixteenth century BC, but with the arrival of the Carthaginians came the Celts who merged with the Iberians to become, you've guessed it, Celtiberians.

In common with most of the other European lands, Iberia had been just a small part of an imperial jigsaw cut out by Rome. It had remained unperturbed for centuries until AD409 when the northern clans, the Visigoths, Ostrogoths, and probably the Gollygoths for all I know, overran Southern Europe, swept through Gaul, poured over the Pyrenees and down into Hispania. They traversed the same mountains as I had just driven but used a lot less petrol and avoided the tollbooths, finally establishing themselves in the third century and taking control. Those Goths, members of an ancient Teutonic tribe, must have been heroic warriors. They whacked the Roman Empire and founded kingdoms in

Italy, France and Spain. From all accounts they behaved like thoroughly good thugs; rude, ignorant and uncouth. It was the Greeks who, having witnessed their dubious social behaviour patterns, coined the name Barbarian. As far as they were concerned, anyone who couldn't read Greek was a Barbarian, so the Goths must have been A-list. You can still find them actually. They come from Gotham, a village in Nottinghamshire. But they are somewhat tempered nowadays. And of course Batman hangs out in Gotham City.

It is tricky to understand how the Gothics who were allegedly so uncultured ended up with a name that is more readily associated with a style of architecture. One that has a predominance of vertical lines, pointed arches and clustered columns rich in stone carving to boot. But art and architectural innovation was all around. Sixth century BC Iberian sculpture included the famous Lady of Elche and Bicha de Balazote from Cerro de Los Santos, which shows Greek influence. There is the Carthaginian sarcophagus at Cadiz. The cusp of BC and AD produced some of the finest Roman temples, amphitheatres, aqueducts, statues, mosaics, painted vases and gold *objets d'art*.

Think of how quiet it must have been in Spain 2,000 years ago. No midget 50cc motorcyclettes, for example, revving their immature little head gaskets off. Why and how does a perfectly likeable adolescent turn into a cultural disease when he gets hold of one of these unwelcome little pests? During the day they scream around town, ripping the guts out of their little squirt of machinery, and then when the sun goes down they get it together to double the effort. Like mosquitoes on speed they tantrum around with balls that haven't dropped, daring you to sleep. At that age I wouldn't have been seen dead or alive on such an instrument. It had to be the deep, throaty gurgle of a Norton Commando, a Ducati Senator or possibly a Honda Emperor. The engine could vibrate a girl's knickers off and awaken a Porsche. And another thing. What about those dustmen? Isn't it bizarre that they wait until five o' clock in the morning before deciding to clean up the town? Chucking dustbin lids on to the ground like puerile percussionists. Perhaps they feel that if they have to get up half way through the night then everybody else should too. They shout to each other as if the street was hosting some kind of Mardi Gras instead of being tucked up in bed.

One thousand five hundred years ago the villages had no vehicles of any sort to contend with, let alone silly mini-bikes, or trash trucks. No airports, trains or bus stations either. Just the gentle rhythm of a few horses clopping around drowsy little hamlets going about their chores. No decibel abuse. No church bells or cathedral clocks, no glass to smash. No pianos or electric guitars, no rock 'n' roll – NO ROCK 'N' ROLL?? No hi-fi or MTV. Just a few crude gut-stringed instruments. Totally unplugged. No whisky, no baths or showers, no loos or stripy toothpaste. No condoms or stockings, and worst of all, precious few gardens.

The story of the garden begins when man gave up being a nomadic hunter and settled down into communal villages. The earliest cultivations were probably developed in the time of the Pharaohs, on the shores of the powerful rivers of the Near East – the Nile, Tigris and Euphrates, where the two major ingredients of life, water and sunshine, were supplied in plenty. This allowed early man to discover the trick of sowing seeds and, with a bit of trial and error, plus the domesticating of useful animals the first farmers emerged. Primitive enclosures made of the thickety thorns of the acacia would have been erected to keep out marauders. The understanding of growing in straight lines to allow for easy maintenance and simple irrigation would have marked the first inklings of practical design. Artistic expression would have inevitably developed gradually.

Two distinctly separate disciplines of growing would have appeared. First, the utilitarian one of vegetables and fruit for food and possibly medicine. The discovery of healing properties in plants was at this time, of course, empirical. And secondly, the ornamental and decorative one for relaxation. The latter being for those with time and money to indulge themselves with such frivolity. No doubt the two met when the more mundane use of water widened its appeal with ponds for fish and water plants as well as antediluvian swimming pools. Vines (*Vitis vinifera*), one of the earliest plants found in civilisation, would have been trained over antecedent pergolas to give shade, and the burgeoning fruit orchards would have found themselves acting as an edible decoration. The Egyptians loved their gardens, and very often their gardeners too it would seem. We know this from the pictures found in the tombs and there are many references in the writings found on papyri.

> I am thy beloved
> I am for thee like the garden
> Which I have planted with flowers
> And all sweet-smelling herbs

We were about to head back to Barcelona when José asked if we would like to see some olives being pressed and some oil being made. To watch the process and learn the secrets that thousands of years of hard labour had taken to perfect. It seemed churlish to pass up on the offer, so off we went to a local press that has taken absolutely no notice of modernisation. It stood proudly turning its back on production methods that would add a couple of noughts to its turnover and probably more to its profit margin.

In the centuries of Lleida's existence nothing much had changed. Certainly not the rickety old olive mill we were let into via some cranky metal doors, the windows of which had travelled from clear glass through opaque and were now solid grime grey. I shook hands with a man who seemed to know only the small but important world of squeezing the best out of an olive. He was a shy and awkward person who found it difficult to hold your eye and probably resented the whole PR side of his business, preferring to be left alone to make his superior oil, where he was safe and honoured among his peers. Outsiders were a necessary evil to which he understood he had to make some kind of gesture, but it weighed heavily on his oily shoulders. However, encouraged by a woman that was either his wife, his agent, the manageress, or all three, he started on his well-rehearsed script that informed us that he was the son of a man that had been the grandson of the grandson of a grower back in the days when oil was oil.

The olives arrive from the pickers and are put on to a weighing machine, and the farmer is told how much oil to expect from his crop. They are then put on a belt which moves up a ramp while a wind machine blows off all unwanted leaves, branches and assorted bits of debris. Next they arrive in a receptacle where three big cone-shaped stones, about a metre tall and all slightly different widths, crush the fruit, pushing the pulp out to the edges of the bowl. The amount of olives these worn-down pestles must have crushed over the years is beyond imagining. Someone with a spade as old as the valleys then shovels up the pulp and lays it out on disc-shaped mats (*carpaccio*) about 50 centimetres across. These are then stacked, one on top of another, until about a dozen of them are ready whereupon they are moved and secured into the press. A much-used timber screw is then tightened down until the oil starts to run from the cracked fruit mash, flowing freely through dipping wooden channels until it arrives at its destination. A thought occurred to me about halfway round: if you squeeze olives to get olive oil, what do you squeeze to get baby oil?

The end of the tour through the cobwebbed old factory shed culminated with a bottle of cloudy, hand-made olive elixir being ceremonially handed to their visitors. Its smart graphics label belied its humble origins. It was the first olive press I had seen and I was happy that it had been an old-fashioned one. Their modern counterparts, with their high-capacity stainless-steel tanks, their computer-controlled surgical environments, would surely prove as dull a thing to visit as a glue factory.

As the time approached to say goodbye to José Victoriano I could see that there was every reason to strike a deal with him. His trees were incredibly old and beautiful in their way, he was a knowledgeable and dedicated dealer and the search for Regis Lautour's olive tree could have easily ended in his backyard. But there lay the problem. It had been so easy that I felt a strong impulse to keep the options open, to look further afield and reassure myself that there wasn't anything better round the corner. I was totally aware of the 'grab while you can' or 'don't miss your chance by dithering' syndromes but I felt that if the trees in Lleida had been around for so many hundreds of years they would still be there in a month or two when I had had a chance to widen my knowledge and convince myself nothing better existed.

Three hours later we were back in Barcelona, the car back in its burrow, Claudia making arrangements to meet an architect friend and me up to my neck in piping hot water trying to think of anything but olives. But of course that was not possible. The next day I was heading for Valencia to meet another of Spain's leading olive tree specialists, Señor Junos.

A friend of mine called Louis Dupont, who has a nursery in Provence and deals in all sorts of wonderful trees and shrubs, had recommended that I make contact with this exceptional expert. He said that by the time I had been with him for an hour or two I would be fully briefed on all aspects of the olive tree in general and *millénaires* in specific. From all accounts he would have more knowledge in his little finger than most dealers would have in both their hands and feet. I fully expected him to be an olive. But that was tomorrow and meanwhile I wanted to find a good tapas bar.

The tapas bar is one of Spain's greatest attributes. Slightly idiosyncratic and tailored to a country that eats both lunch and dinner at least a couple of hours later in the day than we do in Britain. Unsurprisingly, Spaniards need to find a little something delicious to put in their stomach as a gap-filler on their way towards the main meals. Tapas fits perfectly. They are highly appealing and extremely tasty little dishes that have been a way of life in Spain for as long as anyone can remember. Who could resist some fois gras fingers, shrimp bites, small steak squares, Iberian smoked ham and spicy potatoes, cheeses, sardines and prawns tossed in a garlic and oil sauce? And that's before you've decided what you really want. They show up the peanuts and crisp brigade as an unimaginative bunch of bunglers.

It takes practice to understand the tradition of tapas. You have to eat well but selectively because the idea is not to have eaten so much that you arrive for dinner as full as a fatted calf. Naturally all this sociable eating inevitably gets helped along by plenty of wine, cider and beer, so the art of staying passably sober is another layer on the understanding of the game. Tapas bars are also a godsend for students who haven't got the money to apply their rumbling tummies to expensive restaurants. As a food it is difficult to define. Actually it is not so much a kind of food but more a style of eating that is quintessentially Spanish. They are as varied as the people who cook them are. Ranging from the simple like grilled fish, sausage or cheese to the more cultivated offerings like quail, frogs' legs (probably leapt in from France), caviar and young eels. They are nearly always served in little helpings. The bars serve them quickly and expect you to eat them quickly. It's all about instant gratification. Any delay spoils the point of them.

Spanish cuisine is not the spicy, red-hot chilli, neck-sweating cooking of South America. It is much gentler and enormously varied. It is a much-appreciated cuisine that can hold its chin up high among all other European cooking.

Tapas probably originated in Andalusia where copious quantities of fine dry sherry are drunk as an aperitif. Being fairly alcoholic it might have been considered wise to line the stomach with some bread before starting on the fortified wine which would ensure that you stayed reasonably sober. So if you're eating bread why not add something tasty to it? *Voilà!* Tapas.

There are, of course, hundreds of tapas bars in Barcelona to choose from, but a friend, Alejandro, had invited me to visit a couple of his favourites. An architect trained in Bogota, Alej had come to Barcelona like many other South Americans of his profession, including Claudia. I had met him through Claudia, and had found him easy and fun to be with. His notions of architecture were sharp and his drawings beautiful. He could sketch a building on one page and capture the features of a pretty girl on the next, moving seamlessly between styles. He also had a little boy of about the same age as mine so daddy-speak contributed to our friendship. He was quite a bit younger but that didn't seem to worry either of us. His English was good, certainly a lot better than the busking guitarist we encountered in the first bar we went into. A small, round, middle-aged man with a bright blue jersey shooftied around the sawdust-covered floor singing:

Men h'ar clever bits of stubble
Sand by sea
Sí, sí, sí.

It bothered me that Ben E. King and The Drifters' imperishable 'Stand By Me' was on the verge of sinking into an imaginary ocean, but what the hell, the tune was right.

We drank Ostatu rouge and then Sagardi. This was barman showbiz. A two-metre spill of cider piddled strongly out of a huge cask and arched over the barman's head, which he then caught in a thin tumbler and served quickly to his customer. We gobbled down chicken livers in sherry sauce, beef tenderloin tips in garlic, sausages with sweet-sour figs, shrimp, melon and apple salad, a bit of boiled lobster and some marinated salmon. The noise was high and cheerful, and when it was time to move on we handed in our little sticks which were counted and our bill calculated.

By the time we left the second tapas bar we were full to the brim and well wined and walked happily, albeit a little unsteadily, through the old part of town, watching it being watered down by trucks with sprays on their tails. Alej thought it a good idea to go and listen to some music and as much as I agreed I knew it wiser to go back to my hotel. I bade the boy goodnight with promises of a replay soon.

Fighting my way out of Barcelona through the traffic was easier the next morning. The timing was better. People had actually gone to work and hadn't come back for lunch. It was a narrow window but I managed to slip through.

It took about three and a half hours to get to Pobla de Valbona-Valencia and to make contact with Señor Junos, the expert. The temperature rose and a warm spring day took over blowing away any vestiges of winter. The south got ever closer.

After some diligent map reading I arrived on a plot of cleared wasteland on the outskirts of Pobla de Valbona. A lot of development had been going on there. The billboards that announced the extravagant plans for new villas were full of artists' impressions of comfortable homes aimed squarely at the aspiring middle class. There was no clue as to what Spanish commercial gems might have been torn down to make way for the largesse of the town planning department but with luck the clearance and demolition had been sedulous.

The address I had written down took me to a numberless patch on the edge of the abyss. I parked the car next to the only house in the immediate vicinity. It looked promising for no other reason than that it had a magnificent olive tree standing incongruously on the boundary of a limited backyard and was probably worth more than the house. There was also a large plane tree with a sprinkling of gravel and that was it. This small area surrounded an architect-free construction whose windows looked as though they had been thrown indiscriminately at the walls without any pleasure. A wide, square entrance gaped off centre and supported one of those practical but undesirable string curtains. Those things that hang in strands of fluffy nylon that you part with your hands and dive through, half expecting to change dimension.

I called from the cell phone to check and it was answered immediately by a man looking out of a window right next to the car. It took me a moment to cotton on to the fact that we were on the same line and that I could put the phone down and talk to him normally.

Señor Junos walked out of his house to greet me. He was a tall, well-built chap in his fifties. He reminded me of someone but I couldn't think who. An enormous cigar was stuck in his mouth like a zeppelin caught in a vice and he wasn't going to let it interfere with his talking. His broken

English cleverly escaped on exhaled clouds like Red Indians sending smoke signals.

He knew about me because I was a friend of a friend and had fired dozens of warnings of my imminent arrival. He directed me over to the big olive tree and posed in front of it like a confident sheriff. His legs splayed and hands on hips.

'The most beautiful and oldest tree in the region, maybe h'in Spain.' Puff puff. He managed a pretty good English.

'How old is it?' I asked.

'More than two thousand years,' he said. 'But,' he pulled on the baguette burning on the front of his face, 'you won't find many as old as this that are as pretty.' And he was right. It had a wonderful old gnarled trunk that was in very fine condition. The crown had a thick head of healthy leaves. It really was implausibly beautiful and regal.

'Are you selling it?' I wondered aloud.

Señor Junos made a noise something between a snort and a yawn and suggested we went inside.

I was shown into the strangest sitting room I had ever seen. It was the size of a small aircraft hangar and had the atmosphere of a sound stage at Shepperton. In one corner there was a sitting room complete with all the necessary props; a bookcase, coffee table and sofas with a television and video. All laid out next to a dining room with eight carver chairs, plates and glasses. While the walls actually went up into a huge industrial ceiling the 'room' was contained by topping out with a stuck-on frieze at about only three metres. Above a grand stone fireplace was hung a cheerful new carpet depicting peacocks strolling among florid *Magnolia grandiflora*. The dining room boasted an ambitious wood carving which Señor Junos informed me was the god of wind, whoever he was. Perhaps a god known to sailors, or in the context of this dubious bit of chiselled timber, he might have been the god of indigestible green vegetables, depicted as he was, arguing with a bunch of aggravated lions that seemed to have been frolicking among indiscernible salad leaves.

Over the other side of the hangar lay a collection of useful farm implements. A tractor and plough, some large spraying contrivance, an assortment of old metal and wooden machines and a few hand tools.

In the middle of the room, taking up pride of place, was stationed a new mega-bike bursting with two-wheeled cyclesterone. It gleamed and glistened under the harsh strip lighting. It was not a romantic thing; it had just a single saddle adequate for one small bum only. The fairing was beaten back around the body, smoothing out all the awkward bits that bikes have. The exhaust pipes rose up out of the manifolds like erections and the fuel tank moulding resembled a pregnant tummy. A boy-toy. It was nearly a shock to learn that it belonged to Paloma, Señor Junos' younger daughter.

Admittedly the young girl had been mooching about dressed in red leathers with a matching helmet slung over one wrist. Reasonably it hadn't been difficult to associate her with the bi-tyred beast that growled in its sleep over by the drinks cupboard, but I had, and call me conventional, presumed her to be a pillion. Now I realised it was her very own little plaything.

Between the farm equipment and the kitchen was a highly unique washroom. A single door with no lock led into a shared loo space with something for everybody. Two normal sitting-down loos facing one another with no partition between them other than a pair of strategically placed televisions. One male urinal, a communal bidet and 'his and hers' wash basins mingled unashamedly with vending machines for condoms and tampons. More mysteriously, an electric kettle with a picture of an olive on its side was available. The room, in common with the rest of the experience was cruelly lit but impeccably clean.

Next came the kitchen, which was a riot. Quite impossible to work out if this was for real or just for show, it burst with modern high-tech cuisine gadgetry. Standing by a commercial-sized squeezer was a basket big enough to be a laundry collection point for a family of twenty. It was filled to the brim with about a hundred freshly picked oranges. Lined up like ammo waiting patiently in a pinball machine, they were about to be fed into the device below and have the living juice squeezed right out of them. Making tumblers of perfect golden liquid in a few seconds.

Señor Junos steered me over to the table where he introduced his wife Pilar, his son Miguel, who spoke very good English considering, and two daughters: Penelope and Paloma the bike. An assortment of boyfriends, passers by and unknown quantities were waved at in one embracing sweep. We all sat down together while the chief held court and directed proceedings. Generally the family managed to laugh, or at least smile, at the right times, cheer on his rehearsed statements and made sure he had everything he needed. Clearly a statesman in his own sitting room. He poured deep whiskies into two glasses and offered me one. It would have been rude to refuse this hospitality but it wasn't what I was looking for. I wanted to get on, see the trees, discuss the prices, gather info and get out. But things were not to be so simple.

Just to get something going I asked him via Miguel how much he wanted for the fine old tree out in his courtyard.

'I won't sell it,' he said simply.

'Well, how much is it worth then?' I said, genuinely interested.

'I'd sooner sell my children,' he said with a dismissive wave towards the girls. 'I have turned down the equivalent of £120,000 for it,' he added not entirely convincingly. I think he was getting pesetas, Euros and pounds a bit jumbled but whatever way it was viewed it seemed an extraordinarily high amount. But at least he was putting a reasonable value on his daughters' heads.

The whole family being gathered round the table, a fairly high-octane dialogue then took place between him and his grown-up daughters, one of whom had recently married. They wanted him to sell. Another glass of whisky, another fat cigar and the temperature was rising. Maybe they had been discussing all this before I arrived and it just came to a head when they realised I might just be a serious punter. At that price even Latour would stall.

The conversation moved off olives and on to matters of a more intimate nature. It turned out that Louis Dupont, our mutual olive contact and friend, had come down from Provence to attend the wedding of Señor Junos' daughter, Penelope. This was considered a great coup and the family had been thrilled to see him.

The newly married daughter was ordered off to find the photograph album of the wedding. She returned with a huge black velvet bag, which she carried flat in two hands and laid, carefully on the table. She undid the golden pull-cords slowly and the book was extracted from its cover with the reverence one might accord the original manuscript of *Love's Labour's Lost*.

Suddenly I knew who Junos reminded me of: Hugh Heffner. He was much more King Bunny than Don Adriano De Armado, and Penelope would have had to struggle hard to emulate either the Princess of France or indeed Jaquenetta.

'Vows are but breath, and breath a vapour is . . .'

The good book was proudly opened and the glossy pictures spread themselves across two pages and positively beamed out at you. A four in hand with tassels and ties harnessed with traditional splendour waited patiently to get on with the task in hand and pull the open carriage off to nirvana. The happy couple sat looking magnificent and as rigid as shop dummies. Isn't it strange how some people can put on a morning coat and look as if they were born in it whilst others turn into cardboard stiffs.

I wasn't sure whether this little liturgy was just a regular reliving of the recent nuptials or whether it was being laid on as a civil ceremony for my sake. Our mutual friend having been at the wedding was probably enough of a link or excuse to reshuffle the glorious golden moments one more time. Anyway I hummed with approval just in case. It was a fine do although the hiccup in Spanish architecture that was their house made an odd juxtaposition to the late nineteenth-century style of their big day.

The bottle was passed round and was politely turned down by one and all. I was fascinated by the way that the cigar not only stayed in his mouth while he spoke, but also it seemed while he drank. He managed this much like the ventriloquist who downs a glass of water while his doll insults him. Not being one to acknowledge a refusal, he went ahead and poured out another slug of scotch for both of us and rather shockingly downed his in one speedy gulp. He burped and produced a framed photograph of King Juan Carlos and Queen Sofia of Spain shaking his hand and admiring his old tree. It was hard to work out what the King was doing in Junos' backyard, but there he was along with his Queen, admiring the tree as if they had never seen such a thing before. Perhaps he was best man at the daughter's wedding.

'Two kings,' said Junos grandly. 'The King of Spain and the King of Olives.'

Señor Junos has been in the olive business since, as he said, 'I had 24. I now has 52.'

'When I was in my twenties,' he went on, 'old trees were in a small demand but the technology was poor. We would have to dig them out by hand. We had only the tractor to lift them up but the roots were freed manually. The roots are as hard as iron is.'

The conversation turned to my quest and what he could do to help. He said that he thought 2,000 years seemed to be the maximum. Maybe a little more, but after that it was the second growth. By that he meant that the original tree would probably have disintegrated, but a new shoot might well appear from the rootstock.

'When we go to look at my old olives I'll take you to a local park where there is a tree of 3,000 years old.'

'Could we buy it?' I said, sort of automatically. This phrase had started to come out every time anybody mentioned an old olive tree. Soon I would be known as Alex Can-we-buy-it-Main.

'No no,' he said. 'It is a national treasure.'

'How about a cutting? Could we take a cutting?'

Junos looked at me and saw I was serious. He filled his tumbler and then generously poured whisky all over the back of my hand which I was feebly using to cover my own glass.

'It is a national treasure,' he said. 'I can't just go in and take a cutting, help myself, it would be stealing, theft, robbery. Anyway there are only two shoots.'

'Go on then,' I said. 'One for them, one for me.'

He tipped his glass and stared into the already small amount of whisky left barely covering the dip.

'I would have to go in after dark and borrow one . . .' he trailed off.

A silence fell around the table. I looked around and everybody seemed to be in a frozen animation. It wasn't that they were hanging on the suspense of it all, more that they felt they were all there under duress and longing to be given the nod so that they could leave and get on with their lives. They were bored stiff and wanted to go out and live.

'Anyway it gives a good twist to buying an old tree,' I said quietly mostly to myself, resolving to pick up on this again at a later date. 'Shall we go and look at some trees?' I asked, changing the subject and getting up. Time was getting on and I wanted to be back in Valencia before it got too late. If I didn't take the initiative it could mean staying with the Junos family and that wasn't really on the agenda. What would the bedrooms be like? Probably full of wax dummies of Franco, Basque scalps and deranged matadors with horns sticking out of their chests.

After so much alcohol a few worries about Junos' driving fleetingly passed the front of my mind, but once we were underway they soon fell off. I was too busy hanging on with my legs wedged between the back of the front seats and the front of the back seats to give much thought to his ability to control his motor car. His wife had joined us for the gentle little outing as well.

'I tell the ages of the trees by reading the roots,' he said. 'I can guarantee this. It is better than carbon dating.'

Junos may have been an olive maverick but he indubitably knew his subject. I didn't need to ask questions because he was answering everything I could have dreamt up and more.

Suddenly the jeep pulled off the main road and headed into a local park. A large, sprawling area of trees and picnic spots.

In the same way that Spanish hotels don't have carpets in their rooms, just bare floor tiles, the park had no grass, just a covering of dry earth. But there was a small lake and in the middle of it bubbling water sprang enthusiastically up and into a huddle of ducks that gathered round the source, bobbing their heads and wagging their tails. In 1410 St Vincent had blessed the park and its lake, and there is a saying that as long as the water keeps flowing into this pond, Lleida will have something to drink. I think Junos took great solace in this fact.

After a loose conducted tour we finally arrived at the very old olive tree. A three by two-metre metal cage sat forlornly in the shadows of some mighty parasol pines. Inside, a withered, hollowed-out old root supported a pair of newish shoots, one of which was a paltry 60 centimetres, the other nearer to two metres in height. Spindly, undernourished-looking creatures, they could hardly be described as impressive. The fact that they were growing from 3,000-year-old rootstock added a little to the drama but not enough. A freestanding plaque announced the ancient tree's history and how it too had received St Vincent's benison. It should have been hugely moving. The incredible age, the saintly aura and the struggling new growth symbolising eternal perseverance. Not so much the never-ending life of olives, but the incredible regenerating force that came from within. But somehow it was tragically disappointing.

This old, old olive tree was moving inexorably towards his grave because the heavy hooded pines overhead were denying him his rightful light. It was a case of pure misdirected local bureaucracy. They wanted to show off the ancient tree, but they wanted him to be in a shady location, thinking more about the people who came to admire him than the poor old boy himself. Without sunlight, even for the ever-battling, uncomplaining old olive, there is a limit. He can manage without water, he can withstand excessive heat, he can nudge through without nutrients, he can tackle the winds and wrap up extraordinarily well against heavy frosts, but he cannot do without light. And here in the centre of this calm and tranquil park, organised for the Spanish people to enjoy their family recreation, he lingered on the periphery of death. Not because of old age, the new shoots saw to that, but because of darkness being cast over his weakened efforts of survival by the very thing that kept his visitors cool. I could hardly look. It was like watching the polar bear in captivity that was so bored in his pen, deprived of activity; he plunged towards insanity bred from the desperation of something to occupy his mind. Even raiding the dustbins of outpost engineers in Alaska and risking being shot at would be better than the mindless performance of weaving in a bare bear pit on the edge of nowhere.

I felt a determination to try and save at least one of these poor olive shoots. I didn't quite know how it would be done but I was sure the time would come when I would lobby Junos to help.

We moved on to gawp at a series of palm trees that had been planted into the crevices of a stone wall that surrounded another play area. The wall had been cleverly made with planting holes set into its side. Some wag, instead of planting little rock plants like *Aubrieta* or *Alyssum*, had stuffed in some *Phoenix canariensis* into the crevices and now, however many years later, they grew out of the wall like obedient camel necks. What were they eating to make them so strong? All the lime pointing and minerals left by the builders must surely have long been devoured. The surrounding area supported no other visible plant life so the palms must have been surviving on little more than a prayer and a whisper. St Vincent probably had something to do with it.

Back in the Jeep we beat along at a steady 130 kph occasionally peeling off to look at old olive trees. We climbed out. Stared and climbed back in. Different varieties were pointed out but to the uninitiated it was hard to spot the difference.

Every time Junos said they were 800, 900 years old, I said 'not enough, I need older' and on we would ply. We scrambled round field after field until the trees seemed to merge into one endless hedge. Beautiful, old and in great shape, but always they were too young, or so I believed. I now felt that the thing had to be a couple of thousand years old to enter the competition.

'Now I show you the real thing,' Junos announced, and with that pulled his vehicle off the road once more, gathered up speed and shot up the side of a hill like a demented entrant in a four by four wheel competition. It was practically impossible to climb out when he stopped. We were so shaken up, there was precious little that was solid within us.

'These are 1,500 to 2,000 years.' He had parked next to a pair of extremely elderly-looking fellows. Junos pushed me over to the first one and pointed out a dozen characteristics that, as far as he was concerned, confirmed its age. Just as I was taking it all in I was pulled by my elbow over to the other one where the magician performed his tricks again. He pointed to a split bit of bark here, an ancient growth there and a few tell-tale signs that showed excessive age on the roots. At first it was hard to muster much enthusiasm, I was olived out again.

But once I started to absorb the personality of the two old trees I sensed that the gentle atmosphere of calm and tranquillity was once more being generated. It was palpable. A reluctant reverence stole up and gave me a happy shiver. Were they really causing this or was it just my alertness to their portentous legend? Like when you see a mega-famous person coming into a room of unknowns. Does he or she really have an aura or is it just that we have learnt so much about them without knowing them, they seem to grow in stature?

I think Junos knew about this too and we all shared a solemn silence for a few moments. But it was broken by the great man saying that they were for sale. They had, he informed us, been transplanted from a field further up north, had survived without mishap and were a reliable bet for moving to the South of France. Oh, and they would cost the equivalent of £10,000 each. 'Very old, very rare.'

He also added that the variety was the one whose fruit birds liked the best. Consequently they were seldom grown by farmers for crops, but were sometimes added to the orchard just to encourage wildlife.

Nothing like a bit of commercial broadcasting to bring you to your senses. One of these would do. At last I was with a tree that was in contention and could seriously be offered to Regis. It might not be the oldest tree available in all of Europe but it was getting close. Two thousand years of living history and still looking pretty pukka. Anything older was going to be damned difficult to buy. Preservation orders, declarations of national treasures, guardians of villages, living monuments, all these factors contributed to making the quest of finding anything much more ancient than these two trees increasingly difficult. Lies would undoubtedly be told about supposed age, ignorance would offer grander bets, and even some of the other allegedly reliable dealers may say they have something more to offer, but Junos' understanding of the genealogy of his trees was beyond reproach.

We left the two old olives and started back to Junos' headquarters. On the way I asked if we could stop and pick some fresh oranges, without stealing them. Junos said it was no problem but we would need to take a roundabout route and gather some from a field that belonged to a friend of his. People were very touchy about tourists helping themselves and rightly so. We have the same feelings about our cherries in Provence. People park their cars, get out a bag and start helping themselves to the bounty as if it were hedgerow food for free.

Knowing a quick cut across a field Junos took us down a small gravel drive with big open fields on either side. The dipping sun was backlighting the heads of the wild grasses and making them translucent. The track dipped down a small ravine that seemed to follow the route of a long since dried-up stream.

At one point on a low bank, set back a few metres from the trail was a dear little off-white cottage with a washed-out red tiled roof. It had just one window and a slightly battered old door. Down one end a climbing rose scrambled over the gable. Wild flowers had seeded themselves among the big boulders that held the bank in place.

Not far away, sitting comfortably on a craggy bank, was a formidable old olive tree that looked at least a couple of thousand years old. It nestled down against the wind, hunching its shoulders slightly, and seemed to be protecting the tiny building. The big silvery crown which spread itself out far and wide each side of the thick, gnarled trunk was still heavy with black fruit waiting to be gathered, and shimmied against the still dark blue sky. The small rocks that held the bank in place, and around which the ancient roots had crept and curled, seemed to have arranged themselves into a bench seat. The surrounding ground was smooth and dry and there was a battered but clean old pale standing in a hollow.

We seemed to drop into slow motion as we passed the perfect composition, moving frame by frame. It was a flawless tableau, more like a studio set than an actual location.

I was about to ask Junos to pull up when he stopped anyway. Evidently there were some orange bushes behind the tiny building that he knew he could pick.

'Look Señor Junos! Here is our tree,' I practically shouted. 'Right here.' I tapped him on the shoulder and pointed. Then quietly and deliberately I said, 'I want it!'

I knew we had found our grail. 'I will take this one. We can do the deal now, Señor Junos. This minute.'

Junos laughed. 'Sure, you and a hundred others, including me. Don't think we haven't tried.'

'Is it classified?'

'I think so, it is very old. The locals call it the Angel Tree.'

'The Angel Tree, how wonderful, why?' This was getting better and better.

'Look at the shape. Over the centuries it has been blown by the wind into the shape of an angel's wings.'

It was true. The crown of the tree had indeed grown over to one side and spread out into a protective arc that loosely resembled the shape of an angel's wings.

'The local field workers all shelter under this tree when there is a storm. It keeps them dry and watches over them. They believe it gives them guidance and ensures good crops.'

'Their Guardian Angel?'

'Precisely.'

'Could a tree like that be moved?' I asked. 'I mean not necessarily *that* tree but something similar. Would you be able to lift it up and transplant it?'

'Sure,' said Junos without hesitation. 'You would have to be careful and do it slowly. You would have to prune the roots, which would be big and very hard; you would have to cut back the crown. Give it a haircut and do it at the right time of year but it could be done. It is no different in that respect than all the others.'

'Would it survive in Provence?'

Señor Junos said he didn't know Provence but providing it was in a reasonably well-protected place and that the temperatures didn't drop below 12–14 it would probably be all right.

'So you would undertake the work yourself?'

'Sí, of course, but Señor Dingley-Man, this tree is not for sale.'

'No, no, of course not, I fully understand. But would it be all right if I took some photographs, just for the record?'

'Sure. I know Mr Perez, the farmer who owns it, and he would not object. I will pick you some of his oranges.'

As we continued on our journey back to Junos' house I didn't really listen to what he was saying or what Miguel was trying to translate any more. He was rattling on about other trees we should look at before we left. Some of them maybe 2,000 years, blah, blah ...

I had left the ground and was flying high above the Angel Tree watching as she wrapped her wings around her fold. She beckoned me to join and, as I approached her mighty appendage, she welcomed me with such a gracious kindness that I floated down on to her unearthly being like a prodigal leaf.

Here was a tree that appeared to have everything but, damn it, we couldn't have it.

After a difficult ten minutes of saying goodbye and defending myself against Junos' insistence of further hospitality which included drinking at least another bottle of whisky each, I managed to escape without offending anybody. They had been extremely kind and friendly but I wanted to get back to my hotel.

Valencia has both a wonderful climate and the sea. It is also surrounded by orange groves and the Valencians are rightly very happy about this. Everywhere you look you see acres and acres of this pretty bush with its heart-warming blossom ripening into bright round fruits that hang like strange one-coloured Christmas baubles. Orange juice is practically the water of Valencia.

Planning permission is not on the agenda for anyone who wants to develop land that has oranges growing on it, and this should secure this popular fruit's future. But, in places, they are not being looked after properly and they have developed an unstoppable malady know locally as Sad Orange Disease. 'You can try to treat them,' said one observer, 'but it is no good. They are just too sad to recover.' As the orchards are approached, it is hard to miss the devastation as the disease spreads itself across the landscape, sucking the colour out of the picture, leaving a sterile blandness.

The Romans founded Valencia in 138BC. Valentia, as they called it, was to become the most important city south of the great River Ebro with the famous Plaza de la Reina at its centre.

By AD718 the Arabisation was underway and, despite the Christian conquest and the expulsion of the converted Moors in 1609, a lingering influence is clearly evident in such things as place-names, cuisine and rural habitat. In terms of splendour and dazzle it was really the eleventh century when Moslem Valencia was at its zenith. It was then that they built the city walls of whose seven great gates only fragments survive. Rather oddly, today you can find the only remnants in a bar in the Barrio del Carmen neighbourhood. However, the complex system of irrigation channels in the rich market gardens that surround the city are probably Roman and not Arabic. The system and its regulation is still in force. Every Thursday, from eleven to twelve o'clock in the morning, you can go to the gate of the Apostles Cathedral to see the Water Tribunal that still resolves, in an oral and free manner, the conflicts that arise among crop growers.

In 1238 Valencia was conquered by Jaime I, King of the Catalan-Aragonese dynasty who converted it into the capital of a kingdom of the same name but with a Christianised culture. The fifteenth century saw the founding of the university and the silk exchange, and the sixteenth threw in the monastery San Miguel de los Reyes, now headquarters of the Valencian library. By the nineteenth century the city had doubled its population due largely to its agricultural prosperity which was based on oranges, rice and wine plus the annexation of local districts. With the civil war in the 1930s Valencia, a city with long republican traditions, was, for a short while, the capital of Spain as the government abandoned Madrid against the siege by Francoist troops.

With the restoration of democracy and the political system of regional autonomic governments in 1982, Madrid took back its mantel and the Valencian Community was created with Valencia as its capital.

A good look round the city should have been on the agenda but studying the directions to my designated hotel, I realised the place was on the outskirts of town. It took for ever to find and when finally the hotel showed up it turned out to be a recently opened golf club set-up.

'Do you know you can buy fresh Valencian orange juice in tins in the States?' an American asked me in the bar that night.

Little chalets were dotted around the undulating forms of fairways interrupted by spinneys and man-made lakes. Deep incisions of sand did their best to seduce the players from time to time and everything seemed impeccably maintained. People walked around with studs in their dual-coloured brogues with extravagant tongues and they all wore the same jersey. That one that seems to have become part of the golfer's uniform. A sort of cosy pale cashmere with a series of diamonds woven into the front like a slice through a multi-coloured afternoon cake. Flat caps and a singular gait marked them out as committed 'Green' and 'Tee' men.

Feeling a little underdressed without a swollen golf-club bag, I proceeded to check in. The girl behind the reception desk was wearing a white sporty outfit whose manufacture lay somewhere between a bra and a sawn-off sweat shirt, probably found in a leisurewear magazine. Below her exposed midriff hung a pleated gymslip which swished about with a carefree grin. Her legs terminated in a pair of running shoes that had sequential breathing holes and recessed lights for night-time jogging. Her face was as scrubbed and shiny as a polished apple. I felt arthritic just looking at her.

'H'merican?' she asked.

'No no,' I assured her and gave over the passport and credit card. I asked her if she knew what a sporran was. She didn't.

'You have a time for tee off?'

'I'd rather have something a little stronger, thank you,' I said. It had been a hard search.

She smiled at me indulgently. Then lowering her voice, 'I meant what time you wan'ha play golf in the morning?'

Well, I have to admit it was a novel idea and I dare say my swing might have improved no end with her help but it wasn't really my thing.

'No thank you very much, I think I'll probably be off quite early.'

She suddenly seemed to recognise me for the misfit I was. Her brain hadn't encountered people who came to a golf hotel not to play and I fully agreed. What the hell *was* I doing there? There must have been some mistake or misunderstanding in our office when they booked the hotel.

Anyway, the games mistress pinged the bell, an instrument moulded like a golf ball, whereupon a bellhop, who had the general allure of Arnie Schwarzenegger, materialised from the wings. He too was dressed in white and his T-shirt had to work just as hard to cover his chest. He pitched the house smile to perfection. I followed him out of the foyer and slid on to the seat beside him in the caddy car. I muttered something about not being a number and asked him if he had ever seen *The Prisoner*. I was sure it must have been translated into Spanish. I had seen people watching it in Chang-Mai for goodness sake. He had absolutely no idea what I was talking about but kept smiling nonetheless. We zipped down the winding paths with clock golf on one side and tricksy golf on the other. We swung left at the crossroads where The Fairway Bar tussled with The Caddies Rest for the player's attention. A little further on an advertising plaque on the side of the road called out 'Fancy a Birdy? Then drop into The Eagle Room to complete your score card.'

It was a busy place, this. What on earth were the rooms going to be like? Beds made in bunkers, rough carpets in the bathroom. Cards suggesting that if you were feeling a little under par you should down a Ryder Cup of Coffee?

What a weird place. Do men come here on their own and stay in these little boxes, or do they bring their wives and girlfriends with them? If so, where were they hidden? Or was it all a front for a bordello? A sham, a bogus piece of spurious country planning?

After a fitful night tossing and turning, dreaming of encounters with crazy golf club attendants and being run down by careless caddy car drivers, I upped and showered, sliced down to the dinning room and had a pot of Umpires Tea. It would soon be time to go.

Before leaving, however, a fast walk round the recently landscaped golf course and gardens was mandatory.

Just past the caddy Cart Park and beyond the clubhouse, the grounds rolled away over man-made mounds with the dips filled to make small lakes. Tree planting of willows, oaks, chestnuts and *Chamaerops* palms gave an eclectic park feel. Large plant borders had been located at strategic points along the meandering paths. Clumps of *Pittosporum tobira*, *Nerium* and *Viburnum tinus* were supported with *Atriplex halimus*, *Prunus lusitanica* and box *(Buxus sempervirens)*. Beneath these tough and practical evergreens and greys, an underplanting of reliable varieties of sages and *Cistus* interplayed with *Convolvulus cneorum*, *Nepeta* and *Ballota pseudodictamnus*. Somebody had thought about it but had played pretty safe. The maintenance crew hadn't got on top of the job yet but the place was very new and it would take practice to get it right. The irrigation sprays looked pretty against the early morning sunlight and only the keenest and teetotallest golfers had made an appearance. Keeping well out of shot, the walk took me about an hour to complete. I mentioned something to one of the senior staff that I met that it was all looking very snazzy, and she asked me if I had seen the old olive they had just planted. 'It's nearly five hundred years old,' she exclaimed. I said that I had seen it. In the last few days I had seen it about five hundred times.

It was a long haul back to Provence, and it was done in about seven hours with a short break for lunch. Having tasted the tapas you may as well try the paella.

There was a mild despondency settling on my shoulders presumably brought on by having looked at so many trees without finding what was wanted. Apart, that is, from the beautiful Angel Tree. The only one I wanted I couldn't have, and it had spoilt it for the rest.

I was also becoming increasingly aware that the concept of finding the oldest tree that we could buy was running a bit thin. When I had pitched the idea to Regis I didn't really know what I was letting us in for. I didn't realise how difficult it was to 'age' an olive, I didn't understand that the process was to a great extent fairly arbitrary and that the dealers couldn't be expected to know the absolute date of birth. The fact that the scientific process of carbon-dating olives was decidedly hit and miss only added to my depletion. For a while I considered telling Regis all this uninspiring data, but I didn't really relish ringing him and admitting failure. I checked in with Fred and by the time I was home I had kicked myself back into gear and was ready to get back on the case. It was just a dip.

The next day I left a message on Regis Lautour's answering machine saying that I was back from Spain and although I had found few things that might interest him I didn't think the case was closed.

Meanwhile the day job needed attending to.

CHAPTER FIVE

Now, here you see, it takes all the running you can do, to
keep in the same place. If you want to get somewhere else,
you must run at least twice as fast as that.

Lewis Carroll

Regis had rung back early the next morning and I had filled him in on the
Spanish trip. I thanked him for introducing me to the Marqueza de
Wotsit and told him that I had met her goddaughter, Claudia, who had
helped me with some interpreting and what a good evening it had turned
out to be.

I said that I was confident we could find *millénaire* olive trees in Spain
of perhaps 1,800–2,000 years old. That they were movable and one or
two had been magnificent. I said that the exact age thing was full of
conundrums, was subjective, if not illusory. Anything older was likely to
be classified and as such belonged to the government and therefore
unobtainable, legally anyway.

In passing, I told him about the Angel Tree, trying not to sound either
too enthusiastic or too squandered by it.

'You think we should try and buy this one?' he asked.

'We can't Regis,' I said. 'It really isn't for sale.'

'Is it classified?'

'Apparently not, but it soon will be I suppose.'

'How much do they want for it?'

'Señor Junos was adamant that it wasn't for sale.'

'Everything is, as they say, for sale.'

'I will do what I can. I should be back hunting on the tree trail in about six weeks. Next time it's Italy.'

'Is it the season?' he asked lightly.

The small plane touched down in Pisa with the evening sun glinting off its unpainted metal wings. It was a warm evening and the handful of passengers moved unhurriedly across the tarmac towards customs and baggage collection. The collective count on the stress-meter couldn't have been more than one per cent and that probably belonged to me.

I had come to Italy this time ostensibly to meet two specialists I had been told about but had never met. One of them, Alberto, I had spoken to on the phone, but not for ages and ages, the other, Dottori Ricardo, I had yet to make contact with. They didn't know each other but both were in the business of olives one way or another.

I had been warned that moving really old olive trees out of Italy was frowned upon, if not actually banned, and that few nurserymen actually dealt in the game. But I also knew that some of the loveliest trees I had seen had been in Italian gardens and that I owed it to Regis to check it out.

The drive from Pisa airport to the Hotel Santa Maria on the outskirts of Lucca took a little less than an hour. The hotel was only a few kilometres out of town and it made a good stopover point for the first night. I had stayed there a few years earlier with a friend called Maj and I thought finding it would be easy. In fact a lot of looping around the countryside was needed to pin it down. After a few unpolished directions from various locals, the old converted farmhouse finally revealed itself. It was quiet and discreetly comfortable with a tranquil rambling garden.

The long, thin swimming pool lined with dark green mosaic hid in an apple orchard and beyond, a water garden gurgled and tinkled irresistibly. It was full of big golden carp that moved slowly between the white and pale pink water lilies driven by an occasional flip of their tail. They cruised around patiently waiting for someone to drop a few nuggets of fish food into the water. On the margins *Lobelia siphilitica* grew among *Eriophorum angustifolium*, or cotton grass, with its tough upright stems of stiff evergreen rush-like leaves, some clusters of *Iris versicolor* showing its rich purple-veined white flowers, and *Ranunculus flammula* holding up bright buttercup-yellow, cup-shaped blooms. Behind, big clumps of *Aruncus dioicus* (goat's beard) provided a canopy of shade for the *Astilbe* 'Montgomery' with its feathery plumes of deep red, while *Euphorbia griffithii* (spurge) chatted up the stately hemp *Eupatorium cannabinum* probably in the hope of smoking a few leaves.

Inside the building the lift was uncomfortably snug for two people if they didn't know each other well. And although the walls were considerably carpeted, by the time you added a bit of luggage you became rather like a contestant in a weird Japanese game show. But the short squeeze was worth it because when you popped out on to a long landing, the ample bedrooms and bathrooms that beckoned all looked out over the lovingly maintained gardens.

The last time I'd been at the Hotel Santa Maria had been years ago when I was in Italy to buy plants from a specialist nursery.

Maj had been my companion for the journey.

When I was twenty-five I had a well-developed habit of dropping round to a friend's photographic studio when he was working, just in case I could do anything really useful like help the girls change or modify the music, that kind of thing.

One day I had met an Australian model girl when she was in London on an assignment. She was doing a cover for one of the glossies and my chum was doing the shoot. Between takes I had found myself wandering around in her green eyes, doing my best to persuade her to come and see the Grateful Dead.

She was called Maj, and while that name seemed at odds with her lifestyle it had happened because her dotty father, Tom, had actually christened her 'Majestic'. It had been a burden for the poor girl to carry. The name had come, not from a Royalist sense of support or even from a Republican sense of humour, but instead was given by Tom to his daughter in celebration of one his most successful mares. Tom, you see, trained 'Trotters', those lightweight horses that beat round a track in a frantic goose step. They tow a single-seated little chariot behind them on which a jockey perches whilst urging his charge to trot ever faster.

When his daughter was born, Majestic was the current winner of more cups and presumably more money, than Tom could have imagined. The mare had brought fame and fortune to the stables and it seemed only fitting that the great equine animal's name should be indelibly branded on to the branches of the family tree. Not surprisingly, by the time she was four 'Majestic' had detuned her name to 'Maj'.

By the time we had met she was travelling a lot, working all over the world, and at that age it was difficult to sustain any kind of steady relationship, but we remained close friends from there on in.

One day, a few years later, we were having lunch together when I mentioned that I was off to Italy in about a week's time. It was partly to search for some giant *Magnolia grandifloras*, but also to take in a special Ferrari exhibition that was happening in Florence. She was at a loose end at the time so she became my travelling companion. Her interest in Ferraris and magnolias was admittedly fairly moderate, but she loved Italy. She also had an Italian girlfriend, Francesca, who lived quite near Lucca. They had met each other in Bali on a bikini shoot for French *Vogue*. They had laughed at the madness of being taken halfway round the world just to romp around in the surf, scantily clad in obscenely expensive little triangles of fabric. To be treated and paid like princesses, and then appear looking like tainted angels spread over ten pages of a top fashion magazine.

Francesca had later married a much older man, Leonardo, an architect from Rome. Travelling around northern Italy together one summer they had discovered a dilapidated old house in a strange and wonderful location and had decided to take it on as a project. As we were going to be flying to Pisa, and Lucca wasn't far, Maj suggested we should try and meet up with them.

'I'll try ringing but I am not even sure there's a phone,' she had said. 'I haven't seen or spoken to Francesca for ages. They live way up in the hills. Very isolated but it sounds amazing.'

In the event she sent a telegram and Francesca rang back saying she would expect us at such and such a time.

After an uneventful flight from Heathrow we checked into the Hotel Santa Maria. It wasn't quite as smart in those days. More frayed at the edges in the way English country houses often are; showing controlled distress. Back then it had daringly decorated all the upstairs passageways with metallic-looking sixties wallpapers. All chrome trellis with copper leaves. Big strokes of sapphire blue swirls mixed in with shiny black lines. There was even a brilliant red paisley pushing out against a white and yellow gloss background. Probably collectable nowadays but sadly it had all been replaced by something less demanding.

We set off the next afternoon in search of Francesca and Leonardo. Armed with minimal instructions taken from the 'phone and a fair amount of determination we headed straight for the hills.

Following the Serchio River you would have to be a sad person not to be enchanted by the beauty of the landscape and its harmoniously arranged little villages. The valley, studded with medieval parishes and hamlets and surrounded by chestnut forests, has long served as the connection between the plains of Lucca and the trade routes beyond the Alps. One of the simplest and prettiest bridges you could hope to see spans the Serchio. The unusual Ponte del Divolo is made up of a series of small arches that culminate in a final, daringly high and wide arch all reflected in the water. If you kneel you can look through and frame the snow-capped Alps in the background.

Eventually the first recognisable sign on our directions showed up. We turned off the main road and almost immediately started driving along a loose stone track on which we would remain for the next hour and a half. It started to climb gently up the side of the valley, passing small hamlets and smart houses. Woodlands opened and closed on vast open expanses planted with broom, rosemary, thyme and box. Lichen-covered rocks became increasingly evident and occasionally a snake would wind its slithery way over the track. The light was softening and the cloudless sky was dispensing with some of its late spring warmth.

The directions we had constructed were little more than an amateur tracker might have evolved after a memory loss. A scribbled arrow, a bad sketch of a tower, and a questionable fork in the so-called road, but in time we finally emerged up and out on to a stunning sloping plateau.

Looking out at the huge view over the valleys and lowlands below was enough to make your eyes leak.

It was a grand spectacle. The impact was hammered home by the beginnings of a setting sun that bled a crimson stain on to the evening sky.

Down the middle of the plateau a little road wound its twisty way towards the far edge of the mesa. It ended with a small group of houses perched on the tip of the flattened mountaintop. From our map it became clear that this little collection of buildings was where we were headed. Slowly cutting across the expanse, we passed an old man leading a donkey and cart with two small boys sitting in the back. An elderly dog of no obvious denomination sat on the floor. He rested his chin on one of the little chap's knees and dozed to the rattle and bump of the metal-rimmed wheels as they jigged out their route. At the hamlet the road dropped suddenly and steeply and seemed only to be kept in place by the few buildings on either side. Some were lived in, others were deserted. Some were working outhouses, others were unconverted bothies aching for attention. An open gutter divided the road from a cracked and uneven footpath which was constructed of heavy stone, heroically holding on to the steep drop, dealing with it like a skier finding moguls.

The car was parked as carefully and unobtrusively as possible but it still stood out like a moon buggy. It was difficult not to feel you were intruding, and that at any moment we could be jumped upon and locked away. It might have been a scene from *The Avengers*. In fact the inhabitants were wonderfully welcoming, full of smiles, offering helpful if diverging directions, making it all the more sinister.

Dusk was beginning to seep into the frame from the edges when we finally found Francesca and Leonardo's home. A two-storey stone house that was wider than it was tall. It must have been built about three or four hundred years ago but most of the architectural details had been well preserved or reconstituted. All the stone window and door frames were exactly as they should be, the undamaged wall rendering had a mustard-coloured patina and the gutters and downpipes were made of newly beaten copper. It had been renovated and smartened up but not beyond its station.

The front door was unlocked and Maj called out to let them know we were there. There was no answer so we let ourselves in. We went up a few well-worn steps and on to a wooden floor that was suspended from the overhead beams by thick silvery cables and held firm by strong, solid brackets underneath. It stopped short of the house walls by about nine inches all around the room. At the far end the whole expanse of wall had been turned into one enormous window overlooking the thousands of square metres of mega-view set out below. The darkening sky slipped off to the far horizon, pulling the countryside into its skirts. The sun now looked like a big torch with a dying battery.

Built into another wall at waist height was a fireplace. The logs and branches flickered; burning slowly it packed the room with a gentle heat and a condoling smell of cedar.

'Where are they?' I asked but it didn't matter much for the moment, I was too busy taking it all in.

'I'm here,' said a voice from behind.

Turning round, I met Francesca descending the metal staircase that wound down from the room above. The last of the sun caught on her unexpectedly pale skin and long, light blonde hair that she partially held back with a clip. A black cotton sweater, probably one of Leonardo's judging by its size, topped a short black pleated silk skirt. Medium height, she was attractive in an offbeat sort of way. Her mouth and eyes were too big to be classically pretty. She introduced herself.

'Hello, I'm Francesca,' she said smiling. She shook my hand solidly then half-ran into an embrace with Maj. They held one another and laughed at nothing much more than the pleasure of seeing each other again and the instant recall of shared happiness. They kissed and held hands, babbled compulsively for a while and then, with her arm around Maj's shoulders, Francesca announced we were to go out and eat. She hadn't been able to prepare anything because the gas bottles had run out and, besides, she would like to let someone else do the cooking.

'Where's Leo?' asked Maj.

A shadow took temporary tenancy of Francesca's face, betraying a hidden pain, but with a quick check she recovered, smiled and said she would tell us over supper.

We walked down the steep little stone-paved road, with Francesca explaining who lived where and what happened when. As we rounded the corner we came to a small half-hidden trattoria. The terrace was covered by a scrambling wisteria half shading the plumbago that spilt out of the pots beneath. Two of the three tables were taken by what looked like locals with the third reserved for us. The owner, Mario, was a plump old chap with a well-wrinkled brown face. He welcomed Francesca like a benevolent uncle, kissed her on both cheeks, clucked round her and showed us to our places. I thought if the little restaurant was serving as good food as it was serving atmosphere, it was going to be a treat.

It had a set menu, no choice but after a long day it sounded pretty good and turned out to be even better. We started with a small artichoke omelette followed by *Coniglio con Olive Nere* (Tuscan rabbit with black olives), a speciality of the area, that was nobly supported by some rich Chianti. As a midway treat Mario brought us *Faglion all'Uccelletto* which are beans cooked like small birds in the hunting season and one of Francesca's favourites. He added a fresh bottle of white wine from the vineyards north of Florence, and bade us well.

Francesca had enquired with a genuine interest about my work and why I would want to buy trees and shrubs in Italy. It was when I explained that it was mainly due to the availability of mature plants that she had told me about Alberto. He lived near Lucca and ran a company that hired out large trees and shrubs for film productions, TV commercials, weddings and exhibitions. She said she would find his number if I wanted it.

I had contacted Alberto a few days later and he had told me that he had a sizeable portfolio of mature specimens, including cypress, green-oaks, magnolias and of course, olives. I asked him if he would ever sell any of his trees. Only for silly money, had been his answer.

During all the eating and drinking the woeful tale of Leonardo's disappearance was revealed. He had gone to Rome ostensibly for a business meeting but hadn't quite managed to come back. Obviously worried about lack of communication and his well-being, Francesca had instigated a search via mutual friends to find out if he was OK. He was. Very OK. He had shacked up with one of the secretaries from the office he used to work in and had somehow forgotten to call.

Things would be sorted out but meanwhile Francesca had stayed on in the house, lonely but resolute. As the wine took hold, her emotions let go. It was a dispirited and needy girl that sat at the table. She was very anxious that we would stay the night and not head back to Lucca.

'But I only have one bed,' she had said, looking at me first then Maj. In the suspended moment that followed, Mario returned with some chestnut cake. He explained that a soft, sweet flour is made from the chestnuts that grow in the mountains behind Pistoia. With the flour they bake an aromatic flat cake called *Castagnaccio.* An acquired taste. Acquired that is if you could ever get behind an olive-oily rosemary paste with the slightest hint of chestnut when you were expecting something more akin to marron glacé.

We left the restaurant and started back up the hill with a half moon watching over us. As we rounded a corner we almost tripped over a large mound of black fabric lying in the middle of the road. It was difficult to see properly but it seemed to be moving. Without hesitation Francesca walked up to the mound and started to unwrap the cloth, all the time talking quietly in Italian. Slowly a dark old face appeared, of indeterminable gender. With more kind words she started to lift the body, asking us to help.

'This is Bonita,' she said with affection. 'She lives in an old caravan down in the valley.' The old lady kept her eyes closed and said nothing, but her breathing was regular.

We propped Bonita up against the wall, wrapped her black cloak around her and said goodnight.

'Is it all right to leave her there?' I asked. It seemed a bit casual to abandon the old girl but Francesca assured us it was quite normal.

'She is a witch and is always casting spells on people. She was cross with a local farmer the other day and cursed his tractor. It hasn't worked since.'

'Won't she get ill?'

'Oh no, she'll be off on her broomstick soon.' It sounded as if she were only half joking.

We tottered back up the hill, into the house and up to the bedroom.

Three days later Maj and I left for Florence, leaving Francesca in a steady and calm mood. She had decided to pack up a few belongings and go to Milan where friends had organised a studio for her. She would be fine.

Forte di Belvedere, overlooking Florence, boasts one of the most beautiful terraces in the world. Inaugurated as a gallery in 1972 with a successful exhibition of Henry Moore, it has since hosted dozens of highly prestigious exhibitions and events. But to stage a show of Ferrari's, *L'idea Ferrari*, at the Belvedere, was controversial. Was this really to be considered an art exhibition? People were unsure. It would be a first for Ferrari, and a first for the Forte. In fact it turned out to be a very memorable event that was different but nothing more or less than that, and by being staged in such illustrious surroundings it consecrated Ferrari as a major symbol of Italy, and compounding its reputation as an object of admiration. The old place seemed happy to welcome the red silhouettes against the backdrop of Brunelleschi's Cupola, and the prancing horse never whinnied louder. The fact that the country's finest car company and finest city had got together gave credence to both parties. Enzo Ferrari sleeps happily with the spirits of the Renaissance.

Twelve immense glass boxes held together by oxidised metal frameworks had been dotted around the grounds. They had a sculptural relevance all of their own. The substantial, impregnable, rusty red structures stood proud against their classical backdrop and would later stimulate an idea for a greenhouse that I developed with a client. It was known affectionately as the Ferrari shed.

Each box contained a classic automobile of the marque representing six decades of Enzo's inspirational design. Set randomly among these 'cages' were a series of life-size wooden maquettes. The bodybuilders and panel beaters used these to shape the sublime curves of such masterworks as the 512S the 365P and the legendary 250GTO.

Originally developed around 1961–62, the 250, the best Ferrari ever, started life as a shortwheel-based berlinetta, but the bodywork was later lengthened by a slippery wind wizard called Dr Kamm. After coming second in the 1961 Tour de France and third in the Monthlery 1,000-kilometres, it was judged long enough to carry baguettes and became known as the 'Breadvan'. Don't tell me you don't learn important things in gardening books.

The well-oiled timber-framed maquettes fused the technical sorcery of the engineers to the animated creativity of the designers. In so doing they produced a unique sculpture both honourably practical and exquisitely ornamental. The fact that these carvings were only ever intended to be background tools, dummies from which the real thing emerged, made them all the more irresistible to the *tifosi*, the emotional and passionate Ferrari fans. I would rather have one of those in my garden than a Rodin any day. Well, maybe not counting *The Kiss.*

Inside the house most of the rooms were showing plans and photographs. From concept sketches to full-blown working drawings done by highly trained, technically brilliant draftsmen. People who had been prepared to bend over design-boards for hours on end without a computer in sight. The photographs of the flanks and forms of the cars taken by cameramen out of the genre were as beautiful in their abstraction as any Peccinotti shot of a naked human body.

After Firenze it was on to Pistoia to buy the giant *Magnolia grandifloras* for a project back in England. They hung out in groups dotted around the nursery with their roots firmly planted up in enormous timber containers. Some of them stood a good ten to twelve metres high, enjoying the warm weather and feeling protected by the hills that surround Pistoia on the northern side.

Little did they realise that before they could tuck up their branches and put daisies on their roots, many of their number were going to be quite suddenly whisked off to the shivery climes of England. There they would be planted into a colder soil than they ever knew existed, and expected to flourish. Well they have a naughty little trick up their trunk. They undress. They go *Magnolia nudiflorum*. They dispense with their leaves and snigger as the client gawps at a skeleton.

The subsequent procedure is always the same. Client rings garden designer, demands replacements or huge amounts of financial reimbursement, very disappointed, woof-woof, forgotten that they had been warned, etc., growl growl, *et al*. The good client is asked, or even told, to be patient and sure enough, some months later, the brave old *grandiflora* starts up again. Usually. Little leaf buds appear, popping their noses out into the northern European wind, sniffing and sneezing. Bit by bit they acclimatise to the drop in temperature. And then, as spring announces its arrival with heady promises of 10 degrees Celsius, the magnolia slowly unwraps its dark, glossy foliage and spreads out into its new environment. The evergreens will probably remain evergreens from here on in, accepting their lot with good grace, tolerating most of what Blighty can throw at them.

Coincidentally but comfortingly I had been put in the same room at the Hotel Santa Maria all these years later. It had been redecorated of course and the bed had been repositioned, the bathroom modernised and a wide-screen television added, but the view was the same and that was its sweetest asset.

I tried calling Alberto and reached him in his office. It took a couple of minutes to re-establish who I was but not longer. He spoke quietly, without hurry, and I imagined he was a man happy with his lot. There was no sign of excitement about anything but he sounded confident and at ease. I told him about my search for an ancient olive tree, how far I had come and how I hoped I might find something suitable in Italy. Did he have anything, even for silly money?

The trouble was, Alberto explained, that it was now so difficult to find really old trees that were not under government protection, and anything he had he was going to hang on to. He wasn't even sure that if he did sell me his oldest olive he wouldn't get into trouble because he would have to declare it. Besides he didn't want to part with it, he loved it too much. When I asked old it was, he said he thought about 1,500 years or so. Difficult to know exactly. He said that he had some others that had come from Marrakesh, believe it or not. As that city didn't really become a cultivated centre until the eleventh century he doubted they would be more than 1,000 years old. He might do a deal on one of those.

'Are there many companies renting old trees?' I asked. He said that he knew of a few including a young man who had started in Provence and had I not heard of him? He had an Arabic-sounding name and was supposedly bringing 3,000-year-old trees out of Israel, shipping them in containers.

'Which part of Israel?'

'From the Gaza Strip or so he says. He boasts that he's getting about £80,000 for the really old ones, but like everybody else can't really prove how old they are. He hadn't even heard of carbon-dating apparently.'

'Eighty thousand pounds?' I couldn't believe it. 'You must have got that wrong Alberto, surely. Who the hell's going to pay a price like that? Not my client that's for sure.'

'He sold it to a Kuwaiti for between 700,000 and 800,000 francs, that's about £70,000–£80,000, isn't it?' he said.

An Arab boy buying and selling ancient olives under the noses of the Israelis and selling them for a king's ransom to punters in Kuwait? It sounded either inordinately enterprising or confoundingly dumb. I wasn't sure. I wondered if they were the very ones the Israelis had been bulldozing out of the Palestinian backyards.

'Have you seen them?'

'No, but the report is that they arrive pretty beaten up and without much foliage. He also states that you can't see them before you buy them and have to pay up front.'

'Sounds a bit iffy, don't you think?'

'Sí. I'll email you his number and you can check him out for yourself if you want.'

'Thanks. But I know my client isn't in the mood to liquidate his stock portfolio in exchange for a mutilated tree from the war zones of the Middle East.'

I said I would call him later in the adventure and let him know.

When I had been searching on the Internet for olive contacts I had discovered an Italian olive *aficionado* called Antonio. After some initial exchanges we had become e-pals and he told me about a man called Dottori Ricardo Bravatti who lived near Sienna. This was to be my second contact. Antonio had kindly passed me his telephone number and suggested I should ring the Dottori before lunch, say that I was a friend of Antonio's and that we had been discussing old trees, etc.

'Ask him if he can give some leads on buying *millénaire* olives. He might be helpful, he might not, but he will know more about old trees than the nurseries.'

That wouldn't be difficult. All the general nurseries I had talked to seemed unable to produce anything of any substantial age whatsoever. Even some of my well-worn plantsmen in Pistoia could offer nothing very exciting. Stephano, who worked with Zelucci, one of the biggest suppliers in the region, could normally come up with something but a *millénaire* had him stumped.

'You will have to check in with specialists,' he had said, but didn't actually produce one. In fact after a few conversations with plant and tree traders I began to think that the nurserymen were playing their address books close to their chests, well aware of their legal restrictions.

Antonio didn't tell me what kind of doctor Dottori Ricardo Bravatti was or what he had to do with olives, and just gave me his number.

When I rang from the hotel the next morning a young-sounding English woman answered the phone. She said that the Dottori was still asleep, asked if he had my number and what did I say my name was?

I said I would call back later and spelt out my name. Not that it would help anybody.

When later I finally got through to the doctor he asked in a gravel-laden voice what I wanted. No niceties, no polite little entrées, no 'let's make this easy', added to which he sounded much older than I had expected. I told him of my contact, to which he said nothing, and then of my mission in an abbreviated form, keeping to the point. In conclusion I asked flatly if he could help.

'It's possible,' he said, 'but I will need to think about it. Are you near Sienna?'

'Not far,' I said.

'S'OK. I give you an address and you meet me for dinner. It's on the via del Porione just off the Piazza del Campo.'

'Tonight?'

'Tonight at 9.30.'

I carefully copied down the address, and asked how I would recognise him.

'Just sign in.'

The road from Lucca to Sienna is fast with the journey normally taking about three and a half hours. But if you are a visitor on a short stay it becomes virtually mandatory to slip off the motorway and into Florence for an hour or two of unashamed touristing at the Uffizi Gallery.

Even though I had been there many times before, it always comes up with a blast and fits in just as well before or after a plate of pasta and a couple of glasses of *vino verdi*. The Uffizi covers an area of about 8,000 sq. m. and contains one of the most important collections of art of all times, including classical sculpture and paintings on canvas and wood by thirteenth- to eighteenth-century Italian and foreign schools. The Gallery of the Uffizi was also the first museum ever to be opened to the public. In fact the Grand Duke granted permission to visit it on request from the year 1591. Its four centuries of history make it the oldest museum in the world.

Cosimo I de' Medici decided to build the Palace, whose construction was started in 1560, to house the administrative offices (or 'uffizi') of the Government because Palazzo Vecchio, which also overlooks Piazza della Signoria, had become too small to hold them all. But it was his son Francesco I who was really responsible for starting to turn the Palace into a museum in 1581, when he installed the second-floor gallery with part of the grand-ducal collection of classical statues, medals, jewellery, weapons, paintings and scientific instruments in there.

Those untiring collectors, the Medici, were forever adding to the gallery: some of the most important elements to be annexed to the collection came from the inheritance left by Ferdinando II's mother together with dozens of acquisitions made by Cardinal Leopoldo de' Medici in the mid-seventeenth century which were to create the basis for the gallery of prints and drawings of self-portraits currently exhibited in the Vasari Corridor linking the Uffizi to the Royal Palace of Pitti.

If it's a bit of fresh air with a good view you want, try the Piazzale Michelangelo. If you haven't been there you should start planning now. And if your legs are up to it, walk it. The Piazzale itself overlooks one of the most famous and magnificent city views in the world: from here you can see the whole of Florence at a glance, from Forte Belvedere to Santa Croce, the Ponte Vecchio, the Duomo, the Uffizi, Palazzo della Signoria and the Bargello, etc. Higher up, on the other side of Florence, you can see the hills to the north, with Fiesole and the tall belltower of its Cathedral (1213) standing out in their midst.

The square takes its name from the great bronze group that Poggi placed in its centre, a real pastiche of the work of Michelangelo, composed of copies of his David (now in the Academy Museum) and the four allegorical figures Pope Clement VII commissioned him to carry out for the Medici tombs in the New Sacristy in San Lorenzo.

Somewhat daringly, France invaded Florence in 1799, pinched 72 paintings and then promptly abandoned it. But before any Florentines could get their heads together, three days later Austria took over. Austria? For goodness sake. 1800 saw the French invading again and by 1808 Florence was unified with France. In a fit of uncharacteristic guilt the paintings were returned and by 1865 Florence had become the capital of Italy.

In more recent years, towards the end of the war Germany had a shot at making Florence German but had to abandon the idea in 1944. Apart from the Arno flooding in 1966, the only terrible thing to have happened in Florence recently was that terrorist attack on the Uffizi gallery in 1993. Five people died and the gallery was severely damaged.

I parked the car in the shade near the market and headed up to the Piazza del Campo, the great space that is more a heart shape than a square and is surrounded by fine old palaces, shops and cafés. Young couples, many of whom are at the old university, sit beside the Fountain of Joy and kiss each other raw. And it's here that the twice yearly horse race is held. To a casual observer from anywhere but Italy or quite possibly Sienna, watching the horses and riders literally charge round the square, seemingly out of control and out of their heads, is a boggling event. The concession of putting a bit of sawdust down on the slippery stone hardly helps the animals stay upright any more than a treadless tyre would keep a car on a wet track. But the blood, sweat and tears, the honour and passion, prestige and panic, are stitched tightly into the tapestry of Sienna, much like the recalcitrant young bulls of Pamplona. However, the Spanish and Italians would no doubt think we Scots of questionable sanity when some of our number stagger around a country fairground tossing a tree trunk a couple of feet in front of themselves, and wearing a skirt with no knickers just for a little added relish.

A few years ago a friend of mine was visiting Papua New Guinea. As he stood on the edge of the makeshift runway waiting for a small plane to ferry him from one island to another, he heard somebody saying to him, 'Damned annoying this delay, wouldn't you say old chap?' He looked round and at first didn't see anybody, then he noticed a pygmy, in a grass skirt, with a bone through his nose, clutching a leather briefcase. He smiled broadly at my pal and introduced himself. 'How do you do, old boy, name's Johnny.' Trying not to be too fazed by this pint-sized poseur, he asked him what on earth he was doing and how come he spoke English like a Second World War RAF chappie?

'I was sent to Eton, and went on to Cambridge, then joined the British Army on a short service commission. They used to tease me terribly of course, as you can imagine. Not a lot of Pygmies at the college. Bone's a frightful cheat you know. It unscrews so that I can take it out when I go to bed.' He said this pointing at the highly polished little instrument drilled through the centre of his nostrils. My chum resisted asking him if he wore knickers under his skirt.

It was just on 9.30 as I walked up the via del Porione and found the restaurant. The smartly dressed lady receptionist welcomed me warmly and asked me to sign the book. A bunch of waiters hung around ready to help. I started to mention that I was meeting a Dottori Ricardo ... when I was interrupted by the maître d' and motioned over to a table by the window where an elderly man sat with his back to the room. As my guide arrived at his side and whispered something in his ear, he nodded. I moved forward and quickly introduced myself.

He was probably in his early seventies but still had shiny black hair, which was brushed tightly against his head, as if it was being kept in place with shoe polish. His dark suit looked baggy over his thin frame and the white cuffs swamped his slender wrists. His face was a little gaunt and he wore faintly shaded glasses and didn't return my smile. He was no comedian.

'Antonio is an old friend. He rings me and he says, Ricardo I want you to help somebody with a little olive problem. I say I am always helping people with little olive problems. With bad crops, with bad deals, with bad business, why should I help? Because this is different, says Antonio. He's English and wants to know about the beautiful tree. OK, I say to Antonio, you are a close friend, I talk with this Englishman a little.'

He looked at me directly and opened his hands as if to say, OK. You talk.

'Scottish,' I say.

'I don't care,' said the doctor. He spoke our language slowly but well and with a thick accent.

'I am a garden designer living in Provence and I have a client who wants to buy the oldest olive tree that we can find.'

I paused but he said nothing. I had of course started this when I rang him earlier. He just stared at me unblinking from behind his glasses. I went on regardless and explained the story and how far I had got with the quest.

While I talked he ordered dinner and wine for us. He hardly moved in his chair and there was absolutely no reaction to my tale. No little phrases that might encourage me, let alone a sentence.

Dinner arrived bit by bit and he didn't bother to taste the wine, just waved the waiter on. I finished talking and glugged down a huge mouthful of soft, round red wine. I was slightly on edge.

'It is a Morellino di Scansano and comes from Le Pubille. There are few if any, classier wines from this region. This bottle is from a private cellar and not,' he said quietly, 'generally available. You like?'

'It is very good,' I said, feeling like a lout who hardly knew his Chianti from his Coca Cola. I started to sip with a little more respect. There was a sensation of sitting with the Godfather and it was getting stronger by the minute. Who is this man? I wondered. I had a quick flash of the door being kicked open and being sprayed with bullets from the guns of the olive mob.

'S'OK.' He shrugged slightly and then settled down to telling me what he knew, which was plenty.

'The Romans occupied most of the Mediterranean countries for over a thousand years from about 400BC to AD600. They have certainly contributed a lot in spreading the planting of olives from the Middle East to Europe and Spain in particular. I have read that the first olive trees were found around the northern part of the Jordan river more than 10,000 years ago. Archaeologists have found olive seeds that go back around

12,000 years. They were discovered in jars in the old city of Jericho in the West Bank.'

It was my turn to sit silently. He went on, 'I see also a lot of nice old trees in Djerba, Tunisia. The story tells they were planted by Romans. But concerning the origin and spread of the olive, most evidence, botanical and archaeological, points to a centre of origin in the Levant, northern Jordan and Israel, southern Lebanon and Syria. One reference, if anyone is interested,' he looked and sounded cynical, 'is *Introduction, Development and Environmental Implications of Olive Culture: The Evidence from Jordan* by Reinder Neef.'

I started to take some notes.

'Also if you are making a meaningful study of this subject you should read *Man's Role in the Shaping of the Eastern Mediterranean Landscape*, edited by Bottema, Entjes-Nieborg and Van Zeist; it was published by A. A. Balkema in 1990. It is considered important by the serious student.'

Dottori Ricardo took a slow, appreciative draw on his fine wine. He was thinking hard now about the subject on hand. He had become more like a professor giving a lecture, and he delivered it with a smooth, effortless style which was inspiring but oddly menacing.

'The spread of olives and the knowledge of olive cultivation and processing was due in part to the Phoenicians. First to places like Greece, which was a secondary centre of olive origins, and then further west to other Phoenician urban centres such as Carthage in North Africa and other sites in Spain. From these Phoenician centres it is likely they spread to the rest of the Mediterranean world. Some of the earliest olive-processing evidence has been found off the Carmel coast, near Haifa in Israel/Palestine. Pits with crushed olive remains and the baskets containing them have been found underwater at about a metre's depth and several metres from the shoreline. The pits date to late

Neolithic/early Chalcolithic periods as early as 6,500 years ago.'

'Excuse me, Dottori, but how do you know this?' I asked, and still without blinking he told me that he had had time to study.

In prison perhaps? I thought to myself, for extortion? Murder? He pulled me back.

'There is a book, not a best-seller necessarily …'; he paused and I thought maybe he had cracked a joke so I did a sort of non-committal grin that I hoped could be read either way, 'but a must for the thesis "Evidence for Earliest Olive-Oil Production in Submerged Settlements off the Carmel Coast, Israel", by Galili, Stanley, Sharvit and Weinstein-Evron, *Journal of Archaeological Science* 24: sections 1141 to 1150, 1997.'

I didn't dare ask him to repeat that. Anyway without drawing breath he was off again.

'In my research in Jordan, many of the old groves or trees are called "Romani" by the local people, with the explanation that the Romans planted them. While it is more likely that the trees are from the Ottoman periods, olive trees are next to impossible to date, so there may be some that actually are from later Roman/Byzantine periods.'

While he broke for a drink I told him that a few years ago my practice had designed a garden for the King of Jordan. King Hussein, the current king's father. It had been for his country palace about an hour out of Aman. I was busy explaining when the good Dottori interrupted me.

'Of interest to me is the question of which came first, the use of the olive as a food, or for the oil. Unprocessed olives are extremely bitter. While ancient peoples may have had different taste preferences than ours, I find it difficult to believe that people started eating the olives off the tree. I do have evidence that people do eat unprocessed and freshly dropped olives, but only those that have slightly fermented and lost some of their bitterness.'

'If people used the olive for its oil first, how did they discover the knack of processing the fruit?' I queried. 'Of sophisticating it into a cocktail?'

'I never drink cocktails,' he said, his face grimacing, 'so I can't give you an answer.'

Quite suddenly and unexpectedly the Dottori stood up. A couple of waiters who were nearby moved sharply to help him with his chair and without a word he disappeared round the corner. I hoped that he had gone to the loo but I wasn't completely confident that he hadn't taken offence at my dilettante reference to an olive hanging out in the bars of Manhattan and left altogether.

Happily, Bravatti returned to the table after a short time. He sat down, shot his cuffs and put his hands together on the table.

'Just a few days ago', he began, 'I read an old article of an Italian trade attaché, Mr P. Mamoli, dated between 1880 and 1896. He wrote ...' Here the Doctor hesitated while he produced a paper from his breast pocket and read, '"You can see many olive orchards near Derna, Cyrenaica-Libya, more than 117,000 trees. During the Roman age, about 60 to 80 ships sailed from Marsa Susa harbour with a cargo of oil of approximately 1,600 tons a year."'

He lowered the journal and added, 'Perhaps you should look for your ancient olive tree in Libya?'

'Do you think Gaddafi would appreciate me taking his beautiful old olive trees and selling them to the French bourgeoisie?' I said.

'If he makes money, why not?'

The elderly Ricardo looked across the table at me over the top of his glasses, and folded his article and carefully put it away. Then he ate slowly and with pleasure. It seemed churlish to disturb him so I kept quiet and ate too. Presently he dabbed his mouth with his napkin, caught the waiter's eye and called for another bottle of wine. He didn't need a list – he evidently knew the cellar's secrets.

Eventually he continued, 'Also this reportage is useful to attest that olive oil was known and used in times long past. It is useful to know too that unprocessed, just dried olives lose completely their bitterness. It's a very simple recipe, I have tested it too. I used my stove to dry olives: they became sweet and ready to be eaten in a few days. So it's fairly probable that in the past people started eating the olives dried by the sun.'

'And what a good business it's turned into,' I said.

'Sí, sometimes a good business with ingenious people, sometimes a bad business with parsimonious people, but that is not what I am here to talk about. Besides it is regulating itself, and the rules are getting stricter.'

I wondered what kind of an authority on the olive game Ricardo really was, but I was reluctant to ask too much, and while making me grateful for his input to my quest, I didn't want to push it and ask questions that were not on his agenda to answer. I did, however, manage to float an insouciant 'Is your business just olives?'

'No,' he replied, and for the first time that evening he smiled. Well, smiled is a little strong perhaps, but his lips did part over his teeth a fraction, and a hint of light shone from his filtered eyes. He added nothing to his monosyllabic reply and left it at that.

'I think I will restrict my search to Europe,' I said. 'Otherwise I can see myself travelling for months and not even finding what I want, and worse, if I do, discovering that they won't sell it. The transport would be expensive and complicated too, I'm sure.' My voice rose inviting comment if not agreement.

He said nothing. He must be a sensational father I thought, allowing a little sarcasm to tarnish my thoughts.

Coffee was brought with some chocolates and amaretto. My dining partner dug in. He peeled two chocolates from their gold foil wrapping and rolled them through his fingers, from pinkie to thumb, like a gambler with his chips, then squeezed them together and put them in his mouth. I was about to applaud the trick but he started talking again before I had a chance.

'There is a 1,500-year-old olive tree, designated a national nature treasure in Croatia, and it is succumbing to rot and dying, according to local news reports. The tree is in the small town of Kastel, near Split, the regional administrative centre and the main seaport of Dalmatia. Incidentally Dalmatia is a southern coastal, olive-growing, region on Croatia's side of the Adriatic Sea. Half of the tree's crown became defoliated and the trunk split open recently. The tree has been sick for quite some time. Apparently, there was a disagreement among the tree's caretakers how to treat it. I deduced from the news report that a group, who got the upper hand in taking care of the tree, began applying artificial fertilisers and intensive watering at some point in time recently, and that that may have caused sudden worsening of the tree's condition.'

The doctor shook his head and drew on his coffee. 'Emergency meetings are being held by local authorities, and the only expert on treating old trees in Croatia was called to attend to the tree. The tree is, arguably, the oldest living olive tree in the Mediterranean. It was featured on a state poster representing Croatia on the occasion of the European Year of Environmental Protection in 1995. A postal stamp of Croatia featuring the tree was issued and put into circulation only a couple of months ago. However, it would seem that the local expert was obviously not very much of an expert because they have written to me for suggestions.'

'And have you? Suggestions I mean.'

'Sí,' he said in his usual loquacious manner.

'Stop watering and feeding it so much perhaps?' I suggested.

'It is curious,' he said enigmatically.

'Are there any ancient olive trees for sale in Italy?' I asked, trying to guide the conversation back to the point.

'Referring to the age of the trees, many people indicate somewhere an old olive tree that they suppose is the oldest one. Even in the garden of Gethsemane there are eight very ancient olive trees that, according to the Holy Gospels, should be older than 2,000 years. Well, when you see them you can't believe it: they look much younger. But it's true: in the meantime they renew both trunk and root structure so that these young-looking trees in fact have the same ancient roots. The dating of olive trees is particularly difficult to establish.'

'Can you tell their age scientifically?' I asked.

'There are no rings in the olive tree. For the dendrochronological method to succeed, long ring-sequences are needed. Trying to date samples with fewer than 100 rings, on the other hand, is generally a waste of time. Quantities are important. A set of 100 samples is vastly preferable to a set of 10, and single samples are to be avoided except in desperation. One cannot tell from internal evidence whether a single sample has been reused from an earlier construction, cut particularly for the purpose to which it was finally put, or is some later repair. Species are important. Oak, pine, juniper, fir, boxwood, yew, spruce, and occasionally chestnut, have been cross-dated. Olive is hopeless, as are willow, poplar and fruit trees. Large rings in these genera may mean merely that the gardener in the orchards in which they grew was unusually industrious that year.'

'So a lot of it is conjecture?' I said, thinking of my Spanish friend Señor Junos, who reckoned he could read an ancient olive tree's age to within fifty years.

'Sí, conjecture and fantasy.'

At this he finished his coffee, downed his amaretto, did another pair of chocolates and stood up again.

'Signor Dingwall,' he said with a finality that was clearly a replacement for any goodbyes. He buttoned his double-breasted jacket and just before he shook my hand he passed me a business card.

'This is a telephone number of an associate of mine.' He turned on his heel and headed for the door. It all happened so quickly, he had gone before I sat down. So that's what he was doing earlier, he wasn't going to the loo at all, he was paying the bill. Dear old chap, how sweet of him. I was just sitting there wondering where I would stay that night when the maître d' came up to my table and passed me a leather-bound folder. I opened it to find an account of forehead-prickling proportions. The Dottori hadn't paid at all. Well, I supposed, that was OK, why should he? He gave me his time and information. Although I didn't feel I had quite gathered all the material I wanted, I had enjoyed the evening in an oblique sort of way, further to which I had another lead. Had I known the score I might have tried steering him towards a more provident wine although I doubt I would have been successful. The Dottori had been quite the most intimidating man I had ever broken bread with.

I settled up and wandered off into the night. I found a cheap hotel with too many bright lights and too few comforts, but it did the trick. Tomorrow I would start again.

The next morning, with my head firing short of one piston, I sat in the Del Campo drinking orange juice and trying to make sense of the card the Dottori had given me. It was white with small black lettering announcing: *Nicola Pagani – Esperto di Antichità – Certaldo – Tuscany* and her number. Why would an antique expert know about old olive trees? Perhaps she just deals in *old.* If an olive is over a thousand years old, it is an antique, simple. Perhaps it is a front for something more seditious. I was beginning to think everybody was behaving like dubious Sicilians.

I dialled her number and waited ages for it to answer. The call was collected by a woman with a slow voice and out of breath. She announced,

'*Pronto. Villa del Tettuccio.*'

'*Buon giorno, Signora Pagani?*'

'*No.*'

'*Permesso. Parla inglese?*'

'*No.*'

'*Signora Pagani, per favore.*'

'*La Signora Pagani non sarà disponibile per un'altra ora.*'

'*OK. Grazie, Signora. Ciào.*'

I put the phone down a little too quickly but it hadn't been a very satisfactory conversation. I had charged in, assuming English would be understood, but whoever I had spoken to clearly couldn't and although I had got enough to realise that Signora Pagani wasn't available for another hour, it made me realise that perhaps she wasn't going to *parla inglese* either. The Dottori had spoken English so well I had forgotten to check. I had an idea. The guy who had been on reception at the place I had just stayed in had managed to talk to me pretty convincingly, although admittedly it was all hotel-speak. He might have a limited English vocabulary but I thought I would nip back and see if I could make him an offer he could refuse.

Alvaro was about 28 or 29, not very tall, swarthy, a little overweight and had bags of charm. He accepted my proposal graciously.

'Sí, of course I help you, Signor. It will be my pleasure. Whatta ya want me do?'

I explained that I had to try and make an appointment with somebody who may not be able to speak English. If she could see me I would need directions to her house and I would need to explain how I had the introduction, etc.

'This is no problem. You have a probable phone?'

I said I did and waited for Alvaro to deal with his duties. I looked around the little place that I had just spent a solid night in and saw that it was spotlessly clean if low on style. No one had told them how dimmed light was better than a flickering strip. The cruel light that brought out every blemish known to human skin, that denied the body a shadow and denounced romance as an irritant to be stamped out.

'OK, signor, I am at your disperusal,' Alvaro said squintly. I spent the next five minutes giving him the outline of my mission, gave him Signora Pagani's card and wished him luck.

He called up the number, must have spoken to the same breathless woman and then, after a few politenesses and a short delay, introduced himself to Nicola Pagani. He chatted away to her like a long-lost friend, laughed, cajoled and flattered her. After a few minutes he put his hand over the mouthpiece and said that we were invited to lunch, both of us, tomorrow?

'Sure,' I said, smiling, 'why not?'

Alvaro promised me the best room in his patron's hotel, whatever that might mean, convinced me of the practicality of staying there and before I knew it I was ensconced back in the Hotel Paradiso.

After sorting out his worksheet with his boss, Alvaro and I set off the next morning driving through a light rain drizzling out of a pale stone-grey sky. Alvaro knew the road to Certaldo, Nicola's local town, and she had given him specific directions from there to her house which he said sounded quite grand.

Certaldo is an old town of pink brick perched on a hill with fine views of the Chianti countryside. It is also known as the place where the author Boccaccio died. Nobody seems quite sure whether he was born in Certaldo or Paris but it is certain that the famous *Decameron* stories were written when he lived in Florence. The idea, or plot, of these collections appears to be an imitation of those of the Orientals, as given in the *Arabian Nights*. During the great plague that was sweeping Florence in 1348, a party of ladies, all close friends, agree to avoid the danger and retire together to the country. They occupied their time by telling, each in turn, a story for their amusement. They passed ten days in this manner, and each day is occupied with ten stories, helped by three male friends who joined the group.

There was even a story that told of a farmer who would regularly tie his wife to an olive tree to see who would free her.

They were published and were widely popular, making Boccaccio's *Decameron* one of the earliest best-sellers.

We got to *Il Tettuccio* right on time and were met by a fine old lady and a fine old house both in an advanced state of ruin. The gardens too seemed overrun but a phantom form could be discerned through the insipid rain.

Nicola Pagani who must have been nearly eighty if she was a day, seemed unperturbed by the weather as she moved gracefully and deliberately from the front door and across the terrace. Actually she wafted. She was wearing a long, flowing dress and large brimmed hat with flowers pinned into the band. She organised herself down the worn-out steps with one hand touching the damaged balustrade and the other on the arm of a wintry old woman who shuffled along beside her holding a summer umbrella with a large hole in it.

We got out of the car and walked over the weed-plagued gravel to meet her. Alvaro, grinning widely, introduced himself and then me. I shook her frail hand which trembled gently. She spoke English in a soft, slightly distant voice with a rich accent.

'You are welcome, Mr Singwell. I do not have so many visitors nowadays. May I present my assistant, Signora Balena. Is that why you are called Singwell because you sing well?' she said, smiling dreamily as if I were a nightingale. She didn't need to know that it wasn't quite right so I left it at that.

'I am very happy to meet you, Signora Pagani. Thank you for inviting us to your beautiful house. But please, we should go in before you get wet.' I was glad she spoke English. It lightened Alvaro's role.

The party retreated back up the steps and into the house, into a huge hallway with absolutely no furniture or pictures. There wasn't even any glass in the windows, just some fresh-looking voile fabric attached to a metal railing that blew in on the southerly breeze. It was dark, damp and dramatic.

We trundled along a cheerless panelled passageway and were ushered into a large drawing room. The change was startling. It was an Aladdin's cave of treasures lit by two enormous chandeliers, each holding dozens of light bulbs. They glistened like jewels and threw a dazzling pattern across the walls. The floor was covered with faultless Aubusson carpets and the room throbbed with exquisite antiques. There was no evidence of a leaking roof and the multi-panelled glass windows were intact.

Nicola conducted a slow tour, pointing out a selection of her possessions here and there. There were illustrated books and illuminated manuscripts on the shelves, the sort of stuff reserved for accredited scholars rather than the general public. Bits and bobs from the repository of the Medicis, the Laurentian library in Florence and Venice's Biblioteca Nazionale. They covered everything from botanical drawings to scenes from the old testament. Perfect copies of Dante's *Divine Comedy* illustrated by Botticelli to scientific treatises of Leonardo. There was a catalogue presenting over three hundred images of watermarks found in Italian printed maps of the sixteenth century.

On the walls were some fine pictures of Venice, including a weird embossed working of the Palazzo Ducale made from leather, and a Mario Meli depicting a dark city with a row of ominous-looking gondolas lined up beside the Molo Riva Degli Schiavoni with the Basilica di San Marco looming out of the murky mist in the background. Further along the wall she had a lovely picture of two girls wearing floral dresses with feathery collars and smart little hats. Painted in 1903, it was called *Noble Women*. Tapestries and wall hangings proliferated.

She showed me an eighteenth-century inlaid writing desk by Holand, tables by Heurault and Rebener on top of which Venetian glass vied for space with the Majolica ceramics of Deruta. There were nineteenth-century walnut consoles and bureaux as well as a glass-fronted cabinet displaying Tibaldi fountain pens. In a far corner a lacquered chest brimmed with delicate sixteenth-century lace, more valuable than jewellery. Oddball bits like church vents and water-well lids from the fourteenth century slept on the floor along with countless bronze statues, and hand-painted vases.

On each side of the fireplace a series of painted miniatures in oval gold frames hung one beneath the other, while on the mantelpiece a pair of ornate candlesticks guarded a beautiful gilded mirror.

As Nicola settled into her chair she saw me admiring an early French clock and told me that it was a Louis XV brown boulle and ormolu mounted bracket clock stamped Etienne à Paris circa 1750, one of the earliest. It was about 50 centimetres high with strong black roman numerals painted on individual white enamel plaques. The veneered casing was laden with highly ornamental gold relief work.

I went over to Alvaro and closed his mouth. He was looking loopy.

'Sit, sit,' she said pointing to a selection of sofas, day-beds and armchairs. We obeyed. 'Now gentlemen, what is it that brings you to see me?'

I explained that Alvaro had taken up a temporary position as my interpreter but had already added travelling companion to the portfolio. Then I told her the story of my client and our search for the oldest olive tree we could buy. She listened with interest although I suspected that the Dottori had probably enlightened her a little. I couldn't believe he would hand out her card without giving her warning of his actions.

I concluded the outline of my mission and waited for her to say something, which she did after a short delay.

'As you can see my beautiful house is in a poor state of repair and if I am to keep it I must look for ways of raising money. My professional advisers say that I can never make enough from my little, how you say, hobby?' She waved her feeble hand round the room. 'They say perhaps I should look to selling land if I am to save *Il Tettuccio* from falling down. The cost of repairing the roof alone is enough to make me weep, but I have a son, Federico, and four grandchildren who all love the property, who wants to take it over from me when I die. Federico says it is his "dynasty and destiny".' She looked tired and a little forlorn. The door opened and Signor Balena announced quietly that lunch was served.

Alvaro moved over to Nicola to help her up, a gesture she accepted with patient grace and said, 'Come, I will continue while we eat.'

We followed the old girl out of the drawing room and back into the desolate passageway. I was twitching with anticipation, trying to imagine what the dining room was going to be like. A roofless stage with a priceless refectory table? Food piled high on a silver service and eaten at broken card counters? I wasn't disappointed.

A pair of huge metal double doors, thick with engravings and carefully weighted to make their movement possible by the weakest of arms, opened on to a large square room with no windows. In fact it was a room inside a room. A set with tapestries hanging from ceiling to floor, most created with dark bruised reds, purples and rusts, earthy browns and splits of beige. The room was furnished economically in Bugatti. A suite comprising four cobra chairs, well spaced out around an oval table, was complemented by a firm-looking sideboard. The floor was carpeted corner to corner with a thick black stitched rope and the only 'props' were one Venetian canalscape poised on an easel and a three-foot high silver funnel filled with a tremendous bunch of pale pink roses, their soft breath sweetening the scent of the room.

As Alvaro's gasps and grunts subsided we settled into our historical chairs, raising our glasses filled with a light white wine, and proposed our hostess's continuing good health. She acknowledged the formality with a slight bow of her head and knocked back half the contents of her glass in one. She picked up her narrative.

'I want my house to fall into my son's arms but not in a million pieces.'

'Perfectly comprehendable,' offered Alvaro.

'I have much land with several little hamlets, I think we can raise enough money if I sell parts of it, but it saddens my heart so much.'

'Why don't you mortgage some of the buildings, and then perhaps one day your son could buy them back?' I suggested.

'The Paganis never borrow. Never have, never will.' There was a defiant glint in her handsome face. 'But I am telling you this not to elicit your sympathy but because we have many beautiful old olive trees on the estate. Some of them are very ancient and Ricardo thought you might like to buy some.'

So there we had it. Finally it was all clear. Here was a way for her to make a bit of extra cash for the kitty before the land was sold off. The fact that it might be devoid of old olives wasn't going to alter the asking price.

I showed an interest and it was agreed that Fabio the gardener would show me the trees in the afternoon, even if it was still raining.

We ate off exquisitely hand-painted plates made in the Vienna porcelain factory *circa* 1806, depicting fleshy pink cherubs plucking their harps in the faces of growling lion heads, a dark glossy green acanthus-leaved border ran round the edge. Over lunch I told her a bit about my work and what it involved. Then it was Alvaro's turn. He confessed that one day he hoped to take over The Paradiso from his uncle and turn it into Sienna's leading hip hotel. The inheritance thing was obviously getting to him and I half expected him to start bidding for the Canaletto. Nicola in turn talked of her passion for antiques, how she had travelled the world buying and selling when she was younger, and that her own collection was, as she charmingly put it, 'valuable'. She still did a little trading with recognised dealers in Paris, New York, Rome and London, but she considered herself too old to do very much. Her advisers obviously knew better than to try and persuade her to part with anything in her portfolio that she didn't want to sell. Did she have any vintage Italian motor cars? I asked optimistically, but 'No' she said, only the old Maserati that she had been using for years.

The clouds had begun to break up and a wink of sunshine found its way through the gap. The ground smelt fresh and the wetness under foot was a pleasant change from the dry, desiccated ground that had become the norm over the last few weeks.

Fabio was an intelligent man in his mid-forties. He was small and stocky but light on his feet. He carried an air of thoughtfulness and was evidently pleased to be showing us round. As we walked away from the house in search of transport he told Alvaro that he had been at Genoa university studying botany, but had decided on a more mundane career working outside. He had found the idea of research, teaching or working for a big company left him apathetic. He was happy at *Il Tettuccio* and hoped the place would stay in the hands of the Paganis.

As we approached an old barn, Fabio disappeared inside. A few moments later he emerged amidst a cloud of spluttering exhaust and rattling tappets. He had obviously told an ancient tractor coupled to a trailer that they should both do something useful. The old things looked very tired and unconvinced. With an experienced hand he had pumped, pushed, turned and coaxed the oily engine back into life and ordered Alvaro and me to climb aboard the trailer.

The rolling countryside was mostly covered in vines with a few fields growing wheat as a support act and as the tractor chugged along the little-used track startled rabbits belted for cover and birds squawked out their shrill warnings.

As we arrived at the top of a slope, Fabio slowed down his machine and pointed to a group of trees in the distance. With a sign that confirmed we were on course he opened the throttle and we whizzed down towards the distinguished old olive trees planted in a group on the side of the valley.

They were fine trees, in good health and contented with their age, but there was nothing about them that I hadn't seen before in Spain, other than that they were Italian.

Fabio told Alvaro that he loved these trees and had known them all his life. In fact he had played underneath them with his little sister when he was a boy and his father had been working in the estate office. He thought they were probably about, give or take, weighing it all up, a thousand years old. The history of the place had some kind of documentation to back it up although he wasn't sure of its authenticity. This gardener-cum-chauffeur had no idea why we were looking at the Pagani olive trees. He didn't ask and if he had put his brain into gear to figure it out I doubt he would have come up with the idea that they may have been for sale. As I looked at his beloved trees without much inspiration, he quietly said, 'But of course there is an older one at the bottom of the valley. Must be nearly, if not exactly, around about 2,000 years old. They say it was already an old tree when the others were planted.' As Alvaro translated, his voice faltered. 'This is very old no? Jesus he be just a *bambino*.' He mimed a cross and looked heavenward.

'Let's go see it,' I said, suddenly feeling a bit like a cowboy in Montana, and off we steamed across the open land and down into the bottom of the valley, nearly bouncing off the trailer as it jolted against a rock. Tummies full of pasta, cheese and home-grown white wine jostled uncontrollably. Every now and again Fabio would turn round and point something out. 'That's a Black Redstart,' pointing to a small bird not much bigger than a sparrow. 'It's as happy in the countryside as it is in the city.' Then a little further on: 'That's swallow-tail larva on that milk parsley over there.'

A half-hidden zebra-striped caterpillar who was busy munching took no notice. Bellflowers, spiked rampion and purple coltsfoot, as well as several species of orchids, were all drawn to our attention.

From the back of the trailer I could see that the old olive tree that Fabio had been referring to was getting closer. It had a big woolly head of leaves and stood taller than a house. Its big, gnarled old trunk hid a thousand secrets in its wrinkly bark, and the slight breeze that blew up from the mouth of the valley shivered through its branches.

The tractor sighed heavily and we went to say hello to the senior member of the olive herd. It was a fine tree indeed. Certainly very old, but still strong and well balanced. The inside of the trunk was hollowed out by the hard work of survival, but there was plenty of life in the old fellow.

I was standing falling in love with the thing when Alvaro came up to me and said, 'Fabio says the Paganis call this "The Family Tree". They say that when this tree dies, the family dies with it. Each year they gather round and say a private prayer and drink lots of wine from their vineyard.'

'Then it is not going to be for sale,' I said flatly.

'Problemly not,' agreed Alvaro.

Fabio loaded us back on to the trailer and told us that he would show us the remains of a great garden and, if we were good, he would let us see his own private parts. He shot his eyebrows, smiled conspiratorially and whipped the wheezing tractor back into a canter.

In 1450 *Il Tettuccio* was transformed from a small castle into a hunting lodge for one of the lesser Medicis. It is reputedly the work of Bartolmei who had already designed the cloisters of the church of San Marco and the Palazzo Medici-Riccardi in Florence. The strong, square building retained its crenellations and watchtower as well as its central courtyard and covered patrol walks. The garden outside the walls, however, was emphatically created to generate a feeling of contemplation and reflection. The feudal concepts of war and domination having been usurped by more cultural pursuits.

It was a deep shadow of its former self, but the garden still managed to hold on to its spirit. A little enclosed garden on one side of the house still showed signs of eight square beds which would probably have held fruit trees, aromatic herbs, selected vegetables, and roses. On the other side, an old pergola sagged under the weight of a corpulent vine. The decaying columns built of semicircular red bricks known as *pianelle* dated from the time of the villa's construction and each had a different capital. This Fabio explained proudly was in keeping with the 'Alberti principle of *varietas*, which reflected the Neoplatonic concept of the unity of a single idea expressed in a multiplicity of forms.'

Phew – steady on, Fabio.

But having started his educational programme he was not about to be stopped. He led us to a statue of Hercules not far from the house, where the mighty man was in the process of strangling the giant, Antaeus, surrounded by the splashing waters of a magnificent, if somewhat beaten-up, fountain. 'It is,' Fabio informed his willing students, 'an allegory of the power of Cosimo de Medici, the first Grand Duke of Tuscany. And was probably erected in memory of his visit to the villa.'

We were still whirling from this sudden onslaught of historical and cultural facts when Fabio announced in a theatrical flurry that it was Leon Battista, universal man of the Renaissance, who said, 'In villa life you will enjoy pure and airy days, open and happy.'

Alvaro translated the best he could but still managed to come up with something about enjoying hairy plays, but it didn't matter. His role as interpreter had already stretched much further than he could possibly have envisaged and he was managing heroically.

We had just got back on to the trailer when my good companion chose this moment to tell Fabio that I too was a gardener. A professional one at that, working in the South of France. This brought our erudite guide to a sudden stop. He turned and looked at me as if I was his long-lost mother. He came up to me, put his hands on my shoulders and said, *'Plantatio rosae, lilius inter spinas, fons hortorum, hortus conclusus.'* (Just in case you had forgotten let me remind you, 'Rose garden, lily between thorns, fountain of gardens, garden enclosed'.) I smiled milkily back at him and said, 'Quite.'

He turned excitedly to Alvaro and said that we must now go and see his private parts that he had spent many years cultivating.

Fabio had a small cottage about a mile from the villa and as we trundled down the drive we passed a fading old clay tennis court. Nobody had slipped and slithered across its loose red surface for many years and the fencing round it sagged like an old hammock, but there was something very evocative about it. You could imagine smart young things dashing around whacking the ball amidst calls of 'game, set and match!' Huge jugs of freshly squeezed orange juice in the little pavilion and chaps manoeuvring themselves into mixed doubles with their favourite girl.

His home was discreetly hidden under a mixture of parasol pines *(Pinus pinea)* and holm oaks *(Quercus ilex)*. A tall thin cypress tree *(Cupressus sempervirens* 'Stricta'*)* near the front door had a profusion of climbing rose *(Rosa* 'Kiftsgate'*)* scrambling up through it and the terracotta pots spilled over with *Campanula isophylla*. The peeling notes of the local church bells rang out, hung in the still air for an instant, then faded like an elusive dream.

We walked round the side and he let us in through an old arched wooden door set into a high stone wall.

Inside, by contrast to all we had seen so far, was an immaculately maintained, orderly garden of great flair. In the centre three camphor trees *(Cinnamomum camphora)* grew contentedly together forming a focal point throwing shade over a small basin surrounded by ferns and *Iris sibirica*. Mature *Hydrangea petiolaris,* camellias and *Ficus pumila* covered most of the walls, except on the south side where white *Plumbago* and off-white *Bougainvillea* mixed with the evergreen mock jasmine *(Trachelospermum jasminoides)* and bathed in the warmth of the afternoon sun that had at last established itself. The gravel paths criss-crossed one another and were edged with clipped box. Spires of clipped yew *(Taxus baccata)* grew out of borders filled with roses, fuchsias, agapanthus, white lavender *(Lavandula angustifolia* 'Alba'*)* and *Pittosporum tobira* 'Nanum'. In one corner a timber and brick greenhouse gleamed like new.

Nearby, a newly weeded border played host to a contest for space. A comely rose *(Rosa* Regensberg) with its silvery pink blooms hustled the delicate pale flowers of a poppy *(Papaver* 'Perry's White'*)* to move over, while the low-growing *Convolvulus mauritanicus* averted her shy blue eyes.

'Do you know the *Arbutus menziesii*?' Fabio asked. 'It has green leaves, white flowers and red berries, the Italian national colours, and they all appear at the same time.' He pointed to a young tree near to his home.

At the far end of the garden a split in the wall revealed a cotoneaster spilling through the gaps watched by a clump of curious senecios, cineraria and *Teucrium fruticans*. The tall, spiky leaves of a purple *Phormium tenax* drooped over a congregation of rosemary (*Rosmarinus officinalis*), *Bergenia* and *Atriplex halimus*.

We headed up the path that led to the front door, lined with lemon trees in huge pots.

'This is very good, Fabio,' I said, 'cleverly thought out and well balanced.' It was meant as a compliment and I hoped that the translation avoided sounding patronising. 'In the academic gardens, the poet listens under the laurels to the song of Apollo.'

'Fincino,' exclaimed Alvaro, 'I remember that from school, it was Fincino who wrote that.' There was a look of intellectual relief on his face. I noticed that his beard growth had darkened since we had been at *Il Tettuccio*.

The house door rattled, creaked and suddenly sprang open and a very old bulldog half fell into the garden, her short bandy legs slipping on the wet ground as she wiggled in delight, a snuffling rasp escaping from her flattened old face.

'Ah, my wife,' said Fabio. Alvaro spluttered and coughed with schoolboy giggles and we all gathered round to shake her hand.

Late afternoon arrived and it was time to get back to the house and have some olive-speak with our hostess.

I asked Fabio to run us back. 'But,' I wondered, 'could we just drop in and have a look at the Maserati?'

The stables had long since lost sight of any four-legged thoroughbreds but the stalls had been cleared out and in their place a four-wheeled thoroughbred waited patiently instead.

It was the beautiful Zagato-bodied A6G coupé of 1954. One of the earliest production cars Maserati had made.

Before the war one of the greatest names in racing history had concentrated on the manufacture of single-seaters. A few sports cars had been built but there was no such animal as a production road-going Maserati.

The magnificently polished red grand tourer was parked across the stable at a rakish angle, its wheels turned slightly off straight, and looked like it was posing for a photograph. Inside, the creased leather and wooden steering wheel promised a thousand stories. It was a well-used car that had been beautifully cared for.

'It has a 1500cc, six-cylinder engine with a compression ratio of 8:1 and a power output of 125 bhp. The four-speed Maserati gearbox is fitted with the Porsche baulk-spring syncromesh on all ratios,' said Fabio.

So the guy knows his engines as well as his onions. I nodded my head and slipped in behind the wheel.

'Can't be many of these around nowadays,' I said. 'Is it still used?'

'Sure. The old lady drives it regularly. Sometimes I act as chauffeur in the evenings. She can't see so well in the dark and the headlights aren't like modern cars.'

When we returned to the villa, Nicola had laid out a wonderful imitation of English Teatime on the terrace outside her drawing room. Silver teapot and jugs, fine bone-china plates surrounded a beautiful cut-glass cakestand with a copper handle. Dishes of clean cut sandwiches and a variety of biscuits that Fortnum's would have been proud of spread over the heavy brocade tablecloth. There was even some fresh fruit in a huge bowl. The ironwork seats had deep red velvet cushions, and a large canvas umbrella kept the late afternoon sun at bay. Such hospitality was going to make it hard to tell her that I didn't want to buy all her olive trees.

'Fabio has looked after us very well, shown us the olive trees, the grounds and even his own garden,' I said.

'Ah, his sanctuary from the outside world. A universe in which he finds nature to be a thing of endless mysteries,' Nicola said.

She went on, 'He always says there are two types of gardens. One kind is shady, made for contemplation and consecrated to Apollo. The other is less austere and is dedicated to Bacchus.'

'Are these the two Gods that dwell in the shadows of all fifteenth-century Italian gardens?' I offered, doing my best to board the same train of thought.

'Quite possibly, but I think in the case of *Il Tettuccio* there are some others as well.' She paused. 'What did you think of my olive trees? Are they of interest to you?'

I slipped another wafer-thin slice of buttered bread into my mouth and went for it. 'No.'

She watched me, and when I added nothing more her face hardened and she said, 'Why not? You haven't even asked how much I will sell them for.'

'Signora Pagani, it is not the cost that concerns me, it is the age. I have already found some trees that are much older and they would be supplied by people or companies that would organise the transport, offer me a guarantee and oversee the planting.'

'In Italy?'

'No, they are in Spain.'

'Bah! Spain. Who wants to buy from the Spanish?'

'Well, they have quite a sophisticated network for buying and selling very old trees these days. Of course I would only buy from a bona fide supplier and—'

'So the problem is,' she interrupted, 'that I am not a sophisticated supplier, is that it?'

The water was getting decidedly warmer, and I needed to tread it carefully.

'Perhaps if you would consider selling that old tree at the bottom of the valley I could organise something.' I looked her straight in the eye.

She sat back in her chair and let out a long breath. I had a sinking feeling that I had compounded her disappointment in me. I didn't even dare to look at the slice of cake that had my name on it. Thick, gooey chocolate still warm from the oven and sitting on a plate with a knife and napkin.

'That old tree,' she said mimicking me. Then quietly, 'I presume you mean The Family Tree?'

'Is that what you call it?' I bluffed.

She shook her head and stared at the back of one of her hands as if she had noticed it for the first time. She moved it slowly through an arc, seemingly fascinated by its structure.

'I cannot sell you this tree, but perhaps you could ...,' her head turned towards me with a sudden directness, 'adopt it.'

'Adopt it?' I said.

'Sí. You know you can adopt starving children in Africa, you can adopt monkeys in Brazil, prostitutes in Hamburg, probably even homosexuals in Hampsterdam for all I know, so why not an olive tree in Tuscany? Sometimes a noble deed brings much honour to a rich Maecenas.'

Here was a whole new way of looking at things. I tried to imagine ringing Regis and suggesting to him that his courtyard should remain empty save a small plaque which denoted that somewhere in Tuscany he had adopted a very old tree for the benefit of the Pagani family.

'This is a novel idea, Signora. How exactly would we do that?'

'Easy. You take responsibility for the tree, it is yours on an adoption lease but we keep it here. You give us money each year to maintain it and we rename it after your client. It becomes known as, what is your client's name?'

I didn't want to tell her so I made up a name. I could explain my actions later if this bizarre idea proceeded. 'He's called Monsieur Martel.'

'It becomes known as "The Martel Olive Tree" and all who visit will be grateful to the support and interest of Mr Martel. He on the other hand will feel a warmth knowing that due to his kindness and generosity a very old and magnificent olive tree lives happily on in Tuscany, in the beautiful grounds of the *Villa del Tettuccio*. Cared for and cherished by a thankful family.'

What a scam, I thought to myself. Where did she get this one from? An adoption *lease* no less. How long would the lease be, for the tree's lifetime? As I was beginning to believe that olive trees never fully died, this could be a complicated piece of legislative literature to draw up.

'What would happen if you sold the land that the tree is living on?' I asked.

'Ah no, this would not be possible. We would never sell this parcel of land. Never. We love this tree too much.'

'It is certainly an intriguing idea and I will call Mr Martel this evening. I will ask him what he thinks of adopting as an alternative to buying. How much should I say that it would cost?'

Nicola Pagani said nothing. She moved in her seat a little and pulled out a gold flask from within the folds of her dress. Her shaky hand untwisted the cap and she poured a slug of brandy into her cold tea, added a lump of sugar, stirred it up and knocked it back in one. She sucked in, clicked her tongue, made a noise something like 'Taagh' and shook her head. Then straightening herself up she said, 'Enough to pay Fabio's wages plus a little bit more for treatments.'

Obviously I didn't know what that was but an intelligent guess multiplied by God knows how many years might or might not sound like a good idea to my man back home.

I looked at Alvaro, lifted my chin slightly and indicated that it was time to leave. With great good manners, we all said how much we had enjoyed meeting each other, we thanked Nicola for her kind reception and I assured her that I would contact her as soon as I had spoken to 'Mr Martel'. We bade our salutations to Fabio and Signora Balena and left directly.

'What an Exmoredinary day,' said Alvaro as we turned on to the autoroute back to Sienna. 'Do you think your client will want to adopt her olive tree?'

'The idea might amuse him I suppose, but I am sure it won't stop him wanting me to find an actual tree for his garden,' I said.

That night I read my email for the first time in three days and there were two messages from Antonio. First he wrote;

> I have heard of a nursery in Chiusi which has many old
> olive trees in big pots for sale. Since this nursery is not far
> from Montegabbione, I will take some photos with my
> digital camera and send them shortly to you. These trees
> are very old but not the oldest ones in Italy. Moreover I
> know that it's possible to buy olive trees in South of Italy,
> Puglia, but honestly I don't know exactly how and where.

The next message read:

> As promised I have been in Chiusi and I have shot a few
> pictures of some old olive trees that are available in the local
> nursery and the sales department has given me the
> information I wanted. They told me that these trees are not
> so very old, probably only a few hundred years, I thought
> they were going to be much older. As you can see they are
> in pots but as they weigh more or less than 7000 kilos you
> would need an exceptional transport and it would probably
> be very expensive. All the trees are coming from Tuscany
> (Montalcino) and Umbria (Lago di Chiusi). They were
> drastically pruned but they look healthy.
>
> Do you want to go to Sardinia? Because apparently there is
> not just a single thousand-year-old olive tree there but a whole
> hill of them at Villamassargia, in the Province of Cagliari.
> This is S'Ortu Mannu, the Great Olive Grove, and walking
> through it is really suggestive. The huge knotted plants tower
> up, motionless but full of life. The entire community of
> Villamassargia looks after S'Ortu Mannu, takes care of it and
> protects it, but when you look at these olive trees that are one
> thousand years old, we tend to get the impression that really
> and truly, it is the olive trees that protect the village. I am also
> attaching a photograph of the tree that grows out of the
> clock tower I mentioned. Ciao, Antonio

I opened the attachment and looked at the picture of a very old olive tree
growing out of the roof of an ancient clock tower. Underneath he had
written:

This is the one I saw in Spello, near Assisi. It is at least 20 metres up and is popular with the pigeons. The clerk at the information bureau told me that it is hundreds of years old but at the moment she could not give me any more particulars. The entrance to the tower was not allowed so I couldn't go on to see it. Don't expect it is for sale unless you buy the clock tower as well!

I had told Antonio about the Spanish trick of selling their land with their trees and he had thought it comical. It was, as always, delightful to get his messages. He had been kind and helpful at every turn. But unfortunately reading between the lines I couldn't see that there was actually very much to get excited about. First the trees in pots in Chiusi were not old enough, the ones in Puglia were highly speculative and the Sardinian village was definitely not about to start decimating their ancient forest to sell me part of their pride and joy, and from all accounts their protection. Besides which they still weren't any older than the Spaniards.

I rang Antonio that night and thanked him for his introductions and his letters, I told him about my meetings with Ricardo and Nicola and said that I was flying back to Marseilles the next day.

'So you have not found the perfect tree in Italy?' he said a little disappointedly.

'It doesn't look like it, but I have furthered my education. What does the Dottori Ricardo do by the way? What was his profession?'

'Oh, the Dottori is many things to many people. He is a doctor of philosophy, he trained as a lawyer and has protected farmers in court dozens of times. He has also been a political activist. Something that has landed him in jail more than once. Now he lives quietly in Sienna with an English woman thirty years younger than him. He has been known to disappear for days on end with some very suspicious characters and people surmise that he has something to do with the underworld. But who knows. He has been a good friend for many years.'

I rang Regis.

'I'm still in Italy but you will be pleased to hear I have been staying in a very cheap hotel, saving on expenses. But tonight I am in a very expensive hotel balancing the books.'

'Oh good,' he said sarcastically. 'But what about the assignment. Have you found something very old?'

'Yes. She's about eighty and won't sell her tree,' I said flippantly, 'but she might let you adopt.'

'I don't want to adopt an old lady thank you.'

'No. How about adopting a very old olive tree.'

'Why would I want to do that?'

'To warm the coals of your conscience.'

'What conscience?' he said. 'Anyway, which part of Italy are you in? Maybe you could see Hannah my cousin, she is staying in Florence.'

'I've got a friend with a daughter called Florence.'

'Why is it always so difficult to talk to you?'

'Must be the line. I don't think I will have time to meet your cousin, I have to get back to base tomorrow.'

'Tell me more about this adopting thing.'

So I told Regis about the meeting with Signora Pagani, her gardener and her trees. I said that once again the very tree we wanted didn't seem to be for sale. However, she had offered it to us for adoption. A novel idea but not one that would fill his courtyard.

'So if I adopted this tree it would be legally mine?'

'I presume so, although I wouldn't want to hazard a guess about the small print of Italian law, sub-section I: Adoption, paragraph 2: Olive trees; the leasing thereof.'

'Nor would I, but it is an engaging idea,' he said.

The conversation concluded with me agreeing to call him again in a couple of weeks to review the situation. This tree was proving hard to find, but we weren't beaten yet.

CHAPTER SIX

Greece

The fabled rivalry between Poseidon and Athena came to
a head when the Greek gods in council decided to build a
great city in Greece. They promised the renowned
metropolis to whichever of them could provide mankind
with the finest and most useful gift.

With a blow from his trident, Poseidon made a superb
horse spring from the rock. The immortals were
impressed.

Then Athena gave a mighty stab with her spear and a
gigantic olive tree appeared, covered with blossom and
fruit.

The immortals did not hesitate. The city was named
after her, the grey-eyed goddess became its protectress and
the olive the national tree of Greece.

The History of Herodotus, Book VIII

'I had a phone call from somebody in Hamburg yesterday,' I said, 'who has
just bought a property near Eygalieres. I agreed to go and look at it this
evening, if that's OK with you?' It was pretty much rhetorical, but worth

mentioning so everybody knew what everybody was up to. We were sitting on the terrace having breakfast.

'OK,' said Mrs D-M. 'Talking of Germany, I've just been reading a story in *Time* magazine about a blind psychic who says that he can read people's futures by feeling their naked buttocks. He's called Ulf Buck and he's from somewhere near Hamburg. He said backsides have lines on them that can be read just like the lines on the palm of a hand.'

'An arsonist then?' I said, pleased with myself.

'No, that's a torcherer,' said Mrs D-M.

On the way over to Eygalieres that evening the car got a puncture just as I was coming off a roundabout. Slurring on to the grass edge I reached for the 'phone to call for help but then decided perhaps that was a bit wet. Instead I set to and unscrummaged all the tools required from their hidden pockets in the boot, and according to the rules set out in the handbook started to change the wheel. The spare is irritatingly stored underneath the car. This means that the clean clothes you put on to look tidy for a new client get mechanically filthy. It was all a very aggravating struggle but halfway through the battle with a jack that deeply resented being commissioned, a small car drew up with two young guys in it. They look fit and strong. I thought. We'll have this changed in a jiff. They mumbled something about helping, I grinned appreciatively, lied about being a hands-on type, no need for garagist, etc., but if they could give me a couple of moments that would be really great. Then I realised that the bloke was asking *me* for help.

'What?' I said incredulously.

'Which road for Barcelona?' he asked, staying firmly put in his hot hatch. I gazed at them for a moment with the wrench in my hand. Whereupon the youth raised his voice and said, 'Barcelona, which way?'

His companion revved his engine impatiently.

'Right,' I said, 'Barce-bloody-loner. Sure, it's up to the roundabout, turn right keep going for about fifty kilometres, at the second set of traffic lights turn left. You can't miss it.' Barcelona was quite the opposite direction but it made me feel better.

I yanked the spare out and – horror of horrors – it wasn't even a matching posh wheel. Instead it was a pedestrian black metal-rimmed thing with a nondescript make of tyre attached. So when you pay hundreds of extra Euros for a tidy set of alloys, don't expect them to include the spare in the assembly. But at least the tyre had some air in it. Poorly shod, with unpolished heels, I limped on to my assignment.

The Gröbers' house was big. It was probably big before renovation, but looking at it now it seemed an enormous amount of new work had been carried out. This despite there being a planning consent regulation that decrees only 250m^2 can be redeveloped.

A big man with a big waist came out of the house,

'Hello, I'm Klaus Gröber,' he said with a heavy East-German accent and extended his hand. He had a shallow smile that only just managed to reach the edges of his face, dying at the boundary. His eyes were small behind thick glasses and he was sweating and drawing small breaths in the way obesity demands.

'Thank you for coming at such notice.' It sounded as hollow as a five-year-old saying, 'Thank you for supper, please may I get down?' A polite formality with about as much substance as a squirt of air.

The niceties exchanged, he invited me into his home for an aperitif. It was a fine old farm house that had been done over from top to bottom. The whole building had been opened up into four gigantic rooms that reached right up into the pitch of the roof. Three of which had galleries.

The furniture was an esoteric mix of antique French and anything that might have grabbed his imagination. He led me up to one of the attics which he used as an office. On worktops set against the walls sat rows of flat-screen computers, satellite digiboxes, huge plasma TV screens, phones, faxes and music players, all arranged logically and neatly. Speakers were built into every corner and multiple shelves held rows upon rows of CDs, DVDs and videos. In among this collection of mediabilia was a glass-fronted cupboard that held a stack of rifles and hand guns. They were all gleamingly clean and held in place by their own individual mountings. Two small drawers at the bottom of the case held bullets. I don't know that for certain but I bet they did. In the centre of the room a huge black ebony table with an inlaid beech border was cleared apart from one matt-black rotating computer screen and a microphone. A pair of cavernous leather chairs sat each side of the table and he motioned me to sit in one of them, while he landed his bulk in the other.

'How long have you been working in the South of France, Mr Dingwall-Main?'

'We moved here about eight years ago. It took a year or so to get up and running,' I smiled and left it at that.

'My wife is very interested in horses. Do you like horses?'

'Sure. I've met some nice horses. My family used to keep a few when we lived in Scotland. But I live quite happily without them.'

'I detest the things,' he said quietly. It was as if he was remembering a particularly nasty experience. 'But my wife is obsessed by them. Fortunately there is only one here at the moment but that is soon going to change. She has some racers in America and runs an eventing school. Now she wants to organise a polo team down here.' I nodded but kept quiet and listened.

'We have several outbuildings which she is going to convert into stables. Actually she is currently searching for a full-time groom as well as a landscape gardener.' Again the thin smile. 'Your number was given to us by Monsieur Prix, the architect.'

Jean-David Prix is a good friend; we have fought several campaigns together and wouldn't hesitate to recommend one another. I wondered how Jean-David had managed with this one. 'Did he renovate this house for you?' I asked. I hadn't heard him talk of it.

'No. We bought it already done. We have many hectares of ground and would like to construct a lake and also a pavilion. Can you do this kind of thing?'

I said I could and explained that about ten years ago I had done something very similar in Buckinghamshire, England. An American polo team had set up an English headquarters not far from Windsor. They converted a huge metal-frame barn into very slick stables with beautiful wooden stalls, tack rooms and grooms' quarters. They were exquisitely fitted out and no cost had been spared on detail. An equally smart clubhouse and an apartment had been added. It had been my job to create a garden around the buildings, plan the field itself, to design the bunds around it, to organise viewing areas, car parking and the holding pens that the horses used between chukkas. They too had wanted a lake and it had been landscaped in with considerable thought to the balance of wildlife and the retention of water so that if necessary, the playing field could be irrigated without depending on town water.

I had learnt quite a lot about the game during the year it had taken to create the landscape, and could talk easily about handicaps and had mixed with the Rockastocracy, minor royals and fizzy water-drinking models that made up the polo fraternity. By far the most interesting of the collected personnel being the ponies themselves. Ponies by name but in reality more often horses by appellation. The game, having originated in the East where the riders tended to be small in stature, used small stocky ponies, but by the time Westerners had got hold of it, Arab horses had become quite a normal inclusion. Watching the skill of these guys hitting the ball with devastating accuracy while galloping at full tilt down the pitch was good spectator work. The horses seemed to sense exactly what was needed and positioned themselves with minimum communication for maximum advantage.

'The problem is not one of landscaping necessarily,' I said to Herr Gröber, 'but more of planning permission. The authorities can be difficult about lakes in this area, and stable blocks might cause concern with the powers that be.'

'I do not anticipate any problems,' he said quickly, with a sharpness that would have cut through concrete. His eyes had shrunk even more and he looked scary. At that moment a blonde woman in her late forties, whose skin had seen too much sun and had the sheen of cosmetic assistance, came on to the gallery from a small door I hadn't noticed. She too smiled sparingly as Gröber introduced her. 'Ah cherub, meet Mr Dingwall-Main,' and to me, 'this is my wife, Hildegard.'

I stood up and shook her hand. Anything less like a cherub would be hard to imagine. 'Sit down Mr, er ... Dangsale.'

'Alex,' I interrupted, 'it's easier,' and sat down.

'Has Klaus told you we want to build up a Provence polo team?'

'He was just explaining the idea to me. Actually there is a French actor who runs a polo stable very near to us over in Lacoste. The flies from the ponies aren't popular with his neighbours,' I said by way of conversation.

'Really? What is his name?' Hildegard asked.

'François Clément.'

'I don't care for French films,' intervened Klaus Gröber and immediately closed down any further discussion about our local celebrity Frenchman.

Competition was obviously another thing that he didn't care for.

The three of us talked about my work for a while and then discussed what was required by the Gröbers. Klaus had obviously forgotten about the aperitif or deemed I wasn't worth it and soon we were setting off to look round the estate. With each step that was taken and with each word that was spoken I felt increasingly uncomfortable. Here was a man that was doubtless a bully and was already steam-rollering me. I was some kind of tool he needed to further his ends on a project that he wanted to get up and running to appease his brassy wife. He may have overdrawn at the emotional bank and by indulging her whims and wants he could probably pay off his debt.

We stopped and he pointed out where he wanted first the helipad and then the lake. He was puffing and sweating profusely. The short walk across what would presumably be the polo field had been distasteful to him but there had been no suggestion that it might be left to Sabine to express her own opinions or ideas.

An hour later I was on my way home. I had extracted myself from their company as quickly as I could. I promised them a proposal and with a quick handshake had paddled out of there without delay, relieved to be alive. I wasn't quite sure how I would handle it, but I was not going to get involved with Herr Gröber. No way, no thank you.

In the event I sent in a stiff quote for design fees that I was sure would be rejected by Gröber as preposterous, if not downright illegal. If he did accept it for any extraordinary reason I would have to have a rethink. Perhaps subcontract it out, perhaps feign illness, perhaps just say no. I heard nothing for weeks and had assumed my plan had succeeded when a call from Jean-David came through. He told me that Hildegard had found her groom. Actually she had found her groom damned attractive and had run away with him. Gröber, according to the guardian had apparently oscillated between explosive anger and pathetic sadness. He had yelled obscenities at everybody and broken up the house, shot her horse in the head and burnt her convertible, then blubbed helplessly for hours on end like a little boy who had just been orphaned. The house was already on the market and Gröber had left for 'somewhere in Europe' without a word or forwarding address. I felt sure that the good Lord had delivered me from the jaws of hell.

'Come and have lunch in Cucuron on Tuesday,' Regis had said when I rang him by way of reporting in. 'I'll reserve a table next to the pond. It's market day, so park and walk.'

Cucuron is a lively little village set right at the foot of the Luberon mountains and is situated at the third point of a triangle between Regis in Ansouis and me in Lacoste. It has a population of about 800 and is surrounded by dozens of small farms producing cherries, melons, olives and the Côtes de Luberon wines, all of which appear at the Tuesday morning market. The colourful stalls are set up around the huge rectangular pond that occupies most of the centre of the village.

If you go to the St Michel dungeon you can look across the rambling old village roofs towards the Notre Dame de Beaulieu with its thirteenth-century towers, ramparts and doors. Under some of these ramparts, in a cave, lurks an ancient oil mill which is open to the public during November and December when it's olive-picking time, and you can watch the pressing and production in *ye oldy worldy* style. Look south and there is Bosco's country at your feet. On the horizon is the Montagnes St Victoire, so dear to Cézanne, the Alpilles of Daudet, and as far as you can see, the Alpes de Provence of Giono.

I found my client already seated at his table discussing the menu with the formidable lady who evidently ran the restaurant. There are several eateries dotted along the edge of the water, some more tempting than others. This one had a big white starched tablecloth held in place by a carafe of rosé, a basket of fresh bread and a bowl of olives.

Market was over but there were still lots of babies in prams and older children dashing around on bikes. Their mums sat nattering under the rolled back blinds in the dappled shade of the plane trees which rustled in a mild breeze. The usual props of cigarettes, dark little cups of strong coffee, regional newspapers, bags stuffed with fresh produce and brimming straw baskets lined with newly cut flowers abounded. There were cars parked in the way that only the French seem to get away with. No sign of any meter-men clad in municipal uniforms handing out stinging tickets that spoil your morning shop-up. The gentle country rhythm just flowed on.

Regis was, as always, immaculately turned out and dressed in linen. Something he wore with consummate ease and made everybody else look drab. He waved me to my seat, poured out some pink wine for us both and with a quick 'santé' we eased into lunch.

'So tell me more about Italy. Still no sign of the perfect olive tree?'

I told Regis about the trip in more detail and how really the only tree in contention that I had seen was the one that was up for adoption.

'I have thought about this since we last spoke,' he said. 'I am not a great philanthropist. I do not see myself as a patron of olive trees, lining the pockets of impecunious old ladies in their shadowy days of decline. However, I have to say that for some obscure reason I do find the idea engaging. Perhaps because it is so ridiculous, so unlikely. Adoption in my mind, as a word, only applies itself to children, possibly animals and maybe to ideas. It suggests to me the taking in, the offer of shelter. The adopted party lives with the adoptee if you like, under their guidance. I have never remotely considered applying it to something so static as a tree.'

'I think in this case adoption just means offering protection to something that has a life force, a spirit albeit an old one. The benevolence has nothing to do with having the object within your immediate realm. It's a bit like sending money to help Third World children.'

'That's charity. It is compassionate but it does lack the continuing commitment that lies within the deeds of adoption as I see it.'

We ate in silence for a while, but because I was mindful of telephoning Signora Pagani, I pushed Regis. 'Can you see yourself going for it? This adopting thing? It doesn't solve the problem of your courtyard of course,' I said.

'No. For the time being I think we should keep trying to find this elusive old tree that is for sale, somewhere.'

I agreed and told him that I would ring the old lady and decline the invitation. I also mentioned that the next leg of the journey would be Greece. I planned to chase up a few leads on trees that were allegedly 3,000 years old and quite probably for sale.

'That is very old trees,' Regis said. 'Which part of Greece and when?'

'Crete. Where the Mediterranean olive story started. I hope to go in about two weeks' time.'

'My daughter Dominique will be there. She is staying with her boyfriend at his aunt's house. I think it's near Rethimnon. Is that close to where you will be?'

'I don't know Crete so I can't tell you. We fly to Iraklion and are booked into a hotel somewhere around Agios Nikolaos. The only place we could find that sounded comfortable at short notice. Looking at the map the island must be about a couple of hundred kilometres long.'

'I'll give you their number. It might be fun for you to meet them. Give me a ring. Are you taking your wife?'

'That's the idea, and the little boy. I thought they could have a week off while I do the olive thing.'

We finished lunch and I agreed to call him before I left. I felt that Lautour was really hoping this trip would be it. It was getting expensive for him, he still had nothing in his courtyard and he wasn't that confident I was going to find the tree. It wasn't so much that he was really losing interest in the idea, just that he was going off the boil a little bit. And while I needed to be circumspect I knew that it would be clever to crack this egg before much longer.

The most important period in Cretan history is the Minoan period which lasted some ten centuries. It was the nucleus for the creation of the first Greek state, of the first religion and of the first Greek art.

The history started about 4,000 years ago, moved through a time of cultural magnificence reaching its zenith around 1400BC.

By 1200BC Crete had been divided into a number of warring communities leading the island into an obscurity hardly imaginable only a few hundred years earlier. It slipped through the great Classical and Hellenistic periods with very little to report. Between 69BC and AD330 Crete became part of the Roman Empire with Gortyn as its capital.

From those ancient times right up until today the olive tree and its fruit have been the symbol of wisdom, of peace, of health and of power. Due to its Mediterranean climate Crete was predetermined for the development of olive trees which grow everywhere, in both the valleys and the mountainous areas plus they fruit in winter. It was also worshipped as a sacred tree and the oil was offered to both the gods and the dead.

I rang Regis to let him know I was off to Greece the following Saturday and was going without an interpreter. I had made some enquiries and was hoping someone would come forward, otherwise I would have to find somebody when I got there.

I told him I had spoken to Dimitri, a Greek friend of a friend, and that he had told me where to go to see some interesting trees that might be for sale. Not ideal but it was a start. He agreed that the oldest and biggest olive trees probably were in Crete. Probably the most difficult to move as well.

'Did he say *how* old?' asked Lautour.

'Not exactly but the ones I'm going to look at are related to one in Athens that is known as Plato's tree.'

'What do you mean related?'

'Well, from the same family, and I took it to mean of the same generation.'

'But Plato was about two and half thousand years ago so they are no older than the Spanish ones you've seen.'

'The famous three,' I said.

'What famous tree?' Regis asked.

'No, the famous *three*,' I said. 'Aristotle, Socrates and Plato. More brain between them than the whole of China and America put together.'

'Aristotle was his student, not his contemporary,' Regis corrected me, 'and did you read the story he wrote about the trial of Socrates. Immortalising his final days?'

'No. Should I?'

'Of course. You might learn something,' he said.

'I'll check in when I get back.' I was about to hang up when Regis said, 'Hang on a minute, I'll give you Dominique's number.'

The charter-company plane sat on the tarmac like a recalcitrant seagull, tapping its claws on the apron impatiently waiting to taxi out and get with it. The Greek captain turned on the intercom, introduced himself and apologised for the delay, explaining briefly that due to French air traffic control everything was running behind schedule. There was a hint of exasperation in his voice so that we knew it was us against the French and that delays were strictly their territory, whereas had it been up to Greek technicians we would have been well under way by now.

He then surprised us all by telling a joke. He obviously wanted to capitalise on his moment with a captive audience. It was, he warned us, an English joke and apologised to any French passengers who may not understand.

An elderly couple living out their winter years in abrasive contentment saw their relationship as a contest as to who would show signs of degeneration first. One day the husband suspecting that his wife's hearing was failing tested her by asking from the garden if she would like a cup of tea, my dear? No answer. He moved to the hallway and tried again, 'a cup of tea my dear?' this time with a little more volume. Still no answer came, so he moved into the kitchen, and standing behind her with a much-raised voice positively demanded to know if she wanted a cup of bloody tea! 'Yes please,' she said, 'for the third time.'

Well, you have to give him something for trying, although it was slightly bizarre to have a stand-up comic that you couldn't see but was unequivocally in control of your life for the next couple of hours.

Because of all this dawdling, the airline allowed a late-arriving passenger on to the plane. He was about nineteen with a shaven head, covered in third-degree acne, had no luggage apart from a small backpack and was destined to sit next to me.

After take-off he wriggled in his seat like a baby with nappy rash, fidgeting and twitching. His knees jumped up and down and he played air drums with his eyes closed. It was difficult to concentrate on reading while he made imaginary crescendos on the top hat backed with fast little snare drum dalliances. He twisted imaginary drumsticks round his knuckles, threw them up into the air just missing the cabin lights, catching them on the back beat and with an inner rush of satisfied coherence, brought them down to roll into a finale and a thousand encores. Every part of his body was spasming with bonks and bangs that Buddy, Baker and Bonham would have envied. His head protruded and bounced from his hunched shoulders like a vulture on speed and evidently his solo was winding up to a climax as the flight attendant arrived with something he camply referred to as lunch.

'Herbivore or carnivore?' he asked the drummer, his eyes narrowing. The fantasy percussionist didn't answer, he probably hadn't heard him, so our trolley host, leaning over at an angle that allowed nothing for turbulence, tried again. This time, drummer-boy evacuated something from his ears which must have been his music inlet valve, muttered about not eating when he was composing and returned to the last bars of his overture.

We arrived at our hotel well after midnight and were shown to a small white painted 'cottage' which was just discernible in the dimmed garden lighting.

The hotel was made up of a central building which contained the reception and administration block, the dining rooms and bars. From there a series of satellite bungalows emanated with varying degrees of appointment. As ours had been booked late in the day, we were given a fairly regular set-up without frills and no view of a cobalt sea. It was known as 'A Standard Villa' and was fine. It was a work trip and the financing was to be a company expense. It was perfectly comfortable, well serviced and only a few minutes' walk to the swimming pool or seaside.

By lunchtime the next day Mrs D-M in her inimitable way had had us upgraded.

The hotel itself was secluded and protected but across the bay the inevitable mass development of dozens of new houses were being rushed up to meet the insatiable tourist demand. The beach line wrapped itself round a mile of seafront in the south-east corner of the island. A limitless expanse of rendered cement blocks. That fast and successful Mediterranean construction that northern Europe would never get away with. It wouldn't pass planning and it wouldn't last long enough to pay off the mortgage. But down there it is go and changes the landscape overnight. Blink and you've missed the inauguration of yet another hotel, supermarket, condominium or covey of designer villas for the aspiring sun-seeking second-homers. The scaffolding is often a precarious set of wooden poles lashed together with hemp. The builders can knock you up a three bed. en-suite, x 2 recept, garage + pool in about ten minutes flat.

After being hassled by the shrimp for half the morning I agreed to go and get him *another* ice-cream. On my way I passed an assortment of fellow guests including a man lying on a pool lounger wearing a thong, mountain boots, socks and a bright red chest accompanied by a young girl who looked like tomato ketchup. Further on, a lady was reading her newspaper upside down and her husband floated face down on the surface of the swimming pool fully kitted out with snorkling equipment. What was he looking at? There were no other people in the water, no sharks, octopuses or treasure chests that I could see. Maybe he was just practising for the big event like when somebody loses their swimsuit. I overheard a couple talking and she was saying earnestly to him that there was something she needed to get off her chest. Her partner, with a lewd sort of gurgle, said, 'Would that be your bra, love?'

I reached the kiosk and without hesitation laid my order on the line. Junior and I sit confidently in this world knowing that, beyond reasonable doubt, the best ice cream available on any continent is the Haagen-Dazs caramel-covered toffee-on-a-stick. The frisky consistency, colour and taste are so perfectly balanced, the cheeky marriage of additives, preservatives and natural contents so finely tuned, it deserves an award. I bought two, each. On my way back I dropped my ear into the same couple's conversation. 'Poor boy. I think he's very highly strung,' she said. 'Very well strung more like,' gurgle gurgle.

Clearly if a hotel of this size was to have a high level of occupancy it was going to have to take in allcomers. Simply, if they had the money they were welcome. But what some of the visitors would think of the collection of sculpture that was dotted around the gardens was hard to imagine. In a heroic and unstinting show of cultural awareness the hotel had either bought or commissioned pieces from all around the world. A huge solid Minos bull cast in concrete with heavy iron horns but oddly no legs brooded in the entrance courtyard. Near the swimming pool a two-metre archway carved in the shape of a human profile stood acting as an entrance, on the beach a four-metre high man made from rope held a bit of driftwood and between some pine trees a clothes line was hung with metal shirts. Further over towards one of the restaurants you could find giant spheres of cable looking like magnified balls of wool, nearby a big metal box was full of suspended iron fish. Further on there were ladders of glass kinetic shapes and water features. Near our cottage, towering timber-framed pyramids were to be discovered, draped in barbed-wire. In the window of the hairdresser's 'boutique' a crown was suspended above a soldier's kitbag – a reference to the crown of Greece and the battles that had been fought. It sat comfortably surrounded by assorted hair treatments and photographs of clean-cut models, just like mother would like.

The gardens and grounds had been thought out carefully. The meandering little paths made their way through huge shrub borders planted with banks of white, cream and pink oleanders, wild *Pelargonium* and grasses backed with tall dark pencil-thin cypress trees and pines. Sparkling yellow broom mixed in with uncontrolled purple *Cotinus*. Then on they led around the lawns and through the trees that eventually ended up on the main esplanade that ran with the sea on one side and more planting on the other. Clipped *Pittosporum* and myrtle joined a hundred varieties of rose that flowered for all they are worth daring the deep reds and pale pinks of the *Hibiscus* to outdo them. Highlighted by grey *Cineraria maritima* and *Santolina*, periwinkle crept slowly over the low ground.

Each bungalow, cottage, villa, or whatever they want to call them, was surrounded by its own planting. Blue-mauve *Lantana*, with yellow hearts mingled with rosemary while the deep purple-blue of morning glory wound itself up and through the *Osmanthus*. Beautiful but furiously invasive, threatening to strangle anyone who gets in its way. In isolation tall palms towered over smaller olives, cactus and tamarisk, while cream and purple *Bougainvillea* scrambled over walkways and arbours.

The skyline was broken by huge pines with their dry, hot smell and a regiment of parading cypress trees protected the *Ficus* and lilacs beneath them.

In a corner near the kitchen, masses of yellow African marigolds grew with geraniums, *Amaryllis* and carnations in pots, lemon trees and lavender mixed with basil, thyme and mint. The evocative scents clung to the heat of the summer afternoon. A rather stern *Eriobotrya japonica* cast a doubtful eye over some straggly *Teucrium* while the complementing pale blues of *Ceanothus* and *Plumbago* were deep in conference about the behaviour of the young variegated ivies and *Euonymus*.

Arguably, staying at a hotel like this is easier than being Caribbeaned out. Not because of the financial disparity so much as the calm lack of competition. No need to go to the manicurist and botox parlours before hitting the beach. It doesn't matter if you arrive with only two pairs of sunglasses and three changes of bikini. Nobody will have noticed. No secret peering from behind Porsche shades. No wriggling with insecurity because someone else looks marginally more toned or is slenderer or younger, with bigger or smaller bosoms or pecs, slinkier or sexier bums. No need to smirk conspiratorially at some metabolically challenged heavyweight or a provocatively wrinkled oldster. No fuss about spreading middle age or greying hair. No time-wasted speculating about lip enhancement. No, it's just a melting pot of contented mediocrity and none the worse for it. However, I think I'll be looking for ancient palm trees on St Barts next time.

According to Greek legend, Zeus was born on Crete. He was quickly hidden in the Idaean Cave by his mother Rhea, aided by Uranus, to protect him from his father Kronos who had a nasty little paranoid habit of eating his children in case they might usurp his throne. History doesn't reveal whether he ate them roasted, sautéed, minced or raw, but apparently one day Rhea swaddled a long stone to fool him and the old boy swallowed it whole, indicating he must have adored oysters.

Zeus was then lucky enough to be brought up by the Nymphs who employed a special goat, Amaltheia, to suckle him on her milk. When he grew into manhood, or godhood (lord of heaven and earth, the father of gods and humans), he overcame his own paternal problems and started to rule the world, which he governed with eleven other gods. Why restrict yourself to a relatively small island in the Aegean when you and your team could have the planet? Besides he had a useful weapon, The Thunderbolt. A chap could go a long way with one of those.

Any young, virile ruler would inevitably start to think about getting himself a wife sooner or later, and Zeus was no exception. Although he had a legendary amount of girlfriends and mistresses, some of whom were goddesses and others mortal women, his lawful and perpetual wife was Hera.

She was steady and supportive and, despite being driven to terrible jealousy by her husband's continuing infidelity, she stood by her man. One of the errant god's dalliances was with a beautiful girl called Europa, the daughter of the King of Phoenicia.

Understandably, her father was not too keen on this power-crazy, married kid who called himself a god disporting with his daughter and did what he could to keep them apart. However, Zeus was not about to be put off easily and came up with an unusual take on the proceedings. Instead of sending the damsel a field of wild flowers or an orchard of lemon trees in blossom, only to be found out by his wife, he simply turned himself into a white bull and trotted incognito down to the beach at Sidon where Europa was playing with some other girls. He lay at her feet and flirted furiously in the way that only a bull can. Being an old hand at the pulling game he quickly seduced the lovely lady into climbing on to his back. No sooner was she astride than he jumped up and started swimming furiously further and further from the shore with Europa hanging on to his horns for dear life. Rather like Marianne Faithfull in *Girl on a Motorcycle*. Zeus had stolen Europa from under the king's nose.

At the spring of Gortys, Zeus changed himself back into a more handlable shape and the couple made lurve under the shadow of the plane trees. Ever since that time the trees have never shed their leaves in honour of the god and his loved one. Incidentally the bull whose shape Zeus assumed rose to heaven and became the well-known constellation of Taurus in the Zodiac cycle, but you probably knew that.

Time passed and the happy, if decidedly odd, couple had a few children, one of whom they called Minos. This beefy lad with a divine and bovine heritage grew up to become the King of Crete, founder of the Cretan sea-power and creator of the Minoan civilisation.

Europa stayed on Crete and gave her name to a continent. She may well have franchised it out to a chain of late-night supermarkets for all I know. She later married Asterionas, who sweetly adopted her children and all was well.

In his prime Minos married a somewhat wayward girl called Pasiphaë. Fable has it that Pasiphaë was another lass that had a thing about bulls. Talk about following in dad-in-law's hoof prints. They hadn't been married long before she decided she was not being fully satisfied by her husband. She felt him to be a part-time player, an also-ran, and decided to go for the real thing, the full bull.

Now a pretty girl has to be fairly inventive if she is to seduce an unsuspecting half-ton of Sunday-joint muscle, so she had her chum Daedalus, the craftsman and inventor, knock up a cow costume for her. It is difficult to imagine how he cut the hide, but it needed to be fairly long to disguise those human knees which are always a giveaway. Anyway, Pasiphaë got what she wanted and was soon pregnant and the happy package was duly delivered. Whether she was surprised with the alarming little monster that was delivered, with its head of a bull and the body of a man, history doesn't report. One surmises that Minos, although a little startled by the unusual look of what he perceived to be his own offspring, wasn't over-fazed by the event and good-heartedly named him Minotaur. Boy, were they in for a surprise.

The brute grew up living on human blood, shouting, roaring and pouring fear into all around him. Nobody could cope with him and his mood swings, so Daedalus was called up once again and instructed to design a labyrinth. An endless maze of passages and dead-ends, so easy to enter and so difficult to leave. Minotaur was lured into the trap where he stomped around unable to get out. Eventually he was killed by Theseus, but that's another story. Oh, these islands in the myths, it's all complete bull breath of course, but who cares?

As much as I appreciated the help that Dimitri had tried to give me, I knew that if I was going to search seriously for an old olive tree in Greece I needed a proper interpreter, and quickly. Someone who could not only speak good English but would be prepared to help research the subject and find some good reliable leads. A little luck nudged in.

I had checked in with Philippa in the office and she told me that Doug, one of our clients, had found someone to help me.

Douglas Jackson is a Californian ex-professional sportsman who, having retired from first division volley ball competition has, via a multi-coloured route of playing, coaching and managing, arrived at a point where he operates with a team of experts organising the UEFA Super League football series out of Switzerland. From hand to foot ball on two continents struck me as a pretty impressive leap even for a sportsman, and while the former remains his first love, the latter has become his life, for the time being at least.

He had called the office and when my assistant had said that I was in Greece trying to find an old olive tree and an interpreter, not necessarily in that order, Doug had told her about Melina Opidapolous. He said that she helped them with language and hospitality when the matches were played in Greece.

Without delay I had made contact and thankfully she had been free to help. I outlined what kind of assistance I needed, we agreed a fee and she started immediately. Two days later she had not only come up with a handful of references, she had also located the island's leading olive tree authority, Antonios Gonfonaplolis, had organised a meeting between us and told me to meet her at the airport the following Wednesday.

I picked her up just after nine and we set off immediately for our rendezvous with Antonios. It is he who supplies the Cretan transport authority with the wonderwalls of *Oleander* and cypress trees that are landscaped along the roadside for kilometre after kilometre, sometimes interplanted with olives, pines and figs. The general view is pretty good anyway but this courteous enhancement by the authorities makes the M4 look pretty dismal.

Antonios runs a nursery in Rethimnon, having been brought up in a local village some few kilometres to the north. He now lives in Irkilion so that he can help look after his elderly mother who is hospitalised. A good-looking man in the Douglas Fairbanks Jnr mould, he has a daughter who is an architect, and two sons, the elder a doctor and the younger a partner in the business.

We met up in the garden of a small taverna in Pleuriana that belonged to his cousin. Antonios suggested we have an early lunch and then go tree-spotting. A couple of glasses of very cold beer, lots of olives and an enormous plate of Greek salad was dealt with in the shade of a few old, spreading mulberry trees, their part-painted white trunks looking like half pulled-up trousers.

The amiable olive connoisseur was not at all fazed by my quest. He had exported trees to other Greek islands and was currently negotiating with the organisers of the Olympic Games to supply mature olive trees for the 2004 meeting. They needed dozens of them at around 400 to 500 years old, and they would line the streets leading up to the Olympic stadium It was a good order but he was finding the bureaucracy slow and difficult to work with. The trees needed a two-year cycle in which to be lifted and moved, planted into huge holding containers, maintained and established. They would then be shifted again to their final positions. The crowns had to be pruned before lifting and the trees would need a good twenty-four months to grow back. If he didn't hear soon, it was going to be difficult to supply something that lived up to expectations.

He said he saw no great complication in sending trees to Provence providing the preparation was carefully handled, but the thought of how much it would cost made his eyebrows shoot up and down. He would lift the tree and keep it in his nursery for six months to make sure it is healthy and then ship it some time between March to October. He said he would lift two to make sure he had a back-up. He will only guarantee the tree if he is present at the planting. And while this is easily arranged he was concerned about the language problem. It was agreed that Christina might have to come to the party as well.

As we talked, an elderly man hobbled in gingerly, using his stick to negotiate the steps that led down to his regular table. Antonios recognised him as his old schoolteacher and went over to say hello. When he returned he told us that the old boy was 96 and still insisted on driving around far too fast in his BMW. The locals were so worried that he would kill not only himself but others too, that they had taken to sneaking into the car and disconnecting its battery.

Each day the ritual started with the old man calling up the garage to come and fix it. After delaying for as long as they could, the mechanics would turn up and fiddled with wires and pretend to turn the engine over. They would shake their heads and give one another knowing nods and then announce the car unstartable.

The pensioner was going to crack this sooner or later and the safety of the population of Pleuriana would be under threat once again. Meanwhile the charade goes on. It is a little sad to see the once serious and respected teacher, a post that is as revered among its retinue as any priest, lowered to the scale of small-time farce. But as his young cleaning lady and sometime companion, to whom the retired teacher has proposed on countless occasions, said about her imperturbable, antiquated employer, 'He's a cheery old skeleton.'

I told Antonios more about my assignment, starting from scratch to eliminate any misunderstandings he may have picked up. I asked him the same old questions and to a greater or lesser extent got the same old answers.

The big one though was 'Could he find me a tree that is more than 2,000 years old?'

Without much hesitation he said he could.

'The really old trees on Crete are the *Throumbolia*,' he said. 'They are by far the oldest variety. The oldest I know of are about 3,000 years plus. They have been allowed to grow to 30 or 40 metres in height. Nobody prunes them because the middle-sized olive they produce is of a poor quality for oil-making. Although some think it is good for eating. Anyway the yield is low and the economics of picking do not allow for a profit on a tree that is sparsely fruiting.'

'And these are for sale?' I said.

'They are for sale,' he answered, again without hesitation.

'Are they difficult to move? Would they survive the change of climate?' I was going at him like a man late for his train and probably repeating myself.

He took his time and stayed with his agenda without being discourteous.

'For this reason most people in Crete are pulling them out and using them for firewood. A replanting programme of smaller, higher-yield trees, *Kothreiki*, is taking their place. This is the variety, without doubt, that produces the best olive oil in the world.'

'If we did take one of these really old *Throumbolias*, would it adapt to Provence?' Even if I was repeating myself I had to push on with this point. It was on top of my worry list. It made me shiver to think of all the work that would go into lifting and moving it, both emotional and financial, only to witness it dying slowly over a couple of years.

'They are not difficult to move if we use the correct equipment. Sometimes it is difficult to get this equipment up to the tree because of its location. If we have to take down and rebuild walls for example it adds considerably to the cost. But I think the most important thing you must understand about these very old trees you will see this afternoon is this. Because they have not been 'farmed' and are unpruned, they are very tall and very wide. This makes them truly beautiful but impossible to transport. They have to be severely cut back not only to make it possible to move them on the roads, or put them aboard a ship, but also to help them re-establish themselves when they are replanted. The energy that the root system has to find should be restricted to as small an area as possible. Do you understand?'

I said I did because I had heard and seen it before. I added that I would still like to see the trees and he could show me the minimum amount of pruning he thought we could get away with.

'But to answer your question of how it would survive in Provence is more difficult,' he said, 'I am not acquainted with your climate but if the temperatures drop to minus 12 or 14 as you say they do, then it must be a concern.'

'So you would be wary of giving guarantees?'

'Yes, I would be wary.'

'Are there any other varieties that have been prepared and are as old?' I asked.

'Not as old, except possibly the *Vialamota*,' he said, 'but the *Vialamota* is the only variety that cannot be exported. Not even as a small tree. Very much not. It is Greek, it is good and it is staying that way.' He smiled ruefully.

We set off in the early afternoon, thankfully cocooned against the belting heat by the car's air conditioning. The road winds up into the hills and although this is Mediterranean country it is quite different from the South of France, Italy or even the wild lands of middle Spain. But they are not islands and it is the sea and their mountains that give these Greek satellites a special identity all to themselves. The landscape is dry, tough and hard, which could be a description of the people themselves. The craggy grey stone becomes increasingly evident as we climb higher and the determined evergreen ground-cover starts to lose its grip in places and reluctantly slips behind.

The view out to sea with the other islands in the far distance, some wearing small caps of cloud and the miles upon miles of dark blue water, reminds you that life here is isolated and you are very much dependent on the brotherhood of islanders for survival. The heartbeat of a country's existence is pumped as much by its landscape as it is by the customs of its residents and here on Crete there is a tighter sense of identity than you would find on the mainland. And for a visiting northern European the language makes considerably less sense than the schoolbook French, Italian or Spanish you may have picked up. The wines and foods are also a permanent admonition that you are away from home.

After a few kilometres, we pass through his childhood village of Panormom. Antonios pulls up outside a small white terraced house where two bent old ladies dressed from top to toe in black sit outside the doorway looking like inquisitive crows. Antonios stops the car right next door to them. He slides down the window and just gazes at them and they gaze blankly back. It is a bizarre moment but he doesn't let up, just a smile but no words. What are they thinking in that moment, I wonder. Suddenly their blank old faces light up. Slowly a crease in the leathery brown skin is followed by a gentle smile that brims over into a joyous exclamation as they recognise their nephew. They are as pleased as punch to see him. A family gossip takes place while a tractor and trailer and two cars patiently wait for the reunion to relocate or wind up.

As we drive on towards our meeting with remarkable trees Antonios tells us that he and his brother would walk four kilometres every morning to catch the school bus and again in the evening to get home for supper. That's a long way for little legs to walk every day.

The olive was brought, so myth tells us, to the Greek world by Heracles, from the riverside regions of the Black Sea. Historians locate its origins in Syria and in the long narrow valleys between the Taurus and the Lebanon.

No other fruit-bearing tree comes near it in terms of longevity and we probably feel some kind of consolation in that we can count the passing years by a feature of nature which surpasses our own. And the olive tree is, undoubtedly, one of nature's greatest monuments to time. In fact in Greece very old olive trees are referred to as 'monuments'.

He is a unique fellow in the world of arboriculture and as one historian wrote, 'it supplies soap for cleaning body and abode, oil for light, food and medice, and wood for hearth and warmth'.

It is understandable that this tree is so important to the Cretans when you realise that one in twenty cultivate it. Not for the first time did I reflect on this remarkable plant that manages to look beautiful at all times of year. I was in love.

In the Middle Ages, Greeks began 'leaving' their trees to people in their wills. It's a practice still carried out today with pious exactitude wherein there is a law governing the ownership of the olive. It is a tradition in which possession of a tree does not mean that you necessarily own the land it grows on. Boy, that must make for some hectic meetings in the local court, especially as quite often trees are willed to two different members of the same family.

Panos Theodoridis observed in his book *Olives in Greece* that the olive, as part of the landscape, is a coveted prefiguration. The only 'guilty' use that he could identify was the practice of the olive growers of clearing the ground of holly oaks and planting olives, not because they wanted to cultivate them, but because their purpose was to secure some proprietorship. Woodland is difficult to sell, but there is always a market for olive groves. They can be inherited and they can be exchanged.

So is it the tree of life? It must be up there as a serious contender for the title, but others might argue the case for the regal oak or the mighty cedars. Supporters of the conifers could enter the contest. And what of the almond? It too has fruit, or at least useful nuts which can be eaten raw, roasted or covered in chocolate, it produces a fine oil for soaps and flavouring, it has a heart-softening blossom, and the trunk twists fabulously with decades of wind erosion, making it as good a sculptural form as anything else. But the almond badly falls down on longevity; after sixty years it has become decidedly infirm and will soon need to hear the Final Rites. Further, it is not persistent with its foliage and is sometimes difficult to establish. That said, most local farmers would not want to imagine life without an almond tree on their land.

After an hour of driving we finally arrived high up in the foothills of Mt Psiloreitis which at 2,456 m is the highest mountain in Crete. It is around those parts that you find Idaean Andron, the very cave where Zeus was raised, at least it is according to Greek myth.

The car was parked and we started out on a walk across the fields and down little lanes suitable only for a tractor. The sun was hot and the low-slung countryside, craggy with rocks, pines and rough grass, stretched down to the calm deep blue sea in the distance. Little white-painted smallholdings punctuated the otherwise sparse landscape. It was a good opportunity to discuss regal trees with the expert.

I started by checking on Antonios' take of ageing an olive. A 'Monumental' as they are referred to. His answer was much the same as what I had heard before and what I had come to expect, that ageing an olive was no easier than peeling a coconut.

'It is impossible to define the length of an olive tree's life accurately. It is not like other fructiferous or forest trees. Although there is no specific evidence, it is obvious that many of the existing olive trees must be a few millennia old.

'Determining the age of very old trees is difficult as they don't fully retain the wood of their central trunk. This makes it hard for modern technological methods to establish how old they are. So the classical method, which is based on the number of yearly rings, presents many difficulties due to the special format of the tree. That is, when it's old there are no rings because it's hollow.'

I didn't let on to Antonios that I knew this to be the case and that I had heard it all before, partly because there was no harm in the facts being reiterated and partly I didn't want to tamper with his rhythms of explanation.

'A rough approximation of the tree's age,' he went on, 'can be made based on the evidence of its perimeter or the largest range of the central compact trunk, and the definition of the average yearly pace of growth of the tree's radius. This pace differs not only according to the variety but also due to the climatic and nutritional conditions of the ground that existed in the area that the tree lived. It can generally vary by 0–3 mm per year depending on the conditions. Usually, however, it's around 0.8–1.5 mm per year. Therefore a trunk whose largest radius is $R = 120$ cm and has an average pace of radius growth of $r = 0.8$ mm / year will be $T = R / r = 1200:0.8 = 1500$ years old.'

'Does that mean that olive trees have a square root?'

Antonios looked at me in the way a teacher might look at an impertinent pupil that is trying to upset his class.

'Excuse me,' I said sheepishly, 'but you are talking to a man who was allergic to algebra.'

Antonio continued. 'Of course the determination of the trunk's radius is quite difficult since in most cases the trunk of old trees besides being hollow is also unsymmetrically developed and therefore the imaginary cross-section-cut used for measurement is undeterminable. An examination of incisions on trunks and branches reveals that in very few instances is their shape symmetrical whereas in most cases it's actually screwy and has many centres. This is why the determination of age requires knowledge of physiology, of the way that the trees develop and also the climatic conditions of the area throughout a long period of time.'

Quite. The olive tree wasn't the only thing that was going screwy.

'Fossilised olive leaves believed to be 60,000 years old were found in the walls of the Caldera of Santorini.'

I had heard of the island of Santorini or Thera as it is also called but had never been there. An island at the south end of the Cyclades complex. The Caldera is a colossal basin of some 40 square kilometres with water being up to 600 metres deep and the surrounding walls some 350 metres high.

'So the first olive made its appearance in Greece then, and not Syria or Israel,' I said.

'Many countries contend for the wise root of the olive,' Antonios said smiling and sounding like Homer.

'But 60,000 years ago, that takes a bit of beating surely,' I said.

'Well, the first *written* evidence for the cultivation of the olive comes from Evla in northern Syria, and a little later in the Palestine region. It has also been testified that the first inhabitants of Crete of the Neolithic period, around 6000–3000BC, collected and consumed olives. Later on in the third millennium BC, the period of copper, the inhabitants of Crete began to domesticate the olive tree and a thousand years later, by 2000BC, they had begun to cultivate and exploit it by producing what is known to us as olive oil. But, to make things still more complicated, the latest research points towards the view that the olive actually came from Central Africa, and from there gradually moved north towards the Mediterranean, became acclimatised and stayed on. Fossilised olives have been found at the heart of the Sahara, at Hoggar. So it is confusing, this tree of ours, and covered in mystery.'

Central Africa now. What a head-hurter. But as we were currently standing on Greek soil I steered back towards home ground.

'So by the time we get to the Minoan period, olives were quite commonplace?' I suggested.

'Sure. There are plenty of archaeological finds that testify to the major presence of the olive in Minoan Crete. Wall paintings, tools and scriptures prove that the Minoans had produced and stored olive oil since 1700BC. A clay cup decorated with olives from 1450BC that was discovered at the Zakro monument in Eastern Crete shows that during this period the Cretans used olives as part of their diets.'

'But the timber doesn't seem to have survived though, does it? Not like say oak, beech or teak. Is that because it is unsuitable for construction?' I asked. 'I thought it was very hard.'

'Some of it has survived. Various bits of timber that have been discovered from that period are olive wood. It seems they were used for roofs of houses and stairs. Although you can see that olive wood, while strong and hard, is going to be limited on modern constructions. The pieces are seldom long or straight enough. But it works well for small furniture and handicraft objects such as bowls, spoons, boxes, wooden instruments. Did you know that the club of Heracles was made of olive wood?'

'I didn't,' I said. 'That probably explains a lot of things. By the way, what's the difference between wild olive and unwild or tame?'

'Cultivation. The difference is that the wild olive, known as *Olea europaea* var. *oleaster*, is untainted by human touch. It has probably sown itself and lived its life without pruning, feeding or soil ploughing. The cultivated olive as you know is regularly pruned, is grafted, it gets treatments against bugs and maladies, it has the earth around its roots loosened, and consequently produces much more fruit. The wild tree never grows higher than five or six metres and is thorny. The leaves are narrower and sparser and its trunk is smoother and greyer. It is also more resistant to wind than its cultivated cousins and some will tell you it lives longer.'

'So if I am going to find the oldest tree possible I should look for a wild olive?'

'Perhaps, but as virtually all the trees are now cultivated it would make your task virtually impossible.'

'How much further before we see *your* trees Antonios?'

'We are nearly there.'

Today, olive trees, with a population of over 35 million, have spread their much-loved form over the whole of Crete. They cover the small valleys and plains of the island. They move into the shady ravines and climb up the hills. They advance high up Madares and almost reach the snowy peaks of the Omalos and Psiloritis mountain ranges. From there they start their descent again right down to the edges of the sea. They embrace villages large and small. They intertwine with the churches and the squares. They go into the courtyards of the Cretan people and share silently with them their sorrows and joys. In the shade of their silvery-green natural beauty they play host to feasts, festivals and weddings.

But the olive also provides the Cretan people with both their inestimable harvest and their precious golden oil. The oil that has for centuries nourished, healed and sustained the surviving strength of these islanders. The oil that today constitutes the foundation of the economy for its 95,000 agricultural families. For thousands of years olive groves and their cultivation have been playing an important role in the economic, religious, social, cultural and even political life of the people that live in the Mediterranean basin. These trees manage to connect Greek mythology to the present day and the traditions within the culture of the local communities have remained pretty much the same throughout.

We came to a small chapel nestling in among the wild shrubs and trees. It was as simple as could be and the inside was brilliantly clean. The little altar had a small photograph of Mary wrapped in polythene to keep her dry and, next to her in a glass jar, a few hand-picked flowers were just holding on. On the floor one or two half-full plastic bottles of lemonade were arranged neatly behind the door. It was miles from anywhere with no vehicular access yet it seemed to be as used as any village church. It was very restful and we stood quietly for a little while gathering our thoughts. Then after a few respectful kisses to the Virgin Mary, we continued our journey, and Antonios carried on educating me to the wonders of olivology.

'You can see in these old olive trees,' Antonios explained, 'a shape and appearance that implies an undeterminable span of life. A life so long that it should be measured in millennia. These are trees whose size, outward surface, internal hollows and general structure reveal a design that illustrates the turbulent course of their life through time. They deserve proper protection, prominence and development as valuable evidence of the Greek cultural heritage.'

I was again impressed by how passionate these olive guys can get about their subject. Understandably so, and Antonios was up there leading the pack.

'What happens to the wood of uprooted trees, or ones that have died? Apart from craftwork products, is it of any use?'

'They are usually burnt.'

'How do they get so hollow and still live?' I wondered.

'When the branches of the olive trees break off due to the weight of their produce or the snow, or are cut off during the trimming process, the sections that are created cause conditions for the decomposition of the internal dead wood of the trunk and create cavities of various sizes and shapes. This phenomenon of cavities does not seriously affect the development and generation of the tree; it does, however, contribute to the tree's breaking down. In such instances new trunks can develop at the base of the old tree and a cluster of three or four trunks is quite possible.

'In many cases the dimensions of these cavities are such that they can fit up to maybe six people inside. Big enough to have been used as areas for children to play in, as protection against rain or cold, as hiding places in instances of pursuit, and even as animal shelters.'

'Yes, I heard that in Spain they were used as hiding places in times of war.'

In front of us was an old dry stone wall that had crumbled and a big gap had appeared.

'They have been stealing the stones,' Antonios muttered almost to himself.

I said that I hadn't heard the expression 'monument or monumental' as a way of referring to trees before and asked him if it was peculiar to Greece.

'Monumental olive trees exist in many countries of the world. Most of them, however, can be found around the basin of the Mediterranean (Italy, Spain, Yugoslavia, Portugal, Cyprus, Palestine, etc.) where there is evidence that the cultivation of the olive tree has existed since many thousands of years. Many of these trees have been characterised as *monuments of nature* due to their age, their size or their history, and they have been protected and developed accordingly.'

I loved the way that a simple question thrown in would get paragraphs of answer. Amazing that the olive tree could easily supply so much information.

'Monumentally, however, olive trees are also mentioned in non-Mediterranean countries where olive cultivation only began a few decades ago. In China there is an olive tree that is considered as a monument because it was planted by Mao Tse-tung even though there are older trees that apparently had been imported by the French missionaries much earlier in time.

'In Greece of course there are monument olive trees in almost all the areas where the olives are cultivated, but only a few of these have been observed and mentioned in published articles. Of course the most well known are those that are mentioned in ancient scriptures or are quoted in mythology. They were located or still are located in the region of Attica, where the popular myth of the conflict between Athena and Poseidon took place for the name of the city of Athens.'

'Which ones are considered the most famous?' I asked.

'Well there's Plato's. The famous tree where it is said that the ancient Greek philosopher Plato used to teach under its shade. It was mentioned in *Nefeles* by Aristophanes. This tree, until some years ago, was situated on Iera Odos (Votanikos) near today's Agricultural University. It was uprooted, however, when a bus hit it in 1977. The wood of its trunk has been transported and is being maintained in a special conservatory at the yard of the University. In the spot where the tree was, there is now a section of the old trunk with several offshoots, that are protected by a metal railing. Then there is the Pissistratos. This one is more than 2,500 years old. It is being cared for in the courtyard of the Anargyron church in Athens. It has survived from the olive grove of Pissistratos (560–527BC) and it has been recognised by law as a tenable monument of nature.'

'I've heard about that one and I'll have it,' I said facetiously. I was getting a bit tired, frankly.

'Then there's the Kalamata olive tree. Not one of the oldest but has a trunk perimeter of 8 m, diameter 2.56 m. It's estimated to be 800 years old and it was saved in an olive grove that was set on fire by the armies of Ibrahim Passa in 1821–24.

'These are all monument trees that in some way have inscribed on their trunks their troublesome walk through time. Trees whose entire shape and appearance suggests a very long life. There are others of course who are remarkable because of their sculptural forms or because they have huge cavities, but I can only go so far with this before I need to check my files. Look here are the trees.'

My eyes had been so fixed on the ground watching where I was walking, I hadn't noticed the grove of giant trees coming up.

Suddenly they loomed in front of us, about thirty of them and not one a centimetre under 20 metres high. Huge branches linking arms with one another spread out majestically from massive old trunks. Vast clouds of silvery-green leaves mottled the sunshine as it tried to penetrate the floor below. A few broken branches lay abandoned on a deep bed of dry leaves and an eerie silence hung on the warm air. It was as if they had stopped talking and were holding their breath until we went away. And sweet was the sound.

The ancient trees in Spain had been magical too, but their consistent pruning over the years had left their crowns low. And as enchanting as they had been with their endowment and venerable age, the magnitude of the trees that stood in front of me that afternoon in Crete were something else and rendered me unconditionally silent.

As I gazed up, I saw an age of mysteries camouflaged in ash greys, silvers, greens and browns. My eyes were dazzled by the pledges of nature, from the softness of silk to the irritation of bramble. The massive trunks, contorted by the hurting sway of a never-ending life, were fully paid up constituents of a mournful lodge.

I moved calmly among the herd, not wanting to disturb them, stroking and soothing them and trying to understand if it was wise to sequester these beautiful creatures.

I was sure if I discussed my thoughts with Antonios he would accuse me of anthropomorphising. 'The English they not only think their dogs are human but now it's trees.'

'My mother-in-law says dogs *are* human,' I would counter, 'and she's always right. So why not trees?'

Antonios would probably tell me that the Mongolians think nothing of making nice leather coats out of dog skin and the Chinese cook them. Oh, the famished eagle screams, does it not?

With weeping virtue I asked my olive guru what damage he would have to inflict to the trees if he was going to move them.

'First we would need to cut them right back so that they could survive the tr—'

'Trauma?' I interrupted.

'Transplant,' he said, 'then we would dig round the roots with a special instrument. We would bring in a crane to ...' My mind wandered as I stood trying to imagine what these olive elders, these field marshals, would look like with their height reduced to the dimensional requirements of a lorry, even if it was an articulated flat bed. I had terrible doubts.

How bizarre. Here I was, looking at a 3,000-year-old tree as imposing as a cathedral. A more illustrious and exalted specimen you would be hard pushed to find. A tree that was quite possibly the culmination of my search and I didn't want it. I didn't want to degrade it.

'How many do you want?' asked Antonios with a big grin.

'All of them,' I said, as flippantly as I could muster.

For the next half-hour I played a game of pretending to look at the trees closely, to take photographs, to jot down some measurements and finally to mark my first and second choice.

I felt incredibly flat and disappointed. I had thought that Greece would throw up the winner and it might be the end of the chase. When Antonios had said he had trees that he could sell, move and transport that were 3,000 years old, I had allowed myself a wave of excitement at the thought of calling Regis to announce the result. Now I thought that to arrive in Provence with some poor tree that had been reduced in size by two-thirds, had its roots severed and been extracted from its friends was certainly callous if not culpable. Further, it came with no guarantee of survival. I might be murdering it.

As we walked back he asked me more about the client, my line of work, and we talked of families, friends and foes. We also talked of Cretan history, the wars and battles and the terrible pains inflicted by the Turks. Because of this he took a detour to show me the Arkadi monastery that stands proudly on the side of Mount Idi.

One of the most glorious in Greece, the Arkadi monastery is revered in Crete for the holocaust that happened there in 1866. On 8 November about a thousand people – monks, soldiers, women and children led by the Abbot Gavriel – chose to die by blowing themselves up in the gunpowder magazine rather than fall into the hands of the invading Turks.

Hundreds of skulls in all sizes have subsequently been found and are slightly eccentrically displayed on shelves in one of the ante-rooms, lest anyone should ever forget.

It's almost too much to imagine. All being huddled together, with men toughing it out while the women clutch their poor innocent and uncomprehending children. Everybody unanimously surrendering to the wisdom of their holy elders. Sanctioning their decision that suicide is better than to let the enemy take you alive. The private thoughts, the doubts as the moments run out and the end is truly nigh. No more conjecture, no more debate. With your eyes to heaven you call out to your divine protector and hope beyond all hope that the terrible explosion that is about to happen will terminate your lives before you have had a chance to register that a monstrous wounding is taking place. This sacrifice permitted in the conviction that the devil has truly arrived. That rape and pillage, torture and death lurk in the dirty shadows of the encroaching

Beelzebub, and that to die in a haze of self-generated glory – well, this is precisely the only way forward. Dear God, I beseech thee to let my family never know such horror.

The monastery was founded during the time of the Venetian occupation. Its high walls are reminiscent of a fortress and the church, which has a baroque façade, is possibly the most beautiful on Crete. Incidentally, outside, planted in a disused well, is the biggest clipped *Pittosporum tobira* I've ever seen. The dome must be about two metres across and about a metre and a half at its highest point. In beautiful condition, it shines like a glossy beacon in the gravelled courtyard.

Antonios dropped Melina and me back at the car but before leaving he said that he had another tree that he wanted me to see. He thought it might be for sale and was probably as old as any on the island. It was not in such good condition but if old was what I was after, then I should take a look. He couldn't show me that afternoon so we arranged to meet the next day.

That evening we went into Agios Nikolaos *en famille* to have a drink on the quayside. An ice cream and two tiny cups of coffee for about a thousand quid seemed quite good value compared to the plastic space invader and the natural sponge the size of a small pillow that had to be bought afterwards. Thus laden and branded as gullible tourists we sauntered on along the restaurant-infested harbour front. We were soon assaulted by waiters practised in the art of citizen arrest. They block your way as you stroll along the promenade, virtually pushing you into either their eatery or into the water.

It hadn't been our idea to eat but our son convinced us it was the best possible option and should be undertaken without argument. Once coerced and captured, we sat resentfully looking at a menu condescendingly explained by torrid photographs of glossy plates of food. It was reminiscent of the Wimpy bars of old. Now that was a hamburger. Thinner than a pound note, 10 per cent cow, 90 per cent dubious filler/fattener/preservative. It had a monopoly throughout the land until the American hamburger invasion. Anyone who ate meat and had experienced a McDonalds in the States laughed mercilessly at a Wimpy (no wonder they called us wimps) and it wasn't long before the withered little excuse for a burger slipped quietly from the high street, shouldered out by its American counterpart. Out-tasted, out-sized, out-serviced and out-priced by those quarter-pounders. The Germans have got a lot to answer for in giving the world frankfurters and hamburgers.

We chose something like a salad and cheese and were settling down to wait our turn when our little boy spotted a collection of live lobsters mooching around in a glass tank of water. He couldn't believe it when a customer went up to them, pointed one out to a waiter who promptly lifted it out and started off towards the kitchen. As he twisted and turned his way through the tables the waiter stopped and showed it to various ladies who giggled and coloured at his over-rehearsed and ghastly *doubles entendres*.

'You like a big one Mrs?' or 'You want to touch it Mrs? It's very hard.'

'Is he going to take it home and keep it as a pet?' asked Junior.

'No, I'm afraid he's going to cook it.'

Horror-stricken, he refused to eat anything else that evening.

'What are you doing tomorrow?' Mrs D-M asked. 'Do you have any more trees to see?'

'Yes,' I said, and explained that Antonios thought it worth my while to look at yet another fine specimen.

'Dreadful word that. Why do you call them specimens? Sounds like something unpleasant you might find in a glass jar.'

'I agree but it's always been like that,' I said. 'It shouldn't take long, then

I thought I might go and see Regis Lautour's daughter and her boyfriend. They are just next door to where the tree lives. He thought it would be a jolly thing to do.'

'How do you know the boyfriend will be there?'

'Because her father said they were on holiday together, staying at his aunt's house. I suppose I will meet her as well.'

'Is she pretty?'

'No idea. Why?'

'The other one is, you said so.'

'I haven't met this one, what difference does it make?'

'Well, you are probably going off to meet some babe that will be all over you like a runny moussaka.'

'She's twenty-four, for God's sake.'

'Exactly.'

'Exactly what? As much as I would love to think to the contrary, twenty-four-year-olds are not generally attracted to fading fifty-something-year-olds.'

'Some are.'

'Not unless they are Mick Jagger or have enough money to float a Third World economy.'

'She might think it cool to pull one of her father's employees.'

'I am not one of his employees. I am retained as an adviser, thank you very much.'

'Precisely. One of his employees.'

'Listen, the best thing is if you come too. The little one can play around the garden and you can meet them as well. I would have suggested it but I thought the olive bit would be boring for you.' But the offer was politely turned down and I rang Dominique in full hearing distance of one and all and made a, er, date.

While these conversations can just as easily go the other way, with me being the suspicious partner, deeply certain that my wife is 'seeing' the summer school swimming instructor, or having a bit of a time with the frozen food delivery boy, they don't really hold much water.

The next morning wasn't very satisfactory. It started with Melina saying that she had to get back to Athens by lunchtime and that her flight was at 11.30. When I rang Antonios he seemed to regret having said anything about the other tree, and was rather preoccupied. I wondered if he had sussed that I wasn't going to buy any of his trees. Whatever, it was difficult to get enthusiastic. Things got worse when we discovered that the man who 'knew' about the tree we were going to look at wasn't there. His wife said that it wasn't for sale anyway and couldn't believe we even thought it might be. So, I didn't get to see the last-chance olive and Melina very nearly missed the plane. It was time for lunch.

I arrived at Stavros' aunt's place somewhat squandered. It was a fine house built into the side of a hill that sloped gently down to the sea. It was carefully designed and constructed using local stone and wood. A vast timber deck which extended out from the sitting room was held in place by angled stilts and appeared to end in mid-space. The maid who had let me in went ahead and called out for Dominique who was evidently round the corner in the swimming pool.

I was beckoned to follow and she delivered me into a summer house with a fully equipped kitchen, a big marble-topped table and enough chairs for a party.

Just beyond, a tall women wearing half a bikini was climbing out of the water.

'Hi, I'm Dominique,' she said, coming towards me and offering her hand.

She had the same chocolate-brown eyes and a warm, welcoming smile.

'How's the olive tree search?' She spoke quietly and confidently, with just enough accent to remind you she was French.

'It's quite a hunt,' I said, pleased that that had come out straight, 'but I don't think we've found it yet.'

'I heard about a man,' she said, 'who used to row over to a lonely island off the coast of Turkey. There was nothing on the island except one olive tree that survived at the top of a hill.' She stopped for a moment while she sorted out some glasses. 'The thing was that he used to take a donkey with him in the little boat so that the animal could help him carry two panniers of water up the hill to water the tree.' She topped up her own glass with champagne and then poured one for me.

'You like?'

'Thank you,' I said, 'I like.' I was feeling better already.

She turned and set off back towards the pool chairs and I followed closely.

I asked her how long she had been living in New York and what she had been doing there. It turned out that she had been teaching French to teenagers for the last two years and was going to change that soon. She didn't elaborate on what would happen next and changed the subject.

'Stavros will be here soon. He's been working in Paris for a couple of days but managed to catch an early flight this morning.'

'What kind of work?' I asked conversationally.

'He's a male model,' she said, without apology.

I never understood why girls are simply models and men are always male-models. I wasn't going to lose sleep over it though.

'But he only does that part-time. He's studying photography. It fits in quite well.'

'He wants to do fashion?'

She looked down and shook her long red hair free, partially hiding her handsome features. From beneath her covering she said, 'No, he wants to photograph people. Portraits. He's got this thing about really old people.' She looked up. 'Some of his shots are really good.'

We talked a bit more about Stavros which led to me asking where his aunt was.

'She's staying with friends in Argentina. Her boyfriend is a cattle farmer.'

I was about to launch into something about the beef industry in England, mad cows, foot and mouth, the callous treatment of farmers kind of thing when a call from an upstairs window changed the direction. A young man waved hello with a promise to be down in a moment. True to his word, he soon sprang on to the terrace, gave Dominique a tremendous kiss while she tugged at his dark curly hair, then he shook my hand firmly and did a double back flip into the pool. Stavros had arrived.

While the boyfriend torpedoed up and down the length of the pool and Dominique helped the maid get lunch ready, I took myself for a quick walk round the garden. Simply laid out, it was none the less charming. The main axis was a path that sloped down the hill side to the beach below where a motor boat was tied up to an old wooden jetty. Cushions of white *Centranthus ruber* billowed out beneath tall purple *Prunus pissardii*, supported on either side by enough grey *Dorycnium hirsutum* to float a wheelbarrow. Long sweeps of dark green *Rosmarinus officinalis* and the downy-textured pale grey *Ballota pseudodictamnus* followed the path down the incline interplanted with blue *Vitex agnus-castus* and *Salvia uliginosa*. *Verbena*, with its tall, skinny, purple-blue stalks, provided welcome little accents to the dense greens of *Prunus lusitanica*, *Olearia traversii* and *Viburnum opulus*. *Gaura*, with its pretty little pink flowers balancing on long arching stalks like butterflies, had invaded the banks and seemed determined not to let the aggressive grey *Atriplex halimus* have it all his own way. Coming back up towards the house, roses climbed, shrubbed and ground-covered in a grand show of extravagance. Figs trained against the walls had their feet in a bed of lavender mixed with the green *Santolina viridis* and the jagged silver-leaved *Artemisia stelleriana*.

I returned to find that the big table in the summer house had been covered in a pale blue linen cloth and was set lavishly with three glasses each, numerous plates and an assortment of knives, forks and spoons.

The lovers had put on T-shirts and Stavros was busy opening some wine. Dominique showed me to my place and the maid started producing an endless parade of traditional dishes.

We started with *paximanthia* and tomato salad. *Paximanthia* is the coarse, thick, toasted wedges of bread that have been baked overnight in a cooling wood-burning oven. It had been broken into chunks and mixed with tomatoes, onions, basil and salt. Horta, a wild-greens mix that included sorrel, black mustard leaves and a curly-leafed endive, accompanied it. Then came skewered, grilled swordfish, which was served with chickpeas, roasted red peppers and cooked feta cheese.

Another bread, *Horiatiko Psomi,* was put on the table to work with *Tzatziki,* yoghurt, cucumber and garlic dip, and Saganaki, small pieces of fried cheese.

Stavros poured a light, fruity white wine that he described as 'well balanced with a fine bouquet from the vineyards of Mandinia', and lifted his glass to toast 'Dionysus – the god of wine – the god of living and growing things, son of Zeus and Semele'.

Apparently Zeus destroyed Semele after she had asked him to reveal their child as a god. Having dealt her the fatal blow he then saved the unborn child by sewing him into his thigh from whence he later sprang! Weird stories and morning glories.

It was Plato who recorded that the Greek word for wine, Krasi, comes from the ancient word *oinous* which apparently means 'that which fills our brains with false impressions'.

The cook brought the dessert to the table. A small rotund lady with a toothy smile, she had wrapped herself up in spotless cotton chef whites, her greying hair tied back with a colourful bow. In front of each of us she put down a plate brimming with *Kataifi*, a sweet shredded wheat pastry with almonds, aided and abetted by a soft vanilla ice cream. Stavros left the table for a few minutes and returned with a bottle of red wine that he discharged liberally and announced that it was a Náoussa '84 Grande Réserve from Macedonia and Thrace. As he sipped the first taste, his eyes closed and he muttered something in Greek that might have translated as 'fan-bloody-tastic'. I drank a little and melted. Who wanted a pudding wine when we had this? It was robust and dry with a quiet asperity and hit the spot with tremendous confidence.

'This is the best that Greece has to offer,' said the nephew reverently, 'and she doesn't have much left.' A disconsolate afterthought.

The ancient Greeks enjoyed a reputation as great wine producers and the history of the vine dates back as far as 5000BC. No one seems quite sure where wine originated but it was probably Mesopotamia or Egypt or Phoenicia. The Greeks are the ones who spread the vine all over the ancient world, east to the regions around the Crimean and Caspian seas and west all the way to Andalusia. Even the vines of the Rhone valley can trace their provenance to the Greeks.

Crete, not only a mammoth producer of olives, also accounts for one-fifth of Greece's total wine production.

But it is retsina that everybody associates with Greece. A mysterious and acquired taste to the non-Greek palate, it is made exactly as all white wines are made, except that it is lightly resinated; a small amount, about two parts per thousand, of pine resin is added to the must at the start of fermentation. Retsina is also a traditional appellation by law. That means no other country in the world is allowed to produce it, even supposing that they wanted to. One can't imagine Sancerre worrying too much about that.

Stavros turned out to be an intelligent and kind man. He had an infectious laugh and was clearly besotted by Dominique. He generously asked me questions about my work but didn't really hear many answers because he was too busy sliding his foot up and down his girlfriend's long, brown legs.

I reciprocated by enquiring about his Parisian trip. He told me he had been modelling for a mail order catalogue, not very glamorous but extremely well paid.

'I was working with a South American girl called Carmen who wants to be a writer. Well, she already is a writer but she isn't published. Yet.'

'An aspiring Isabelle Allende?' I asked, immediately annoyed at my predictability.

'Not at all. In fact she thinks magical realism is dead,' Stavros said.

He told us that he had been reading a short story by the Chilean author Alberto Fuget that Carmen had recommended. It's about two young Latin-American film-makers who take their movie to Hollywood hoping to win an Oscar. It doesn't of course and their hopes of acceptance speeches and gratuitous sex fall flat on the formica.

'Fuget's writing shows that life's secrets are more likely to be revealed in a bottomless cup of bad gringo coffee than in a burst of iridescent butterflies,' he said. 'You know, a lot has changed since Marquez's *One Hundred Years of Solitude* and the never-never land of Macondo. There is a new school, a new voice coming from the south. There's even a book of short stories by 18 authors called *Macondo*. The word is a fusion of "McDonalds", "Mac" computers and condominiums. Latin-American writing is no longer cute.'

'"The light rain of tiny yellow flowers that fall through the night in a silent storm",' I said quoting Garcia Marquez, 'it's like comparing rap to soul, or Damien Hurst to Casper Freidrich. From a malignant wilderness to a sublime landscape.'

'Well, the world gets more polluted every day,' said Dominique, 'terrible wars, crowded highways, more and more developments built with laundered money. People find it hard to write pretty songs when they are in a gutter full of grief.'

'But the artist shouldn't just create what he sees before him, but what he sees within him,' I said, affecting an Indian accent and letting my head wobble. 'Gabo said, "If you say the novel is dead, it is not the novel. It is you who are dead."'

The wine flowed on wickedly and we talked of the world and his wife. We discussed her parents and the houses near Ansouis and in New York. Stavros explained about his education in California and how he was now studying photography. But he didn't get far because Dominique felt she needed to ask a couple of questions about Carmen. They were not so much literary related but more 'did you sleep with her?' related. He convinced her he didn't and we were all jolly happy. I rolled out of there and headed back to the hotel.

'Was she beautiful?'

'Nah, tubby little thing with dirty hair, but very polite.'

With a couple of days to fill before going home, it was decided we would 'do' Knossos.

Knossos was one of the four palaces which flourished in Crete during the second millennium BC. The island had become the centre of the refined Minoan civilisation, of what they call the Palatial Period, and the palaces had resulted from the needs imposed by a centralised economy and social organisation. The other palaces were: Phaistos, Mallia and Zakros. The impressive edifices were built in around 1900BC in strategic positions, ensuring direct connection with the rich hinterland and the important sea routes of the Aegean and Mediterranean.

These buildings, or collection of buildings, served many purposes. They were not only the axis of a highly stratified society, they were also the seat of administration and justice. Important as commercial and manufacturing centres, they were also in control of the economic and productive activities of a wider area.

Stored in the palaces' vast magazines were goods destined not just for local consumption by royals and residents, but for redistribution and trade. While the chateaux were at the same time workshops and ateliers, they had a further use in that they were dedicated to the cult of the Mother Goddess, and were simultaneously major shrines and centres of religious life.

Architecturally, the Minoan palaces were developed from the inside outwards, starting from the large court which comprised their structural focus as well as being the axis of their entire life. The walls were covered with plaster and decorated with paintings in the most important rooms. These fine buildings were all destroyed several times, probably by violent volcanoes but nonetheless were faithfully reconstructed after each catastrophe. Not giving up easily, they went on to stand proud for some 600 years.

Uniquely for that era the palace was not protected by fortified walls since there really was no threat of external invasion. The sea, remember, was well guarded by Minos's fleet.

At that time Crete, though small in area and population, became the first naval power in world history and the 'Thalassocracy' of Minos has remained legendary.

Thalasso is the Greek word for sea, hence Thalassotherapy. The treatment of the body by submersion in sea water and quite possibly being whipped senseless by seaweed.

The complex plan of the Palace of Knossos plus the fact that the labrys, or double axes, the most sacred symbol of Minoan religion, is scored lots of times on the walls and pillars, prompted the notion that this building was *the* Labyrinth, home to the dreadful Minotaur.

Late getting started we arrived just in time for the midday sun to smack the back of the neck with full velocity.

Thousands of tourists, most of whom looked as though their batteries were running low, queued happily for an hour to get in, then queued again to gaze at some ruins and wrecks, some reconstructed bits of past glory, all the time obediently listening to their guides. Herded and heaved from spot to spot the wilting mass did exactly as they were told, glassy-eyed and sweating.

The climax was to see a reproduction of a wall painting (the original is locked up in a museum vault in Ag), then stagger off back to the waiting bus.

'I've seen this place before on *Scoobie Doo*,' exclaimed junior excitedly. 'It's where Shaggy gets kidnapped by a Roman ghost.' Such is the art of learning. TV, the teacher of worldly things.

Maybe it was because I was exhausted, a tiny bit hung over and far too hot, but I found the place knossoly tiring. Perhaps on a calm spring evening with only a few other people and a dedicated guide it would be very different, but as things were, I was glad to be heading back to the beach and the sea for the rest of the day.

The next morning our taxi, the mandatory Mercedes, arrived to take us back to the airport. It came complete with an oversized cab driver in a deeply opened shirt, dark glasses, dangling trinkets and greasy black hair. The lines of a recent combing were held satisfactorily in place by gel. He had a hundred-carat mouthful of grin and leered winningly at Mrs D-M as she slipped into the front seat. He looked as if the sun had melted him a bit, his composure was of a congealed jelly that had been moulded into the driving seat. He probably smelt of sweaty gorillas but fortunately he had employed one of those little deodorisers that conveniently hang from the rearview mirror. I couldn't be certain but I think it was Gardenia Rhapsodie.

Along the route we got stuck behind a flatbed truck that was hurtling round the corners just a bit too fast to overtake without death. Of course it didn't stop our pilot hanging out on the edge and trying. He perched an inch behind the lorry, waiting for a suitably mad moment to go for it. An unusually mesmerising experience heightened by the fact that the flatbed had a horse standing on it. The poor creature had no supports, no bars or screens to secure him safely, just a rope round his neck scruffily tied to the back of the rusty old cab rack. He lent into the corners like a pillion on a motorcycle, his legs gently bending at the knees to absorb the bumps and potholes. With his mane and tail flying in the back draught it would have been magnificent if it hadn't been so foolish. Finally passing, we were looked down on from the driver's seat by something resembling the Minotaur himself. He was probably taking his equestrian catch off to be barbecued.

The plane out of Crete was delayed by an hour so I went shopping. There were only two places to spend money; one was an unremarkable coffee bar, where Mrs D-M was trying to persuade Shrimp to eat something without sugar in it, the other a tourist shop with a dire imagination. Thinking altruistically I set off in search of some jolly little reminder of my visit that I could pass to the support group back home. The shop was not very big and hopelessly over-packed with Cretabilia stocked on glass shelves from floor to ceiling. Being pretty certain that drying-up towels with maps of the island along with chess sets made from the Greek gods were not what was wanted, I reached miles up for a particularly clever little bottle of local olive oil in the shape of an amphora. Quite unexpectedly it slipped out of my fingers. I tried heroically to catch it again but as my other hand was busy fondling my wallet the bottle landslided its way down through pottery plates, fake silver goblets and ashtrays with Greek motifs. It bounced carelessly off a bowl, knocked out a doll in traditional dress and then, gathering speed, it smashed through three layers of glass shelves and came to a terrible conclusion on the tiled floor in a cacophony of blinking shards.

The oil, completely losing its dignity, behaved like an ocean wave breaking against a rock face. It smeared itself over seven-tenths of the shop, leaving the shattered glass to bring about as much trouble as possible. Glinting like snow on a freezing night, the thousands of diamonds with razor-sharp edges stunned everybody into a mixture of wonderment and concern. Just how many bits of glass is a horrible little bottle of oil made up from, for goodness sake? Enough to worry you about children's feet, animals' paws and your own fingers. The well-trained molecules quickly find somewhere to conceal themselves. Lurking in the fabric of the floor it waits till the vacuum cleaner has finished, the brush put away and the cloth thrown out, then 'twinkle twinkle, here I am again'.

The oil had oiled its way across the floor, over the shoes of fellow shoppers, into the low-slung bags of browsing ladies. It had smeared the packets of coffee and chocolates and smudged the cigarette lighters and pens. The ones with pictures of girls in one-piece swimsuits that fall off when you hold them upside down.

The manageress, a bent old woman who hated her public, came out from behind the till like a snake that had cornered its prey. She came up to me and opened her mouth wide enough to swallow me.

Actually none of this happened at all. It was just a game I played to help pass time. I hypothesised it.

You imagine some dreadful scene that you have brought about by your own foolishness and just as you are having a terrible time with it all you drop it. You haven't done it at all.

You are able to look about you and see all is calm. People are behaving normally and the till lady, an attractive Greek girl, is smiling at her customers, wishing them a good flight home. It's a rewardingly satisfying game and the fact that you end up thanking your Maker is all part of it. It's important to remember to thank your God for the simple things as well as the majors. I'm not a religious man, but when the cards are up, the boats out to sea and the numbers seemingly called in, I do occasionally, rather guiltily and apologetically, throw together a prayer. Nothing too Catholic, no huge portrayal of sanctimonious platitudes, and while playing down the Christian foreplay, I mutter a j-pegged supplication rather shiftily to the great Totem pole in the sky. I mean, how can that great benefactor out there deal with all the prayers that must be coming at Him or Her by the million a minute? By what criteria exactly does He decide who or what is right or wrong? The Moslems, the Christians, the East or West, the Black, the White. Each thinks theirs is the right on, up front, bona fide, no-arguments, correct doctrine. Yet we know, don't we, that without conflict there would be no tomorrow. There may well not be a tomorrow *with* conflict, but remove discord and you have an unimaginable game of chess where all the pieces are the same colour. It's like John Lennon's song 'Imagine' – romantic, appealingly wistful but ultimately a non-runner. Sad but true.

Then quite suddenly out of the blue your minor petition, your mini-prayer, seems to get answered. Well, without getting reborn, or feeling it necessary to report a sighting or having received a coming of the Lord, you might gently, without fuss, remember to thank whoever is out there for gathering up your sticks and running with them. It was probably one of the lieutenants rather than the high command but nonetheless somebody picked up the 'phone and replied. Or was it just a recorded message on an answering machine? 'You are through to the Prayer Answering division, Section 3, A–F, Multicultural, Standard replies. Please leave your supplication after the tone. For further help contact Dept 2317, subsection 29, in room 101 by pressing no. 2 on your handset.'

We were delivered back safely unto Marseilles and within a couple of hours the team was in bed and asleep.

But still without an old olive tree. Maybe a little prayer ...

CHAPTER SEVEN

The Angel Tree

Then gently scan your brother man,
Still gentler sister woman;
Tho' they may gang a kennin wrang,
To step aside is human.

Robert Burns

It was raining hard and the valley was blotted out by a darkness that promised heavy weather for a few days. The temperatures were low and a tough southerly breeze blew the wetness around like a deranged showerhead.

We had just managed to finish planting up a garden near Gordes before the storm broke. It had been running as a project for over a year during which time a swimming pool and tennis court had been installed. Terracing, paths, driveways, steps, gates and walls had all found their way into the grounds along with irrigation and lighting. A multitude of trees, shrubs and plants of all denominations had been worked into the design and the whole thing had been executed just about on time and not far over budget. The clients had been due down from Paris and the final push had succeeded in getting 95 per cent of it ready for their arrival. In the last few days the electrician had crashed his lorry as well as his confidence, one of the gardeners had misplaced his motor bike in Avignon after a bit of a night and the metal worker had broken his foot, but we limped on and the garden materialised regardless.

The team had worked well with no big arguments, no tantrums or oversized huffs and considering that most of us were working together on two other projects at the same time, there was a silent sense of professionalism ekeing through the ether.

Actually that's not quite true. Heiner, an immigrant labourer from Dusseldorf who was on somebody's payroll somehow, managed to swear at me in German, French and English and had been, for the most part, spectacularly truculent. He told me to bugger off back to the other poofs in England, to get a life, and most sensationally, to go screw a razor blade. Sweet chap. You give the bloke a job, pay him well and on time, smile sweetly and what do you get? You get Heinered. He was so blunt, imaginatively rude and devoid of any social skills that he became an absolute integral part of the show. It's very important to have a Heiner around, it keeps everybody else calm. Nobody could match him.

Quite often a few days are taken off after a project is finished. If the client is happy that is. To allow a bit of time to wallow in the warm waters of a job well done.

But on this occasion there wasn't room for such luxury. I had been back from Greece for two weeks and hadn't rung Lautour.

For the first time since I had met him I felt reluctant to make the call. I had no good news for him and another expense account. At the outset of this olive idea I had warned him that my costs were likely to be high, probably more than my fees. I had given him an estimate the best I could manage and he had agreed it. But as each trip had been concluded with no solid result, presenting an invoice was becoming less and less amusing for both of us. There is a dullness that seeps into the relationship between client and designer, consultant, call it what you will, when things go too slow. The spirit of the engagement loses a little of its lustre. It may not directly be anyone's fault as such. It could be third parties, weather, slipping stock markets or illness, it doesn't matter really. The point is that the initial excitement and anticipation, the bang that both sides get out of a commission or of buying something new, big and expensive, wilts with the realisation that it ain't gonna happen yet awhile.

I decided I would leave the call until the end of the week and spend the interim thinking about what should be done next. I wanted to be able to say something positive to Regis. God knows what it was going to be but something had better turn up.

I spent most of the next day driving down to a site near Montpelier and back. I was nearly home when the cell phone rang. It was Señor Junos.

'Hi, want to talk to you about a tree beyond trees,' he began, and paused.

'Hang on.' I pulled over and stopped. 'Go on.'

'Ho Kay. It is 2,300 years old and is known as the Angel Tree.'

'The Angel Tree?' I said suspiciously. 'Are you talking about the same angel tree that we looked at but wasn't for sale?'

'The same.'

'But now it is for sale? I thought you said it definitely wasn't.'

'Ah well, now this is the difficult bit.' He paused again.

'Señor Junos, please excuse me but I feel as if I have done nothing but think, sleep and live olive trees for the last few months and today I have been driving since breakfast time. I am exhausted and unless the Angel Tree *is* for sale there isn't much point in talking about it. I am sorry.'

'Ha, Señor Dingley-Man you are fading so quickly. You came to me to help you find a tree, and now I think I have found one, a very special one, the very one you wanted, and you have no interest. I will sell it to somebody else,' said Señor Junos.

'So it *is* for sale?'

'It might be.'

'What does that mean?'

'You will have to buy some land as well.'

'How much land?'

'And the small house. It is only on one floor. What you would call a hottage.'

'A cottage?'

'Sí, a hottage,' he said.

'How much land?'

'Minimum half a hectar, maximum 25.'

'Twenty-five hectares of land is a lot. It's nearly 75 acres. It would require some kind of ongoing maintenance. Half a hectare on the other hand is a containable small freehold, something that could easily be looked after by a helpful neighbour or a local. Anyway, if it's so old why is it not classified?'

'That's a long story which I will tell you not on the phone.'

'It's hot?'

'What is hot? The weather? Sí, s'very hot for time of year.'

'Are you saying that the Angel Tree would be an illegal purchase? That it would be breaking the law?'

'Señor Dingley-Man, you not thinking I would do some things illegal surely. I hope not. Hit is my reputation, my profession. I am a well-respected specialist.' (Actually Señor Junos' English wasn't this good but I paraphrase badly to help make the point.)

'How much?'

'In Pesetas or Heros?'

'Euros.'

'Seventeen thousand heros.'

It was a hell of a lot.

'That includes the tree, land and little house?'

'Sí, but it depends on how much land, but not lifting up of the tree or the transport.'

'OK. I'll tell the client about it.'

'Oh, and there's another thing. A local woman collects the raindrops off the leaves after a storm and bottles it. She gives away the water to people who have depression and it makes them much happier.'

'Do you think that's true?'

'Sí sí, it's definitely true. She gave me a bottle, I have it here and I am not at all depressed.'

'What, are you saying she wants some kind of compensation for loss of trade?' I said.

'No, I am not saying that at all. I am saying that your client may want to continue with the commodity,' he said, 'as a little benefit.'

'Maybe.' I could just see Regis out in torrential downpours tapping the rainwater as it ran off the leaves, then decanting it into cute little bottles to sell to The Body Shop. 'Can you email me a proposal tomorrow?'

'Day after. Tomorrow is my anniversary.'

'Thank you, Señor Junos, I appreciate your trying so hard, and happy anniversary.'

'Thirty-five years, same woman, can you say that Señor Dingley-Man?'

'No. But how about thirty-five women, same year?'

'Yea yea, buenos noches Mr Dingley-Man.'

The changing fortunes of war. Ever since getting back from Spain I had been deliberately pushing the Angel Tree out of my mind. It was a non-starter, just a fantasy. Instead I had been digging around in Italy and Greece and trying to sort out where to take the pursuit to next. Suddenly and completely unexpectedly *that* tree was back in contention.

We had heard about this wheeze of the opportunist vendors before. How they capitalise on the sale of an old tree by unloading parts of unwanted land, and now it had reared its head right under our noses. I wasn't certain that it smelt completely fresh but it couldn't be entirely dismissed either. The point for the moment was that the most appropriate tree I had met was very possibly up for grabs, that is if we wanted to play the game.

The Angel Tree. I said it over and over to myself. There was some kind of magnetic morality to it. A tree with a superior sanctity. It was a little ethereal, a little mystical and of course, a little expensive. But it was also very, very old which added sagacity to its being as well as wonderment to behold. Goodness be, it even had supplementary medicinal properties as a bonus. But would Regis really want to buy a Spanish cottage and a heap of hectares just to get it? I wasn't at all sure. I also knew that I would probably be turning round and going back to look at it again if we were to comprehend the full pregnancy of Junos' proposition.

The rain was still drumming on the windows at lunchtime when the phone rang. It was Regis.

'Oh hi, Regis, I was just going to call you,' I said.

'Well, I hope so. I heard from Dominique that you had met so I do know that you got there all right. But she didn't seem to think you had found a tree for us. Is no news good or bad news?'

'Well, I do have some good news as it happens. Do you remember the Angel Tree that I talked about?'

'Yes, I think so, you mentioned it and said it wasn't for sale? But that was in Spain surely, not Greece?'

'That's right. I thought it categorically wasn't for sale, but now with some provisos it seems it may well be. It is a beautiful tree, Regis, and I think perhaps we should try and get it. I am going to email you some photographs I took.'

'So that means you didn't find anything in Greece?'

'I did and didn't,' I said, sounding oblique, 'But I'll explain more later. Suffice it to say that I left Crete thinking that it was too complicated and too expensive and quite possibly unreliable in terms of survival.'

'What are the provisos? With the Spanish tree I mean?' he said cutting back.

I explained the deal might mean buying some land and possibly a little house that goes with it. I told him that this is now where olive entrepreneurs are at.

'What on earth am I going to do with some useless land and a cottage in the back of beyond, somewhere in Spain, tell me that?'

'Well,' and I said it slowly, 'I have an idea about that.'

'I thought you might. And?'

'How about taking the cottage apart, stone by stone, transporting it up here to Provence, complete with surrounding rocks and boulders, etc., and then reassemble the whole thing somewhere in your garden? There isn't enough room in the courtyard but perhaps on the slope down to the lake. We could totally replicate the little tableau; tree, boulders, bank and cottage. We could have something else in the courtyard instead. It would be a story.'

There was a silence from the other end. I liked to imagine that Regis was thinking what a great idea but in reality I suspected he was thinking I'd lost the plot. Seen too many olive trees for my own good.

'There's somebody at the door, I'll call you back.'

And with that he'd gone.

Well, that's slipped down like a ton of olives, I said to myself and resignedly got on with something else.

The inter-office phone rang.

'Madame Sanot is on the 'phone,' Philippa said. 'Shall I put her through?'

'If you must.' Madame Sanot, a client, had been a queen-size pain in the neck for the last few months. She could complain about complaining. If I had been able to rewind the tape I would have turned down her commission. But I couldn't and although the job was to all intents and purposes finished, she still managed to keep the irritation line open.

'Good afternoon, Madame Sanot, how are you?'

'On the plant plan, you put *Cistus creticus* 'Eriocephalus' and in fact the *Cistus* that has been planted in the garden is the *skanbergii*.' She wasn't one for pleasantries.

'They are both pale pink with grey-green leaves and grow to about a metre in height,' I said. 'The nursery must have substituted them. They often do this if they have run out of the exact one we want.'

'Don't they tell you?'

'Usually, yes.'

'Well, don't you think you should have told me? I am the one that is paying for it.'

'You've been charged the same price.'

'That's not the point. If I am shown that I am getting one plant on the plan and then find I have a completely different plant in the garden, I think you as the designer ought to be held responsible.'

'The point is that they are virtually the same, and we probably thought that you would be quite happy with the substitute.'

'Probably thought I wouldn't notice, more like.'

'I will do what I can to replace it with the correct plant.'

'Don't. I prefer the one that has been planted; it has slightly smaller flowers. But you simply can't go around counting on people accepting just any old thing you know.'

'Of course, Madame, we try to avoid that.'

'And another thing. You said the ...'

Before leaving the office I checked the email. Nothing from Regis. That wasn't a surprise, he hardly ever used it. There were a few anagrams from my pal Don:

Evangelist – Evil's agent
Desperation – A rope ends it
A decimal point – I'm a dot in place

But before I could get to anything else the phone rang. It was Lautour.

'Hello Regis.'

'This is going to make it very expensive, isn't it?' he said.

'You mean bringing the tree with the little building, etc?'

'Yes, your Señor Junos has obviously smelt a good profit if he can persuade the farmer to part with it.'

'I expect so. But it could just be the tree we've been looking for,' I said.

I went on to explain all the details that Junos had given me including how pretty the tiny cottage was, and reiterated the story about the mystical water. I was entranced by the fact that someone should collect the rainwater that dripped off its leaves and hand it out, believing that it acted as a healing potion, curing illness and depression. I just hoped it wouldn't lose its potency if it were brought to Chateau Lautour.

'I came to you originally because I wanted help with our courtyard. That is what our problem was. I wasn't envisaging that your suggestions would entail buying land in Spain, let alone a house, and worse that you would ignore the central point of the commission.'

'A very, very small house,' I interjected.

'When we first spoke I simply wanted some outside advice on how to create an attractive, perhaps even a little unusual, solution to a fairly undemanding problem. You had some interesting ideas and I thought we could work together. Now you are putting forward a very expensive, arguably mad proposal that doesn't even fill the brief.'

'OK, Regis, I take your point. It is probably true to say that this has all got a bit out of hand. Believe me, if I could have bought this Angel Tree for you without the add-ons I would have done it. Ten years ago the man who owns the tree would never have dreamt up such a scam, nor would his family or friends. But the recent demand for these old olives by the rich ex-pats has manifested a highly inventive greed in the peasant farmers. They have rows of fruit ringing in their eyes. But you can't really blame them.'

'Listen, I am not looking to fight with you and I understand how this situation has evolved. I even thought the idea of adopting was quite captivating in its way but as we discussed, it didn't solve my courtyard problem so I dismissed it. Now you are introducing another scheme, which is even more difficult to reconcile.'

He took a draw on his drink, and I waited for him.

'So last night I discussed this whole concept of the Angel Tree with my wife at great length. In the end, and after much contemplation, we decided it would make a formidable folly for Chateau Valois. It would be unexpected and we like that aspect of it. If you can quickly come up with an effective alternative for the courtyard, one that isn't going to be hopelessly expensive and take forever to achieve, we'll go for the Angel Tree and its little Cabanon and put the whole thing on the estate somewhere.'

I couldn't believe my ears. Madame et Monsieur Lautour were going to buy the Angel Tree. Trunk, rock and cottage. I was lost for anything to say for a moment until Regis said, 'Are you there?'

'I am, I am,' I said. 'This is great news, I'm just taking it in. Frankly I wasn't expecting you to say yes. I thought you would tell me that you didn't want to pursue it. But really I'm very pleased. I'll ring Junos immediately.'

'You understand of course that this is subject to me actually seeing and approving of the old tree and its little house. Also making sure that there are no legal problems, etc. But if it is as good as you say we'll do the deal on the spot. You just have to set it up and I'll sign. I'll call my lawyers tomorrow and alert them to my rash behaviour.'

'I am sure you will love this tree, it is so special. I hope Junos hasn't sold it to somebody else,' I said, suddenly worried by the possibility.

'So do I,' said Regis, 'oh, and by the way Dominique is pregnant.'

'She's not! Is she really? What wonderful news. I would never have guessed it the other day when I met her. Stavros must be feeling very noble. Are you happy about it?'

'Yes, we are. She is ecstatic and everybody is very pleased for her. I think Stavros will look after them both with great care.'

I put the phone down slowly and let it all sink in. The months of searching seemed to be over. The best tree I had seen, the Angel Tree, the one that I had most wanted, without doubt the most interesting and appealing, was actually going to come and live in Provence. And on top of that, the Lautour family was about to open a new division. Quite a day.

I rang Junos the next morning or at least I rang Miguel and told him that our client was, in principle, interested in buying the Angel Tree and its appendages. I listened as he told his father who was, predictably enough, completely over the top about it all and said that we should have a drink immediately.'

'Get the whisky out!' he shouted from the background, 'and let's do business.'

I said to them that Lautour wanted to come and inspect the tree, etc., before committing to anything. That he wanted me to come down first and prepare the deal with Señor Junos and to make arrangements for our client's arrival.

Regis Lautour's small aircraft landed at Valencia airport at a little after 10 a.m., as scheduled. I sat in the back of the big Mercedes waiting for him to disembark.

Before long, wearing an immaculately cut, lightweight pale grey suit with a deep blue shirt and tie, Lautour's tall, thin figure emerged through the plane's door. He had somebody with him who was also dressed in a suit. He carried a briefcase and they quickly descended the steps and walked towards the car. I went to meet them while the contracted chauffeur loaded up the luggage.

'Good morning, Regis.'

He smiled and introduced me to Sam Montague, his Anglo-French lawyer who, he told me, spoke fluent Spanish. A good-looking man with greying temples but perhaps carrying a little too much lunch. We shook hands and his gentle manner and kind eyes were reassuring. I was glad the boys had arrived and that the whole thing could now get fully under way.

Hire a fast car and driver, Regis had said. Not that easy, they don't have fleets of Jaguars or Mercs sitting around outside the Hertz rental office in Valencia. He didn't want to waste time, he just wanted to see the tree and whatever else he was buying, do the deal, shake the hands and get out of there. The hard work of organising the lifting, transporting and planting of the tree could be left to me. The legal formalities of the transaction would be handled by Mr Montague in Paris and Lautour's secretary would pick up any necessary public relations.

I had arrived at the airport early, giving me a bit of time to just relax and reflect. To dwell a while on the whole process.

There had been a lot of background work to do before the boss had arrived. I had had to sort out exactly what we were buying. How much land was involved, mark it out precisely so that Regis could visualise his holding and make a thorough inspection of the little house. To find builders that would undertake the dissembling of the building carefully and sensibly. The correct labelling and marking of the main stones, window frames, roof beams, etc., was paramount otherwise there would be a bunch of French brickies looking at a heap of rubble, wondering what on earth it was, let alone how to turn it into a charming little Spanish cottage.

It had been agreed that the deal would be done in three payments. One-third on signing, one-third on a successful delivery to Lautour's chateau and the final payment when the house had been erected and the tree planted. We had tried to persuade the Spanish builders who were responsible for taking the cottage apart to come to Provence and reconstruct it. Believing that it would be the most logical if not the cheapest way to ensure a smooth transition, Regis had made them a good offer, but they had declined. They didn't want to be stuck in a country without their families, without their language and probably without their tortillas. On top of which they didn't need the work anyway.

There had been meetings with Señor Perez, the farmer selling us the package. He had to be assured that the money would be paid on time and that Regis was an honourable purchaser. We needed to be confident that the whole Perez camp fully understood exactly what was happening and when. To be sure that everybody concerned was in agreement with the purchase and that any formalities connected to the mayor or local government offices were in place. To discuss things with the Perez family was in itself a convoluted process as most of them were either not talking to each other and/or were very reluctant to gather together in one place. It had to be decided who would lift the tree, who would transport it, and who would oversee the masons, etc.

On this point Junos said that he thought it would be better to involve the builders and transport people after the deal had been signed, arguing that the fewer people who knew what was going on the better. I supposed he was right and paid attention to my own specific duties. If the tableau was to be authentically reproduced in Lautour's garden, I needed to be sure that the position of the tree in relationship to the house was correctly recorded. The rocks around the tree roots would have to be put back in exactly the same pattern and the wild flowers growing between the cottage and the olive needed to be lifted lovingly, planted up in temporary cases and looked after at all times. Dozens of photographs and measurements had been taken; marks made with spray paint and ground plans drawn up.

Despite Junos' desire for secrecy, each day I found myself drawn into discussions with more and more local people who would happen by, spurred on by rumours of a mad Frenchman who had bought their tree.

Some showed an infectious enthusiasm, others were genuinely perplexed as to why anybody would want it. Some of the more scurrilous locals sniffed around the fringes of the transaction, hoping to score by proxy. When Señor Junos' son Miguel and his good English weren't with me the conversations had been necessarily abrupt, but when Miguel was helping, which was most of the time, we found ourselves drawn into endless conversations about what we were up to. While we determinedly didn't say very much, word had spread that Señor Perez had sold his soul to a Frenchman.

I had two concerns during those furtive days. One was that we might be making a fundamental error here. Was it that we were crashing into a community and removing one of the cornerstones of its fabric indiscriminately? Did we have the right to do this? There was a thin slice of guilt lining my stomach and I wasn't sure it wasn't getting thicker. I comforted myself with the thought that perhaps the farmer would put some of his new-found wealth to good purpose among his neighbours. My other concern was that a man from the ministry would turn up and slap a classification stamp on the tree and kill the whole deal. I eyed each new spectator with suspicion and caution and just hoped for the best.

The evening before Regis was due to arrive, Señor Junos had set up a meeting with the vendor, Farmer Perez, so that we could get everything as ready for Lautour as possible. It was done quite formally. There was no sign of whisky, beer or any other alcohol. No wife or children, and no third parties except his son Miguel. It was just the four of us sitting at an overlit table with some paper and pens. Junos' manner was more serious than I had seen before and he chaired the meeting totally professionally.

Señor Perez was a small, thin man and didn't look very robust. He smoked heavily and seemed nervous about the proceedings. He and Junos obviously knew each other well but he appeared a little intimidated by his friend. His fingers, deeply stained with nicotine, fiddled among themselves and he was shy of looking me straight in the eye. He wasn't your first-choice business partner, but I reckoned it was all OK if Junos was handling everything. At least I hoped. A shiver ran down my back as I thought about what the hell I was up to. Here I was somewhere in the middle of Spain with a bunch of fairly unsophisticated people whom I didn't know from Adam, jauntily committing Regis to a grown-up amount of money. Deeply entwining him into a pledge that involved an incredibly old tree that might be ten minutes to dead on a plot of useless land and a house half the size of a teapot. Gulp.

A survey map was laid out on the table and the six-acre plot of land that had been agreed in the sale was carefully outlined with a yellow marker pen. A contract of purchase, drawn up by the local notaire, was put in front of me to consider. It looked normal enough although I couldn't understand much; it had all the right appearances. It was up to Lautour's lawyer to verify and authenticate the document. It had already been signed by about a dozen people on Perez's side, probably beaten into submission by the greedier members of the family. I asked a few questions about the local authorities. I also said that I thought Perez should sign a piece of paper stating that the tree was not classified as a monument. He looked to Junos with a startled expression as if I had uncovered some deeply hidden secret, but our intrepid olive dealer quickly agreed on Perez's behalf. Next Junos put forward his official invoice for the pruning, lifting and transportation of the tree. He also produced an undertaking to obtain quotes from builders for dissembling the pint-sized cabin. He told me that he knew a local contractor who would send an estimate for cleaning up the site after the tree and house had gone. It would be levelled off, some topsoil added and left to its own devices. If a maintenance contract should be required, or if it were to be let, he himself would make sure it was organised.

I tried to imagine what would become of the barren, asset-stripped six hectares after we had been and gone. There wasn't much in the way of other trees, no other buildings, and only a dried-up stream. There was one bit where there seemed to be quite a good planting depth with reasonable soil. The oranges that were growing on the parcel of land that butted up to the angel plot seemed healthy and content. Maybe the neighbour could be persuaded to take it on. Maybe Regis could turn it into a theme park.

We concluded our meeting believing everything had been covered and were ready for the boss to come and stamp the deal.

I had slept jaggedly that night. My agitated mind pierced with thorny thoughts and an eviscerated conviction that all was not quite as it should be. I dreamt that the Angel Tree refused me shelter and had me banished to the earth's fiery bowels. There all the trees were burnt-out skeletons with long, charred branches that wrapped round my tired body and slowly started to tighten their scratchy grip. In the hot shadows hookers with two heads and four bosoms urged me to taste the tapenade of temptation. I awoke at five tied into a knot of strangled pillows and sweaty sheets.

With Lautour and Montague secured in the back seat of the car, we eased on to the main road and were soon hurtling towards our rendezvous with a very special old wooden character.

Junos had another talent. He was a showman. He had absolutely no intention of letting the Angel Tree go without a song and dance. He had told everybody about the imminent arrival of Regis Lautour, and how the millionaire lover of beautiful trees was going to add the Angel Tree to his formidable collection of ancient trees that he had built up. He had seduced the local paper, television and radio stations with a story of great human interest, and promised them exclusive rights. He had set up a table and stacked it with some heavy-fisted bottles of red wine. Big banners declaring the name of his business were strung between temporary poles and he had loaded Miguel up with cards and brochures. In the background Mozart struggled his way out of a pair of public address speakers which he had to share with a microphone.

The little cottage had been cleaned out and the main room boasted a small trestle table covered in an olive-green cloth on which were arranged all the legal documents and plans. Four red chairs, two on either side, waited patiently for the dignitaries to land on them. A summit meeting of world leaders could hardly have been better prepared.

I don't know what kind of reception Regis had been expecting but I was pretty certain it wasn't anything like the one that awaited him. As his car arrived the considerable gathering that had blocked the small road moved sideways to let him in.

'What's happened here?' he asked. 'There must have been an accident or something.'

I strained to see. Nobody had mentioned any plans to make a 'do' out of the situation so I was as innocent as Regis.

Then I saw Junos, resplendent in a dark green frock coat, breeches and riding boots. He had on a white shirt with ruffles down the front and a huge cigar in his mouth. He walked boldly towards the car with an expression on his face that might have been worn to welcome the pope. He opened the back door of the car, stuck his hand inside and bending over said to Sam Montague, 'Señor Lautour, this is a special privilege and—'

Sam cut him short and hissed at him in Spanish that he was not

Lautour, and that the gentleman getting out of the other side was the man he wanted. Junos didn't drop a beat; he thanked Sam and quickly changed course and with a deferential bow introduced himself to Lautour in front of the Mercedes radiator and a throng of some forty very curious people.

Regis was polite and gracious. He smiled gently to the ever-growing crowd of people that had come to gawp and shook hands with those immediately around him. But at the first opportunity he instructed Sam to tell Junos to cool it and let him look, unhassled, at the tree, the house and the land that he was here to consider.

Junos was not a fool and he did exactly as he was instructed. He gently cajoled the people to give Regis space and took up his post as tour master. He spoke mindfully and explained with Sam's translation how the magnificent old tree had got its name, how he could tell its age and what a bit of local lore it was. He pointed out the shape of the 'angel's wings' and drew Regis's attention to the extraordinary patterns that could be discerned in the bark.

Regis stood back and looked hard and long at the tree. He ignored the cameras and questions that the press were determinedly pushing at him. And though, like reporters everywhere, they were not going to slink back into the shadows just because Regis wanted some space, with amazing dignity and cool he managed to go about his business unfazed. He was clearly delighted with the tree and stood contemplating it with his hands together in front of him. Probably unintentional, but they were in a praying position.

A few moments later Junos guided him into the little cottage that stood a dozen metres from the tree. With its terracotta tiled roof, off-white walls and climbing roses it was as sweet as honey. Ducking to avoid banging his head on the low doorway Regis found himself in the small room occupied by the table, chairs and paperwork. He stopped and stared at the arrangement. Another surprise for the poor man. Thinking he was just having a quick glance round the little house he found it set up like a magistrate's office. The pressure on Regis to buy was almost overwhelming and he had only been there a short while. Again with perfect decorum he didn't bat an eyelid but threw a sideways glance at me wrapped up in a wry smile. He was taking it all in his stride, maybe even slightly amused. He quickly looked around and nodded and shook his head according to Piers's interpretation of Junos' selling points. It was like being shown round a one-car garage in Chelsea and being told by over-achieving estate agents that it was worth half a million quid. The villagers pressed forward, the front row peering in through the windows with the insatiable curiosity of cows, a herd of old flatcaps, rolled-up sleeves and washed-out floral dresses. With hardly enough room to move without hurting each other, the team squeezed back out into the unsettled morning weather. Sullen clouds were gathering in the east and rolling slowly across the sky on a southerly breeze.

Miguel, obviously on his father's instruction, had persuaded Mozart to play a little louder while he started uncorking the wine and pouring long quantities into the paper cups supplied by the management. With the well-known suck and pop of a bottle losing its virginity the gang slowly turned its attention away from Lautour and towards the altogether more important task of wine-tasting. With the dispersing of humanity, Regis was at last able to move forward and start an inspection of the land.

By the time Lautour returned from his walkabout, Mozart had handed over the speakers to a lively recording of a Spanish folk band. Already half a dozen elderly couples, ennobled by the seductive charms of a Herculean red hooch, had started to collide into each others' arms while trying to call up some long-forgotten dance steps.

I had left Regis to walk the fields with Sam and Junos on his own to let them discuss the ins and outs of the business and strike the deal if that is what Regis still wanted. I had nothing more to add to the story – he was either going to do it or he wasn't.

He found me sitting on the ground under the Angel Tree, sipping bravely on some of the meanest, most single-minded adolescent red wine I had ever had to wrestle with. The novelty of the visiting millionaire had waned a bit with the assemblage and he was able to join me unmolested.

'OK,' he said.

'OK what?'

'I've told Junos that I will make a contract with him. We have agreed a price and how it's going to be structured. Sam has insisted on one or two clauses, made a couple of suggestions, but basically we are ready to sign. Señor Junos is very keen on making an announcement and wants me to say a few words, via Sam, to the locals. I have reluctantly agreed.'

'Great,' I said and smiled at him. I felt like giving him a hug but as he hadn't introduced himself to Junos' evil little brew yet I thought it best not. I was shaping up well for a bout of the old tired and emotionals. The next time I lean against this exalted old tree, I said to myself, we will be back in Provence.

Regis winked and tapped the tree. 'I want to light it very carefully so that we can see it from miles away,' he said, 'it should be quite a good walk from the house and I think we'll put a fridge full of champagne in the little Cabanon.' With that he headed off to sign the papers, presumably write out a cheque and prepare for his address.

As Regis went up to the microphone, an antique piece of equipment rescued from the ravages of a bad night on the rock 'n' roll circuit, it squawked and shrilled and pumped feedback through the speakers with a screech that made hands reach for their ears. Miguel fiddled and fussed and persuaded the recalcitrant lollypop to behave itself.

As the sprightly crowd realised that the honourable guest was about to speak, they gathered around him in a warm blanket of muffled giggles and chatter.

Regis stood next to Sam who tapped the microphone and introduced him formally to the local community. There were a few whistles and a round of applause. Sam said that he would of course translate for them and they could ask questions after Regis had finished if they wanted to.

'Ladies and Gentlemen,' Regis began. 'It is an unexpected pleasure for me to meet you all in this convivial fashion today. I had no idea that the sale of this beautiful old tree would cause so much interest.' The microphone sounded hollow and gave Regis' voice a slightly detached tone. Bit by bit the background noise subsided.

'As most of you know, I think, we are going to move the Angel Tree to my property in Provence, and with Señor Perez' permission we have petitioned the *petit cabanon* to come along to keep the old olive company.'

It was meant to be light-hearted but nobody smiled. There was a sort of suspense, good-humoured banter had been replaced by short gasps and bewildered faces that looked at one another in disbelief as they realised what Regis was telling them.

Lautour continued. 'It has taken a long time to find such a wonderful old tree and I can assure you that it will be looked after to the highest possible standard.'

I could hear people muttering about '*el arbol del angel*'. With horror on their faces and with a creeping chill I began to realise that these people had had no idea that Regis was planning on taking their tree away from them. They must have thought he was just buying the property and was here to introduce himself to his new neighbours. Their celebration was nothing more or less than a welcoming party given in good spirit and sponsored by Señor Junos. It had obviously never occurred to them that somebody might actually come and remove not only their beloved tree but the little house as well. I groaned and went to find Miguel. I needed to speak to Junos.

Mr Perez and his family were standing directly in front of Regis as he talked. Most of them stood silently looking down at the ground with an inebriated apathy, but old Perez was gazing up at the speaker. He looked tired and beaten, and tears ran down his face cutting through the wrinkles like a burn through bracken. He twisted his cap in his shaking hands and a more consummate sadness was hard to imagine. There was no music now and as Regis continued, aware of Perez' discomfort and the odd atmosphere that was rising like steam from the warm earth, he directed his speech towards the more general aspects of olive trees. Their place in history and how the French were beginners compared to the Spanish when it came to making olive oil. I could see he was faltering. At that moment the grumbling sky decided it was time to stop threatening and get on with some proper action. A slow spitting changed quickly to a steady rain and people began to move away from Regis and towards the spreading shelter of the old olive tree.

Regis stopped talking and stood watching as everyone started to jockey for position under the tree. The younger ones joined hands and made a necklace round the trunk, others looked forlornly up into the crown. A bunch of old ladies huddled together sharing a sadness. One of them seemed to be catching the rainwater in a glass jar as it dripped down through the branches. Soon even those who had really just come along for a party were caught up in the extraordinarily moving silence that prevailed, and took comfort from beneath the benign old branches.

Out of the uneasy silence a small man weaved his way through the crowd and stepped out in front of Lautour. He looked tense and desperate.

'You can't take our tree, Señor. She belongs with us.' It was Perez. 'I make a mistake, Señor, a terrible mistake. I have been bad with greed. This is not my tree to sell; it is in the soul of all of us here. She is our Angel.' His voice was low and cracked with emotion.

His hands reached out towards Lautour; his sorrowful old face pleaded a forgiveness that was painful to watch.

The Mercedes driver had appeared with an umbrella and stood behind Regis and Sam, doing his best to keep them dry. The rain was quite hard and the visibility had dropped to a misty twenty metres. Miguel wrapped the microphone up in a plastic bag and did his utmost to stop the wine from getting watered down, which some might have argued would have improved it no end. I went up to Regis and Sam who were standing with expressions of bewilderment and impatience respectively. I suggested they took cover in the little house and I would try to find Junos and get some kind of explanation.

I set off in the direction I had last seen Junos. My stomach was churning and I felt cold. I had, it seemed, managed to orchestrate a fair-sized catastrophe. On one side I had a mob of people who would hang poor Perez if he let the Angel Tree go, probably from one of its branches. On the other, I had a client with a baffling set of financial and emotional problems to sort out. It shocked me that I hadn't thought the whole thing through more wisely.

Meanwhile Perez had been bundled into a nearby car whose wipers beat a steady rhythm, allowing the nosy a refreshed peep of the poor man every couple of seconds. He sat in abject misery, refusing to talk to anybody. Then, much as they had arrived, the clouds moved on and the rain pulled up. People were talking among themselves in hushed tones as if witness to a heinous crime. Nobody wanted to leave in case they missed a further scandalous episode. Not many had been soaked because the Angel Tree had done as she had always done: she had protected them from the storm.

I found Junos in a cloud of cigar smoke, talking fifteen to the dozen on his cell phone in the middle of a row of orange bushes. I hovered until he saw me. He muttered something into the mouthpiece and came over to speak to me.

'Señor Dingley-Man, believe me I thought Perez had told everybody about the tree being taken away.'

'Señor Junos, you must go and talk to Señor Lautour. He is waiting in the Cabanon. He is very disturbed.'

'Sí sí, I go now,' and with that the ringmaster headed off.

Twenty minutes later Regis and Sam were back in front of the microphone, the sun had hurled itself into the fray and this time it had been Señor Junos who had called everybody's attention saying simply, 'My friends, please listen for a few moments to Señor Lautour. He has some important words to say.'

The crowd obediently stopped talking and turned once more towards this stranger in their midst.

Regis, standing very straight with one hand in his pocket, the other free to gesticulate, looked calm and unruffled as he started.

'I came here today as a formality. I came simply to see a tree, a little house and a few hectares of land. To satisfy myself that they were what I wanted and to confirm my intention of purchase and of course to pay a deposit to Mr Perez.'

Everybody had started to listen intently.

'I have spent the last few weeks planning the tree's arrival at my chateau. Organising the planting arrangements with my garden designer and considering the complications that might arise with the transport of both the tree and the little house. I had not considered the possibility that there might be any resistance to the scheme. Mr Perez had assured me that everything was in order, that he was very content with my offer and that he had the full backing of his entire family.'

A few people shuffled and looked over towards the car where Perez still sat hypnotised by events.

'I realise now that it was completely misguided of me to think that I could just walk into a community that has known this magnificent tree for thousands of years and remove it without causing any emotional wounds. Mr Perez has said eloquently, in front of all of us, that he has made a mistake and that the tree is not morally his to sell. I now say to you that I too have made a mistake and that the tree is not mine morally to take away. I know this from having witnessed the old olive fulfil its duty this afternoon for its congregation. I see how deeply it is integrated into this local population and to remove it would be both disgracefully arrogant and shamefully unaware.'

Regis took stock for a moment and had a long sip of the red ruin that had burnt holes in everybody's brains that day. As he did so, there was a spontaneous round of applause.

In the last half-hour Regis Lautour had faced a truth. Previously he had only thought about the tree for his own ends. He had not considered any social implications. The fact that anybody might be deprived by this single-minded act had not occurred to him. He had led a moneyed life and was used to getting what he wanted when he wanted it. He had paid people well to oil the mechanics of his welfare. He had seldom paused to consider the consequences of his actions. He was not a bad man – he was extremely conscious of people's feelings. He celebrated nature, whether it was the reinstatement of the parkland at his chateau, his birds of prey or the search for an ancient olive tree. He had always treated his employees fairly and would happily indulge them but only if it did not affect his direction.

That day in front of a simple Spanish group of country folk, he saw, quite possibly for the first time, that he couldn't always get the material asset he wanted just because he could afford it. I too was reflecting and considering my motives. I had introduced him to an idea without really thinking about the details. Junos had shown me a tree that fitted the bill and I had automatically assumed that if he had sorted out a deal to put forward, then everybody must be happy. Particularly as it had taken so long in the coming. In my enthusiasm to get the extraordinary tree for my client I hadn't stopped to ask pertinent questions about how the locals might feel about it being extracted from the jaws of their commune. Junos for his part, ever the entrepreneur, had not made any suggestions that it might cause upset. He had read it that money was the main line and if Perez was happy to sell, he was happy to broker the deal.

Regis put down his glass, tried not to grimace, cleared his throat and continued, 'Now I have a little problem. I have already signed the papers with Señor Perez agreeing to buy this smallholding. I am, if you will, the proud owner of the land you stand on. So, I want to make a deal with you, my neighbours. My eldest daughter is going to have a baby in about six months and I have decided that I am going to give this property to my first grandchild. In exchange for the ongoing protection you are assured of from the Angel Tree, I would like you to welcome my daughter, her child and husband into your community and offer them the same safekeeping.'

This time the applause was wrapped into a roar of approval. Caps were thrown up and cheers of Bravo, Bravo, climbed into the air. The cameras clicked and the reporters text-messaged the story through to their news desks.

Miguel determinedly bullied the wretched red virus into soggy cups and passed it round to the willing conspirators. The music staggered back into life and foot-tapped out a jig that was irresistible to practically everyone.

I felt wrung out and uncomfortably chastised. The Angel Tree belonged to us, or at least Regis, but it was staying firmly put. Whether he approved of the concept or not, he had adopted a tree after all, but at least it was on his own land even if it wasn't in his own country.

With one quick decision Regis had made sense of the whole thing. He had turned a flop into a flyer. A very small person would soon arrive into the world and be the privileged owner of one of the most beautiful olive trees that could be found anywhere. He had spotted the error and had elegantly erased it. A smooth bit of operating seamlessly done and with no outward sign of discomfiture. Quite a christening present from one hell of a grandad.

It didn't take any more than that little speech to put the party back into the people, and with re-found abandon they attacked the criminal little poison as if it were vintage Bollinger. The music rent the air and the sun seemed happy to join in. Somebody wrapped one of Junos' banners round the trunk of the tree and tied it into a bow and things looked set to run until empty.

I spoke briefly to Regis who told me that he would be leaving soon but before he went he wanted to talk to Perez. He wanted to make sure that he had recovered and was not blaming himself unduly.

It transpired that Perez had led a tragic life. His wife had run out on the family when the children were little and he had battled bravely to bring them up on his own with precious little money. It had been hard enough but when his son had died in a motorcycle accident when he was 17, Perez had lost the will to try. His eldest daughter, now nearly 30, had struggled to keep the home together but it had taken its toll. She had left Perez and the younger daughter to fend for themselves and later married a man from the south. His sister and her argumentative husband had moved in with him and later their ancient mother. After years of dispirited existence, Perez saw the Angel Tree as his salvation, his deliverance from a life of purgatory. When Junos had advised him to push up the price by including the empty little house and a bit of land into the package, he had gone for it. Like a man with a winning lottery ticket he thought his life would be so transformed that it wouldn't matter what his neighbours thought of his actions. Besides the tree was his, it was on his land, he could do whatever the hell he wanted. He would be immune to their criticism.

What Regis found was an old man torn by the day's events. Emotionally ripped by the exposure of his selfishness, and inappropriately elated by the realisation that he had backed a winner after all. The conundrum of life had left him bereft of any correctly assembled thought.

Regis had done his best to balance the old man's equilibrium and when he had left him, he had felt confident that Perez would be just fine. Doubly so when the cheque had cleared and his bank account had shaved and put on a tie.

I declined Regis' offer of a lift back to Valencia, saying that I wanted to stay on and talk to Junos. He understood this without question and we agreed to meet up in Provence the following week.

'You'd better have a bloody good idea for the courtyard, young man,' he said, waving a finger at me through the back window of his limousine, 'or you'll never work in Provence again.' His smile was enigmatic and his wave perfunctory. The day had played itself out, concluding with a generous final act. Both spiritually and financially. But, and it was a big but, Regis' courtyard was still without its ancient olive tree. I let out a huge sigh and shambled off to find Junos, yet again.

'Señor Dingley-Man, I want you to—'

'Alex, please,' I said. I was fed up of being a Dingley-Man. I was fed up of most everything.

'Alex is good,' he said. 'So I too must be Pedro, then everything is good.'

'Fine. Where's your son?'

'I'm here,' said Miguel as he came into the room. We were back at the table with bright lights, cigars and whisky bottles.

'Good, because I want you to ask your father to do a very big favour for me. I want him to do something that is probably illegal, and I want it done tonight.'

CHAPTER EIGHT

Capers and Legends

Happiness is not an ideal of reason but of imagination.

Immanuel Kant

The new moon shone like the edge of a highly polished soup spoon high in a bright uninterrupted sky. The bad weather had moved off and it was as if the night were happy to collude and conspire with me.

Junos pulled the Jeep off the road and parked it carefully behind a hedge not far from the main gate to the park. Miguel and I sat in silence waiting for him to say something. We were his accomplices and had agreed to obey orders and keep quiet. He pulled out a pencil torch, unwrapped his home-made map and started to explain his plan. It was three a.m.

'The gates will be locked so we must climb the fence here; there are no big obstacles and it is near to the main path that runs down beside the lake. The olive tree is over there near these big pines. There shouldn't be anybody else about, but just in case keep your clothes buttoned to the neck with the collars up and your hats pulled down.'

I was dressed in a dark green boiler suit, green rubber boots and a rather fetching black bonnet. The other two looked slightly more at ease in their army fatigues that they probably used to go shooting or hunting in. Unless of course they did this kind of thing on a regular basis, but I rather doubted it.

When Miguel had asked me what the favour was that I wanted, I had prevaricated. I had run round the edges hoping to get them totally sympathetic to my request, to lead them in via a glass or ten of whisky and to let it pop out when I thought they were ready for it.

'Well,' I had said, 'Regis certainly handled that with panache. I think we are all quite lucky he didn't instruct Piers to sue everyone of us.'

'Sí sí, he is quite a gentleman,' said Junos, knocking back a shot. Miguel nodded.

'Just think, he came all that way to see the tree he thought he was taking back to his garden in France, and he has left empty-handed and out of pocket.'

'Sí sí, he really is quite a gentleman,' said Junos toying with his empty glass.

'What is it you want me to ask my father?' said Miguel.

'Well, I was thinking that because Lautour behaved so considerately and didn't give us a bad time, maybe we could give him something, you know, to let him know that we all appreciate what he did?'

'Not a 2,000-year-old olive tree,' said Junos quickly. 'He may be a good man and all that, but business is business, I can't start giving away *millénaires* to millionaires.' He chuckled throatily and lit a cigar.

'No, no, of course not. Well, not exactly. But maybe we could give him a cutting?' I said.

'An old olive tree cutting?' asked Miguel, catching on.

'Yes exactly,' I said, 'after all a small branch, or twiglet, is meant to be a sign of friendship, so why not a cutting from a very old tree that we could plant up in a small pot and give to him for his courtyard?'

'Sí, Señor Dingley-Man, Alex, I think this is a very good idea.' He was obviously deeply relieved to be moving away from any extravagant concepts of supplying Señor Lautour with a tree for nothing. Despite the largesse of our client's performance he wasn't about to invest his cut of the action into the Regis Lautour benevolent fund. 'Sí, you must choose a tree tomorrow from the *millénaires* I showed you and I will dip it in the hormones powder, plant it up and *voilà*.' He slapped his knee with delight at his French and filled my glass. I hadn't got to the main point yet, but I let it run for a moment, and allowed his scotch to tickle my tonsils.

'Not just any old tree,' I said, 'I have one specific *millénaire* in mind.'

They both looked at me and in the harsh strip lighting of their hybrid sitting room, cum kitchen, cum dining room, cum workshop, they looked like a pair of grotesque china dolls.

'You mean a cutting from the Angel Tree?' Miguel offered.

'That's certainly a thought,' I said, 'but I don't think so. He can get that at any time he wants. No, I was thinking of something much older.'

'There isn't something much older, señor,' said Junos puffing so hard I couldn't see him.

'Ah, but there is, señor,' I said. Now was the time to pull my cards. 'I am talking about the old tree in the park. The one you showed me that you said was probably 3,000 years old. That withered old trunk with a guard-rail round it, the one that St Vincent blessed in fourteen something. Don't you remember? We talked about taking, or borrowing as you put it, one of the regenerated stems. You said you would have to go in after dark and—'

'Sí sí sí. I remember, señor. But I am trying to forget. It was not a good idea. If I was caught in the middle of the night trying to take a cutting from the oldest olive tree in Spain, I would be castrated and locked up.'

There was a terrible thud followed by a groan that seemed to come from inside the ground. Junos had misjudged his footing and had fallen off the five-bar fence and landed clumsily on his back, fortunately on the other side. The side we wanted to be on. Probably attributable to a wealth of whisky and getting tangled up with his elongated pruning secateurs that he had brought with him. Miguel nimbly followed and helped pick up his semi-winded father and put him back on to his feet. I followed cautiously. I hadn't felt so naughty since one night at school when me and a bunch of cohorts got up in the middle of the night, bicycled over to another nearby educational institution, our chief rival in all sports activities, and meticulously carved the words 'up yours' out of their first eleven cricket square.

Junos, once recovered from his mishap, was soon back in charge of his regiment. At one point we crept past a little tent which had a hurricane lamp still burning on the inside. The silhouettes, as clean as black paper cuttings on the sidewalks of Montmartre, were managing a position that I had never seen before, let alone experienced. *And* in a tent at three a.m. Impressive performance. Not something that's on my 'Dr Ruth's educational sex video', I can tell you. But despite a suppressed wonderment and desire to linger for the finale, Junos growled about how they shouldn't be there and that we had work to do.

The frogs were burpeling and fracking as we approached the lake. They fell into a disorganised silence as we lurked passed. The ducks took no notice and apart from an occasional flap of wings all was quiet. The brilliant moonlight showed us up as an asinine mob as we tried to pretend we weren't there. You could have spotted us from a hundred metres, but we persisted nonetheless, heavy with stage whispers and bent-over postures while creeping along on tippy-toes.

Then the moment of reckoning was suddenly upon us. There in the moonbeams stood the ancient olive. The rusty cage looked more like a prison than a protective housing. The empty shell of the tree's trunk was collapsing with a fatigue buried deep within its structure, but, mystically, from the obstinate old roots rose the long, thin saplings of another generation.

Junos rather ineffectually pointed his pencil beam at the tree and put his finger to his lips and made a theatrical shushing noise that woke up a crow.

Like safe crackers, or jewellery thieves we laid out the tools of our trade with an aching silence. Cardboard tube to stash the cutting in, cotton wool to wrap round the secateur blades and a pair of gloves to avoid fingerprints. A bit dramatic that bit, I thought. I couldn't quite see the forensic department of the local police station over-involving themselves in the scurrilous activity of an olive pruner, but better safe than sorry. And that was it. No other props required.

Junos moved over to the edge of the cage, knelt down, put his hands together, bent back his fingers and cracked them in a suitably criminal fashion. Miguel wrapped the cotton wool carefully round the blades of the long-handled secateurs and passed them to his father. The idea was not so much to cut the sapling with a clean snip, but to tear it gently away from the root with a 'heel' on it. That is, the point at which it parts company with its parent should include a small section of the root covering or bark. However, as the old tree was about 75 centimetres away from the edge of its protective barrier, and therefore just out of arm's reach, it had been deemed commendably sly to cover the blades with cotton wool (you don't want to bruise the poor thing) and to pinch the sapling at its base vice-like, then with a confident tug extract it in one.

And that is exactly what happened. It came away clean as a whistle, a delicious heel of bark correctly in place and, before you could say Topkapi, it was in the bag. Actually, I was just a tiny bit disappointed that an alarm hadn't gone off, that no napping guards alerted to our escapade hadn't winched themselves out of the pine trees, and that we hadn't had to flee down secretly learnt paths disguised as evergreen bushes. Instead we walked briskly back the way we had come (the light was out in the tent by the way), managed the five-bar fence without crisis and were soon sitting in the secure confines of Junos' jeep.

The team leader took a subterranean draw on his flask, and then just managing to contain an internal explosion kindly passed the dripping, overworked utensil to me. Needs must and I too drew on the burning mouthpiece and let the tension go. Miguel had his own brew and for a moment we sat in a contented stupor.

We had done it. From under the noses of the enemy we had pulled off a magnificently brazen caper. By the time this adventure had been told a few hundred times we would have dodged our way through minefields, incapacitated fighter planes, drilled holes into supply cans and slit the throats of frightful thugs.

Having kissed the cutting goodnight I climbed into one of Junos' spare beds and crashed headlong into a soft feathery sleep.

The next morning Junos drove me and the oldest olive cutting in the world into Valencia station, bought me a single ticket to anywhere in

Provence and bade me a fond farewell. The last few days had been quite a campaign and we parted company with a mixture of affection and a hope of never clapping eyes on one another ever again. The sapling had been dipped in hormone powder as promised and planted up in a five-litre terracotta pot. A long bamboo cane held it upright and we had wrapped brown paper round the whole thing to disguise and protect it. I clutched the orphan close to my heart so that she could feel the beat and take comfort.

As the train trundled along I made a few sketches of ideas for Regis' courtyard and when I thought I had solved the problem I rang my chum Don in London and asked him if he had time to do an illustration for me.

'Of what,' he asked cagily.

'Of a courtyard garden. I've done some sketches and made notes and got some photographs to help. It won't take long but I *really* need a good presentation drawing to sell the idea to my client.'

Don knew perfectly well that the 'it won't take long' bit was wishful thinking, but he knew he could probably do it quicker than most. He had, after all, done a lot of this kind of thing before. I also knew he could do it considerably better than most.

After a round of negotiation that involved lots of bottles, several lunches and quite possibly a couple of air tickets, a deal was struck and the valiant chairman of the Chelsea Arts Club signed on.

I wasn't sure what kind of reception to expect from Regis when I rang but he was just as friendly and polite as always.

'Good, I was hoping to hear from you. When did you get back?' he asked.

'Yesterday. I have a few ideas for the courtyard and was going to suggest that I come over next week when I have the drawing finished to show you.'

'Come on Thursday. If I like your ideas you can stay to lunch.'

'Well, count me in for the weekend then,' I said breezily and hung up.

Meanwhile back at the house, one of our ongoing problems looked like it might have found itself a solution to be friends with.

Mr Deblanc was, according to my wife, a short little man with a big tummy that moved around with its own agenda. It wobbled and shook as its owner marched purposefully hither and thither. His ruddy face bristled with a massive moustache of which at least a quarter seemed to find its way into his mouth, lending him a fine substitute for chewing gum. Put him in the right clothes and he could have probably got away with playing Asterix, but as it was he dressed immaculately in a company suit and tie. He conducted himself with a shy, cultivated authority that made you want to put your arm protectively around him, or so Mrs D-M said. He worked for the EDF, the French Electricity Board.

I had never met Mr Deblanc and I intended to keep it that way, for a while anyway. Nonetheless he had been prevalent in our lives at the time that I had returned from Spain. To me he was a shadowy figure of whispered conversations; to the Mrs he was an omnipresent force that brought great promise.

We have two concrete pylons on our property. They were put up in 1952 and have cursed the general landscape ever since. We loathe them and have done the best we can to disguise them with careful poplar-planting, but when the trees begin to get tall enough to truly hide the damned things, along come the EDF and ignominiously prune off the top two metres. They don't ask and they don't do it considerately. We can't plant climbers up the frame of the thing because they might interfere with the mechanics, we can't paint them because that might damage the EDF's property and we can't use them as adventure climbing poles because that might kill us.

When we first saw the property we thought long and hard as to whether we could live with them but the estate agent continuously assured us that they would be knocked down and the lines buried underground within ten years. But we figured he would say that, and we were not about to hold our breath. After deliberation we went ahead with the purchase. For the budget we had set ourselves, the property gave us a lot of positive factors. It was a charming old house with plenty of character, albeit in need of some serious attention, a good position slung in a hammock of land on the valley between two medieval villages and backed up by a breathtaking view out across the Luberon Valley. The only hiccups were the pylons. The cost of moving them was high and the money had been needed for more pressing projects. But, every year, it had come up for discussion and the last time we talked about it we had started to seriously consider investing in their removal.

Mrs D-M rang the EDF and made a tentative enquiry. They said they would send somebody round to look and discuss the cost. A few days later Mr Deblanc turned up at the house, introduced himself and inspected the problem.

Back in the kitchen Mrs D-M made Mr Deblanc some coffee while he watched her every move with a goofy expression on his face, smiling and nodding. His moustache had bristled with appreciation.

'Is it going to be terribly expensive?' she asked imploringly. 'I probably can't afford it but I am so worried that the energy is bad for my baby.' She can get very inventive when necessary.

'Of course. I fully understand,' Deblanc had said soothingly and had reached out to tap Mrs D-M's hand. 'You leave it to me and I will see what can be arranged.'

For the next three Thursday afternoons, Deblanc had found it necessary to drop round and explain his progress. The first time was to say that he had discussed the matter with the relevant engineers and hoped to have more news soon. Mrs D-M smiled sweetly and Deblanc left in a haze of rosy sunshine. The next Thursday, Mrs D-M put on a little lipstick and had the coffee ready. Deblanc, now that he knew the ropes, hopped up on to one of the stools in the kitchen and detailed the intricacies of his job to her, while she listened as if she had never heard anything so exciting before. On the third Thursday, Mrs D-M had now dressed in a short cocktail dress, overdone her eyes and opened a bottle of red wine.

'Now Mr Deblanc' she asked with a little exasperation, 'whenever are you going to remove my pylons?'

'Soon!' Deblanc said breathily. 'I have just heard that they are going to be taken down this winter.' He put his arms up in the air and with a huge grin, '*Voilà!*'

'Really?'

'C'est vrai! There is a programme to bury all the wires from Menerbes to Lacoste, starting in December. We have to get permission from the participating parties to go over their land but we don't envisage any problems. Your pylons will be banished by next spring.'

'At no expense to me?'

'Absolutely none.'

'Mr Deblanc, you are my hero,' and with that gave him a big kiss on the cheek. He coloured a little and then said he would pass by again next week with some forms to fill in and help her write a letter to the authorities.

Mr Deblanc had remained a regular visitor and I had stayed well clear on Thursday afternoons until those pylons tumbled.

The drawing arrived from Don in London the day before I was due to have my meeting with Lautour. He had illustrated the brief perfectly in his own incomparable style.

The idea had been to keep the theme uncomplicated. First another mature plane tree had been planted in the eastern corner to partner the existing one on the other side. Under the new arrival a group of big box plants had been clipped into geometrical shapes: cones, cubes and pyramids, giving a tight disipline to the corner. The restored walls that enclosed the courtyard now had two large plastered panels let into the stone work between the columns, and the smooth finish had been painted in a washed-out pale green. Against these were trained young olive trees in the *espalier* style, their young branches spreading out sideways in a controlled configuration. Below them, growing through a chromium-plated metal puddle, *Ophiopogon nigrescens* admired the reflection of their black arching leaves. The floor had been laid to olive-wood boards except where a fine gravel path cut through from the house on its way to the ornate iron gates that were flanked by six pencil-thin cypress trees. In the very centre, sitting on a circle of broken black slate, was an amphora about a meter and a half tall. Into this old olive-oil jar, rescued from an ancient mill, would be planted the olive cutting that I had so carefully brought back from that park in Spain. To continue its heritage and magnify its legend.

The simplicity was stunning and when the implication was understood the sapling grew in stature and became living sculpture, horticultural marvel and *objet fantastique* all in one go.

The big plane tree in the corner supplied some shade for the little olive in the daytime and made an ideal spot from which to light it at night.

The next morning I stuck the cutting into an old zinc watering can I had bought for Regis so that he could ceremoniously irrigate his mini-monument; then I put the drawing under my arm and headed off for Lautoursville.

Rottcodd, who looked suspiciously at my luggage and asked if I would like to leave it outside perhaps, showed me into the library.

'No thank you,' I said. 'I'll just hide it here behind the chair. It's a surprise you see. For Monsieur Lautour.'

He nodded his frail old head, raised an eyebrow and gave the watering can and little plant a look that suggested he wasn't at all sure his employer would be impressed.

I smiled weakly and handed him my jacket, hat and the watering can. 'Would you leave those in the hall, I'll keep the plant with me.'

'I'll tell Monsieur you are here,' he said and left the room while I busied myself getting the artwork out of its carrier.

Shortly, Regis came hurriedly into the room.

'Alex! Good to see you, I hope you haven't been waiting too long. I was just in the cellar checking in a delivery of Léoville-Barton that arrived this morning. It's the '64; I bought it at auction. How are you?' He shook my hand firmly and seemed genuinely happy and relaxed. But then I would have been too if I had been stacking bottles of exceptionally fine claret into the bins in my cave.

'You had an easy journey back from Spain I trust?'

'Oh, a little turbulence over the Pyrenees but nothing serious,' he said, shrugging it off. 'But what a story that was. Goodness me! I have been telling my friends how serendipity has managed to play a major role in my grandchild's future. I rang Dominique and she is thrilled. She can't wait to see the little house and, of course,' he paused for effect, 'the Angel Tree.'

I felt great relief roll over me. I had been ready for this meeting to be full of recriminations. To be hauled over the coals of his discontent.

Instead he was accepting the whole thing in his stride, was even pleased with the outcome and ready to move on.

'A glass of champagne?' he asked and without waiting for an answer he took a bottle from the cold bucket and unscrewed the cork.

'Perhaps I'd better show you this drawing first,' I said, producing the illustration and laying it on the table.

'No, I'm sure we will enjoy it more with a drink in our hands.' He poured two flutes, passed one to me and put on his glasses.

As is usual on these occasions I remained silent for a few minutes while the client absorbed the image.

'Hmm. Hm-hm-hmmm,' he hummed as he looked and said nothing for a while. Then slowly, 'I think this is good, but explain what this is in the middle, this little sprig?'

I took him through the concept, explaining the panels on the walls, the black plants, the shiny puddles, the olive-wood floorboards and the slate, then brought him to the ancient olive jar, positioned to show off not only the pot but also its contents.

'But the contents are, shall we say, a bit insignificant, aren't they?'

'Ah, but that's the point you see. This little sprig, as you call it, is a cutting from a 3,000-year-old olive tree. Probably the oldest tree in Europe, maybe anywhere in the world. It is a national treasure, guarded by railings and growing in a cage in a park. The cutting has been liberated from the base of the old tree's trunk.'

He continued examining the illustration and listening. After a slow draw on his glass of champagne he stood upright and looked at me.

'This is a great idea, but how the hell do you ever get the cutting? It would be impossible and probably illegal. I am not sure I understand the point of making this beautiful drawing and showing off a marvellous notion if you are unable to produce it?' He was much more serious now and his voice carried a hint of impatience. I thought he was about to snatch my champagne and pour it back into the bottle.

'Excuse me a second,' I said, and dug around behind the chair, then turned to face him.

'Because, Monsieur Lautour, here is that cutting.'

I held out the little pot and its extraordinary inhabitant and passed it to him.

He took it from me as if it were made of thin glass. His face was a series of expressions that moved from disbelief into astonishment and out to excitement.

'Do you mean to tell me this is the genuine thing? This is actually taken from the 3,000-year-old tree? How on earth did you get it? Does anybody know?' Without waiting for the answers he put it down on the table and stood back to admire it.

'A singular treasure,' he said quietly.

We looked at the healthy sapling in silence for a while, as is normal with Regis. He must have been thinking about its ancient parent as much as I was. The timescale and the wonderment of survival. The precious plant that had left its progenitor and come all the way to live in Provence, and was now about to continue a legend for who knew how long.

Regis walked over to me, put his arm round my shoulder and said, 'I think you had better stay for lunch.'

Epilogue

All you need in life is ignorance and confidence, then success is sure.

Mark Twain

Known now as the Junos Olive, the young plant has caused much interest within the Lautour family and among friends and visitors to the chateau. It is growing happily in its new, slightly crazy surroundings and is cared for like a wanted child.

In time the sapling will outgrow its old jar and will be planted in the centre of the courtyard. The ground was prepared beneath the black slate for just this purpose. Once replanted, there is no reason why the little olive shouldn't grow up and live for hundreds or even thousands of years in its protected position.

Inspired by all the recent olive shenanigans, Lautour has started a new olive orchard of some 41 trees. Forty of them are puppies of about twenty-five years of age, but one is much older. He sits in the middle of the plantation, forming the central axis from which all the others emanate.

He is approximately five hundred years old, was born and brought up in France and oversees the juniors like some benevolent old schoolmaster who wants only to indulge his pupils gently with kindness, understanding and encouragement.

FACTS

Common name: Olive

Related species: Wild Olive (*Olea africana*), Oleaster (*O. europaea* var. *oleaster*)

Distant affinity: American Olive (*Osmanthus americanus*), Fragrant Olive (*O. fragrans*)

Origin

The olive is native to the Mediterranean region, tropical and central Asia and various parts of Africa. The olive has a history almost as long as that of Western civilisation, its development being one of civilised man's first accomplishments.

Archaeological evidence suggests that olives were being grown in Crete as long ago as 2500BC. From Crete and Syria, olives spread to Greece, Rome and other parts of the Mediterranean area. Olives are also grown commercially in California, Australia and South Africa. There is some disagreement over when the trees first appeared in California. Some say they were introduced in 1769 when seeds brought up from Mexico were planted. Others cite the date 1785 when trees were brought in to make olive oil. Virtually all US commercial olive production is concentrated in California's Central Valley, with a small pocket of olive acreage outside Phoenix.

Adaptation

The olive requires a long, hot, growing season to ripen the fruit properly, no late spring frosts to kill the blossoms and sufficient winter chill to ensure fruit set. The tree may be grown as an ornamental where winter temperatures do not drop below -12°C. Green fruit is damaged at about -3°C, but ripe fruit will withstand somewhat lower temperatures. Hot, dry winds may be harmful during the period when the flowers are open and the young fruits are setting. The trees survive and fruit well, even with considerable neglect. Olives can also be grown in a large container, and have even appeared in shows as bonsai.

Description

Growth habits: The olive is an evergreen tree growing to 50 ft in height with a spread of about 30 ft. The tree can be kept to about 20 ft with regular pruning. The graceful, billowing appearance of the olive tree can be rather attractive. In an all-green garden its greyish foliage serves as an interesting accent. The attractive, gnarled branching pattern is also quite distinctive. The trees are tenacious, easily sprouting back even when chopped to the ground.

Foliage: The olive's feather-shaped leaves grow opposite one another. Their skin is rich in tannin, giving the mature leaf its grey-green appearance. The leaves are replaced every two or three years, leaf-fall usually occurring at the same time that new growth appears in the spring.

Flowers: The small, fragrant, cream-coloured olive flowers are largely hidden by the evergreen leaves and grow on a long stem arising from the leaf axils. The olive produces two kinds of flowers: a perfect flower containing both male and female parts, and a staminate flower with stamens only. The flowers are largely wind-pollinated, with most olive varieties being self-pollinating, although fruit set is usually improved by cross-pollination with other varieties. There are self-incompatible varieties that do not set fruit without other varieties nearby, and there are varieties that are incompatible with certain others. Incompatibility can also occur for environmental reasons such as high temperatures.

Fruit: The olive fruit is a green drupe, becoming generally blackish-purple when fully ripe. A few varieties are green when ripe and some turn a shade of copper brown. The cultivars vary considerably in size, shape, oil-content and flavour. The shapes range from almost round to oval or elongated with pointed ends. Raw olives contain an alkaloid that makes them bitter and unpalatable. A few varieties are sweet enough to be eaten after sun-drying. Thinning the crop will give larger fruit size. This should be done as soon as possible after fruit set. The trees reach bearing age in about four years.

Culture

Location: Plant olive trees in full sun. Non-fruiting trees are available which can be planted in areas where fruit may be a problem. Strong winds will 'sculpt' the trees, but otherwise they are quite wind-tolerant.

Soils: Olives will grow well on almost any well-drained soil up to pH 8.5 and are tolerant of mild saline conditions.

Irrigation: Because of its small leaves, with their protective cuticle and slow transpiration, the olive tree survives even extended dry periods. Irrigation of young or newly planted trees is recommended.

Fertilisation: Fertilising olive trees with additional supplies of nitrogen has proved beneficial. Many growers in the Mediterranean countries apply organic fertilisers every other year.

Pruning: Proper pruning is important for the olive. Pruning both regulates production and shapes the tree for easier harvest. The trees can withstand radical pruning, so it is relatively easy to keep them at a desired height. The problem of alternate bearing can also be avoided with careful pruning every year. It should be kept in mind that the olive never bears fruit in the same place twice, and usually bears on the previous year's growth. For a single trunk, prune suckers and any branches growing below the point where branching is desired. For the gnarled effect of several trunks, stake out basal suckers and lower branches at the desired angle. Prune flowering branches in early summer to prevent olives from forming. Olive trees can also be pruned to espaliers.

Propagation: None of the cultivated varieties can be propagated by seed. Seed-propagated trees revert to the original small-fruited wild variety. The seedlings can, of course, be grafted or chip-budded with material from desired cultivars. The variety of an olive tree can also be changed by bark grafting or top working. Another method of propagation is transplanting suckers that grow at the base of mature trees. However, these would have to be grafted if the suckers grew from the seedling rootstock.

A commonly practised method is propagation from cuttings, 12–14 ins long, 1–3 ins wide. Cuttings from the two-year-old wood of a mature tree are treated with a rooting hormone, planted in a light rooting medium and kept moist. Trees grown from such cuttings can be further grafted with wood from another cultivar. Cuttings from grown trees bear fruit in about four years.

Pests and diseases: The olive tree is affected by some pests and diseases, although it has fewer problems than most fruit trees. Around the Mediterranean the major pests are medfly and the olive fly, *Dacus oleae.* In California, verticillium wilt is a serious fungal disease. There is no effective treatment other than avoiding planting on infested soils and removing damaged trees and branches. A bacterial disease known as olive knot is spread by pruning with infected tools during rainy months. Because the olive has fewer natural enemies than other crops, and because

the oil in olives retains the odour of chemical treatments, the olive is one of the least-sprayed crops.

Harvest: Olive fruits that are to be processed as green olives are picked while they are still green but have reached full size. They can also be picked for processing at any later stage up through full ripeness. Ripe olives bruise easily and should be handled with care. Mould is also a problem for the fruit between picking and curing. There are several classical ways of curing olives. A common method is the lye-cure process in which green or near-ripe olives are soaked in a series of lye solutions for a period of time to remove the bitter principle and then transferred to water and finally a mild saline solution. Other processing methods include water-curing, salt-curing and Greek-style curing. Both green-cured and ripe-cured olives are popular as a relish or snack. For canned commercial olives, black olives are identical to green olives. The black colour is obtained by exposure to air after lye extraction and has nothing to do with ripeness. Home production of olive oil is not recommended. The equipment required and the sheer mass of fruit needed are beyond most households.

Commercial potential: Commercial olive production is a multimillion dollar business. In the Mediterranean region olives and olive oil are common ingredients of everyday foods. There is also a growing interest in speciality olive oils, often produced commercially from small groves of olive trees.

Cultivars: Over the centuries mankind has produced and propagated myriad olive varieties. Today several dozen varieties are grown commercially around the world. Some representative olive cultivars are listed below.

ASCOLANO: Very large, ellipsoidal fruit. Skin colour very light even when ripe, stone very small. Fruit is tender and must be handled carefully. Contains very little bitterness and requires only moderate lye treatment. Excellent for pickles, but needs proper aeration during pickling to develop 'ripe' colour. Tree a heavy bearer, widely adapted.

BAROUNI: Large fruit, almost as large as Sevillano. Trees spreading and easy to harvest. Withstands extremely high temperatures. The variety usually shipped to the East Coast for making home-cured olives. Originally from Tunisia.

GORDAL: Medium to large, plump fruit, ripening early. Resembles Sevillano. A popular pickling olive and principal cultivar in Spain, producer of most of the world's table olives.

MANZANILLO: Large, rounded-oval fruit. Skin brilliant purple, changing to deep blue-black when mature. Resists bruising. Ripens early, several weeks earlier than Mission. The pulp parts readily with its bitterness and is exceedingly rich when pickled. Excellent for oil and pickles. Tree spreading, vigorous, a prolific bearer.

MISSION: Medium-sized, oval fruit. Skin deep purple changing to jet-black when ripe. Flesh very bitter but firm. Ripens rather late. Good for pickling and oil, specially ripe pickles. Most widely used for cold-pressed olive oil. Tree vigorous, heavy-bearing. More cold-resistant than other cultivars.

PICHOLINE: Small, elongated fruit. Skin light green, changing to wine-red, then red-black when ripe. Pulp fleshy, firm-textured. Tree vigorous, medium-sized, bears heavy crops regularly. Cured olives have a delicate, subtle, lightly salty, nut-like flavour. Usually salt-brine cured. Popular in gourmet and speciality markets.

RUBRA: Medium-small, ovate fruit. Skin jet-black when ripe. Ripens 3 to 4 weeks earlier than Mission. Best suited for oil, but is also used for pickling. Tree large, precocious, often producing fruit the second year. An exceptionally prolific bearer. Very hardy and reliable even in dry situations. Originated in France.

SEVILLANO: Very large fruit, bluish-black when ripe. The largest California commercial variety. Stone large, clinging. Ripens early. Low oil content, only useful in pickling. Used for making Sicilian-style, salt-brine cured olives, also the leading canning cultivar. Tree a strong grower and regular bearer. Requires deep, rich, well-drained soil. Will not stand much cold.

So now you know.

BIBLIOGRAPHY

France

The Cambridge Illustrated History (1994). Colin Jones, Cambridge
University Press.

Spain

Gatherings from Spain (1846, this ed. 2000). Richard Ford, Pallas Athene.

Wild Flowers of Spain (1987). Clive Innes, Cockatrice Publishing Ltd.

Barcelona (2001). Robert Hughes, The Harvill Press.

Tapas (1998). Ann Wilson, Könemann.

On Bullfighting (1999). A. L. Kennedy, Yellow Jersey Press.

Casa California (1996). Elizabeth McMillian, Rizzoli International
Publications Inc.

England

The Garden (1966). Julia S. Berrall, Thames & Hudson.

Titus Groan (1946). Mervyn Peake, Eyre & Spottiswoode.

Greece

The Olive - 'Kallistephanos' (2001). Marina Lykoudi and Vassilios Simantirakis, Bank of Attica Library, Ephesus Publishing, Alimos.

The Olive in Greece (2001). Panos Theodoridis (text) and Dimitris Talianis (photos), Topio Publications, Lesvos.

Monumental Olive Trees in Greece and Crete (1990). A paper by Dr Nikos Michelakis.

The Food and Wine of Greece (1990). Diane Kochilas, St Martin's Press.

Italy

Gardens of the Italian Villas (1987). Marella Agnelli, Weidenfeld & Nicolson.

Touring in Wine Country: Tuscany (1996). Maureen Ashley, Ed. Hugh Johnston, Mitchell Beazley.

Maserati: A History (1976). Anthony Pritchard, Arco Publishing Company, Inc.

Middle East

Wielding the Axe (2000). Michael Browning and Larry Kaplow, Cox News Service.